Oregon
Atlas & Gazetteer™

REF 917.79 OREGON
OREGON ATLAS AND GAZETTEER
2007

Grid numbers refer to detailed map pages

1 inch equals 44 miles

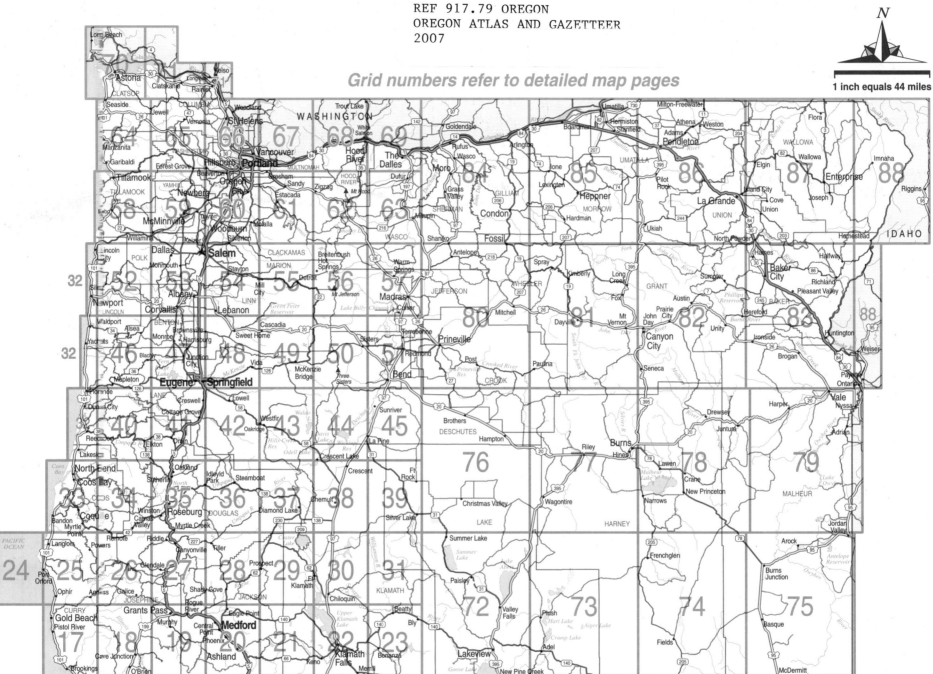

© DeLorme

Important Notices

DeLorme has made reasonable efforts to provide you with accurate maps and related information, but we cannot exclude the possibility of errors or omissions in sources or of changes in actual conditions. DELORME MAKES NO WARRANTIES OF ANY KIND, EITHER EXPRESS OR IMPLIED, INCLUDING THE WARRANTIES OF MERCHANTABILITY AND FITNESS FOR A PARTICULAR PURPOSE. DELORME SHALL NOT BE LIABLE TO ANY PERSON UNDER ANY LEGAL OR EQUITABLE THEORY FOR DAMAGES ARISING OUT OF THE USE OF THIS PUBLICATION, INCLUDING, WITHOUT LIMITATION, FOR DIRECT, CONSEQUENTIAL OR INCIDENTAL DAMAGES.

Nothing in this publication implies the right to use private property. There may be private inholdings within the boundaries of public reservations. You should respect all landowner restrictions.

Some listings may be seasonal or may have admission fees.
Please be sure to confirm this information when making plans.

Safety Information

To avoid accidents, always pay attention to actual road, traffic and weather conditions and do not attempt to read these maps while you are operating a vehicle. Please consult local authorities for the most current information on road and other travel-related conditions.

Do not use this publication for marine or aeronautical navigation, as it does not depict navigation aids, depths, obstacles, landing approaches and other information necessary to performing these functions safely.

Table of Contents

DISCARD

SIXTH EDITION. Copyright © 2007 DeLorme. All rights reserved.
P.O. Box 298, Yarmouth, Maine 04096   (207) 846-7000   www.delorme.com
Printed in Canada

Index

continued on next page

⊕ Unique Natural Features

ABERT RIM – Valley Falls – Page 72 B4 Largest exposed geologic fault in North America. 30 miles long, rising 2,500 feet above Abert Lake. Viewpoint on 640-foot vertical cliff.

ALVORD DESERT – 20 mi. NE of Fields – Page 74 B2 Over 60 square miles of caked mud in summer, covered by water in winter. Annual rainfall only a few inches. Plants unable to survive.

BIG HOLE – 13.5 mi. NW of Fort Rock – Page 39 A6 Huge volcanic explosion crater created by steam. 1 mile in diameter, several hundred feet deep. Similar to Hole-in-the-Ground (see this section), but filled with trees.

BROOKINGS – Brookings – Page 17 D2 Referred to as "The Banana Belt of Oregon" because of unusually mild climate. Temperatures year-round between 50–70 degrees Fahrenheit. Flowers bloom all year. Most Easter lilies in U.S. grown here.

BROWN MOUNTAIN LAVA FIELD – 27 mi. E of Eagle Point – Page 21 A6 Jumbled piles of broken lava cover 10 square miles. 15,000 years old, relatively new volcanism for Southern Cascades. Visible along State Route 140.

CEDAR GROVE BOTANICAL AREA – 8 mi. SW of John Day – Page 81 C7 60 acres of Alaska cedar isolated several miles from nearest colony. 1-mile trail to grove.

COLLIDING RIVERS – Glide – Page 35 B8 North Umpqua and Little rivers clash head on at right angles in amazing display. Scenic wayside.

COLUMBIA RIVER GORGE – Hood River – Page 68 C4 Only sea-level river cutting through volcanic rock of Cascade Mountain Range. Part of 253,500-acre National Scenic Area. Important transportation corridor. (See Parks/Forests/Wilderness Areas.)

CRACK-IN-THE-GROUND – 10 mi. N of Christmas Valley – Page 76 C2 2 miles long, 40 feet deep and 10 feet across, result of tension fracture in earth's surface. Formed when layer of basalt collapsed under pressure of new surface lava flow. Path through crevice. Unusual wall outcroppings.

CRATER LAKE – Crater Lake National Park – Page 29 A8 At 1,932 feet, deepest lake in U.S. Formed thousands of years ago when volcano, Mt. Mazama, erupted and then collapsed. Water collected forming lake. Phantom Ship rock and volcanic cone Wizard Island in lake. Boat tours. Rim Drive (see Scenic Drives and Bicycle Routes—Mountain Biking) circles crater. (See Parks/Forests/Wilderness Areas and Hiking.)

CROOKED RIVER GORGE – Terrebonne – Page 51 A7 River cut through lava flows. 403 feet deep. Scenic and colorful sedimentary rock formations.

CROWN POINT – Crown Point State Scenic Corridor – Page 67 D7 Promontory of Columbia River basalt rising vertically about 725 feet above river. Panorama of Columbia River Gorge. (See Historic Sites/Museums and Parks/Forests/Wilderness Areas.)

DESCHUTES CANYON – 5 mi. SW of Culver – Page 51 A6 Deep canyon consisting of basalt lava flows over 13 million years old. Towering rock walls 600–700 feet high. Deschutes River runs through center.

DEVIL'S PUNCH BOWL – Devil's Punch Bowl State Natural Area – Page 32 C1 Bowl-shaped rock formation fills at high tide, when ocean thunders in through cavern below.

DIAMOND CRATERS – 40 mi. SE of Burns – Page 78 D1 Large lava pool, 6 miles in diameter, formed about 25,000 years ago. Continuing, numerous eruptions created many diverse formations, including small volcanoes and cinder cones. (See Scenic Drives.)

FORT ROCK STATE MONUMENT – Fort Rock State Natural Area – Page 39 A8 Circular, fort-like volcanic outcropping, 325 feet high. Believed to have once been volcanic island in ancient lake. Wave-cut cliffs. Cave located in side once sheltered people 10,000 years ago. (See Parks/Forests/Wilderness Areas.)

GLASS BUTTES – 12 mi. SE of Hampton – Page 76 B4 Rising 2,000 feet above countryside, one of largest known outcroppings of volcanic glass, iridescent obsidian. Mostly streaked with red or brown. Once supplied arrowheads for American Indian tribes within radius of several hundred miles.

HAYSTACK ROCK – Cannon Beach – Page 64 A1 World's third largest, free-standing monolith, protruding 235 feet out of surf. Protected National Wildlife Refuge. Tide pools.

HELLS CANYON – 5.5 mi. SW of Imnaha – Page 88 C2 Deepest gorge in North America with average depth of 6,600 feet. Snake River winds through gorge. (See Parks/Forests/Wilderness Areas.)

HOLE-IN-THE-GROUND – 7 mi. NW of Fort Rock – Page 39 A7 Vast, open volcanic explosion crater about 1 mile in diameter and 300 feet deep. Created by steam. No trees grow inside.

HORSE RIDGE NATURAL AREA – 16 mi. SE of Bend – Page 45 A8 600-acre, pure stand of western junipers. Undisturbed in original, natural condition.

JOHN DAY FOSSIL BEDS NATIONAL MONUMENT – 28 mi. W of John Day – Page 81 B6 Last 40 million years of Age of Mammals recorded here. Plants and animals fossilized in deposits of volcanic ash. Three separate sections with headquarters at John Day Visitor Center. Viewpoints. Fishing. Trails. Over 14,000 acres.

KALMIOPSIS WILDERNESS – 8 mi. W of Cave Junction – Page 18 C2 Several rare and unusual plants exist in wilderness including Kalmiopsis and Brewer's weeping spruce, both pre-Ice Age relics.

LAVA BUTTE – 19 mi. NE of LaPine – Page 45 A6 Recent cinder cone rising about 500 feet. Formed by volcanic activity. Paved road to top. 360-degree view of Cascade Mountain Range. Trail around crater at summit. Observatory building with displays. One of over 400 cinder cones in Deschutes National Forest (see Parks/Forests/Wilderness Areas).

LAVA CAST FOREST – 14 mi. NE of La-Pine – Page 45 B6 5-square-mile, lava-covered landscape produced by volcanic activity over 6,000 years ago. Lava trees and tree molds. 1-mile interpretive trail (see Hiking). Located in Deschutes National Forest (see Parks/Forests/Wilderness Areas).

LAVA RIVER CAVE – 17 mi. N of LaPine – Page 45 A6 Tunnel-like caves, formed from hot lava creating tube, then draining out. Tours of 5,200-foot-long main tube, Oregon's longest known, uncollapsed lava tube.

LESLIE GULCH – 18 mi. NW of Sheaville – Page 79 C7 Narrow canyon almost 10 miles long, varies in width from 20 to 300 feet. Towering red spires and sheer rock walls. Pinnacles as high as 2,000 feet rise from canyon floor. Opportunities for wildlife viewing.

MT. HOOD – Mt. Hood National Forest – Page 62 B3 At 11,235 feet (3,424 meters), highest point in Oregon. Dormant Cascade volcano last active 1907. Visible for hundreds of miles. (See Parks/Forests/Wilderness Areas.)

MT. THIELSEN – 4 mi. SE of Diamond Lake – Page 37 C8 Known as "Lightning Rod of the Cascades," needle-like spire on top of 9,182-foot (2,799-meter) mountain struck by lightning often. Lightning creates carrot-shaped "lightning tubes" and glassy rock formations at summit. Mountain, remains of former volcano, stripped to central plug by glaciers.

MULTNOMAH FALLS – 25 mi. E of Portland – Page 67 D8 State's highest waterfall at over 610 feet. Located along Columbia River. Trails.

NATURAL BRIDGE – 10 mi. N of Prospect – Page 29 A5 Created when Rogue River drops into hole in volcanic rock and emerges again 200 feet downstream. Interpretive trail.

NEWBERRY CRATER – 14 mi. E of LaPine – Page 45 C7 Volcano, Mt. Newberry, collapsed about 10,000 years ago, forming crater 8 miles in diameter. Volcanic cone and lava flow divided crater, creating two lakes.

OREGON CAVES NATIONAL MONUMENT – 12 mi. SE of Cave Junction – Page 19 D5 Single cave began forming over 200 million years ago when region was covered by ocean. Guided tour through 0.6 mile of limestone and marble passageways. Different levels and galleries with varied formations. Temperature ranges from 38 to 45 degrees Fahrenheit. Called "Marble Halls of Oregon."

OWYHEE RIVER CANYON – 20 mi. SE of Rome – Page 75 B7 Reddish-brown canyons rise 1,000 feet over 100-mile area. Remote, high-desert setting with exciting whitewater *(see Oar/Paddle Trips)*. Many geologic formations.

PAINTED HILLS – 8 mi. NW of Mitchell – Page 80 B3 Hills formed from volcanic ash deposits banded with bright red, brown and yellow earth. Short trails provide viewing opportunities. Located within John Day Fossil Beds National Monument *(see this section)*.

PILLARS OF ROME – 2 mi. NW of Rome – Page 75 A6 100-foot-high towers of rock rising from desert floor. Named for resemblance to Roman ruins.

THE PINNACLES – Crater Lake National Park – Page 29 B8 200-foot-high, needle-like, pumice spires created by same volcanic eruption as Crater Lake *(see this section and Parks/Forests/Wilderness Areas)*. Exposed by erosion.

ROGUE RIVER GORGE – 12.5 mi. N of Prospect – Page 29 A5 River roars through narrow gorge gouged from volcanic bedrock over centuries.

SAND DUNES – Reedsport – Page 32 C3 53-mile stretch along Oregon coast provides level surface required for dune formations. Sand, formed by rocky sea cliff erosion, blown inland from ocean for up to 2.5 miles by prevailing westerly winds. Hiking trails. Located in Oregon Dunes National Recreation Area *(see Parks/Forests/Wilderness Areas)*.

STEENS MOUNTAIN – 17 mi. SE of Frenchglen – Page 74 B2 9,773-foot (2,979-meter), massive mountain covers area 30 miles long. Formed 15 million years ago. Valleys and U-shaped gorges cut 1 million years ago by glaciers. 1 vertical mile above Alvord Desert *(see this section). (See Scenic Drives—Back Country Byways and Bicycle Routes—Mountain Biking.)*

STEINS PILLAR – 5.5 mi. NE of Prineville – Page 80 C2 Elongated rock pillar. 350 feet tall and 120 feet in diameter at base. Protrudes high above trees.

TALLEST SUGAR PINE – 13 mi. E of Tiller – Page 28 A3 265 feet tall with diameter of 7.5 feet. Said to be world's tallest. Contains enough lumber to build five average-size houses.

THUNDEREGGS – Succor Creek State Natural Area – Page 79 C8 Official state rock. Egg-shaped, russet-colored nodules or geodes, usually filled with opal or chalcedony. Can be collected in many areas of state, but found in abundance in gulches and canyons east of Lake Owyhee. For more information contact: Oregon Department of Geology and Mineral Industries, 800 Northeast Oregon Street, Suite 965, Portland, OR 97232.

TWIN PILLARS – 8 mi. NE of Prineville – Page 80 C2 Remains of eroded volcano, 200 feet high, towering above pine forest. Reached by 8.5-mile trail from Wildcat Campground *(see Hiking)*.

WILLAMETTE FLOODPLAIN – William L. Finley National Wildlife Refuge – Page 47 A6 682 acres of flat, largely unplowed, native grassland and ash woodland. Grassland rare since most converted to pasture and farmland. Threatened and endangered plant species.

Campgrounds

To locate private campgrounds in this Atlas, look on the appropriate map for the campground symbol and corresponding four-digit number. For more information contact: Oregon Tourism Commission, 775 Summer Street NE, Salem, OR 97301-1282, 1-800-547-7842.
Public campgrounds, located in state and national forest land and in national parks, can be identified by the symbol indicated in the legend. For information on camping in state parks, see Parks/Forests/Wilderness Areas.

	NAME, LOCATION	TENTS	RV'S	PAGE & GRID
2000	Adel Store & RV Park, Adel		●	73 D5
2005	Agate Beach RV Park, Newport		●	32 C1
2010	Albany Trailer Park, Albany		●	53 C8
2015	Alsea Bay Trailer Park, Alsea Bay	●	●	32 A2
2020	Arizona Beach, Gold Beach	●	●	25 D5
2025	B&B RV Court, Detroit		●	55 C7
2030	Bay Shore RV Park & Marina, Netarts		●	58 A1
2035	Bayport Marina, Warren	●	●	66 B2
2040	Belknap Springs, McKenzie Bridge	●	●	49 C8
2045	Bend Keystone RV Park, Bend		●	51 D6
2050	Big Spruce RV Park, Tillamook	●	●	58 A1
2055	Blue Lake Resort, Sisters	●	●	50 A2
2060	Boardman Park, Boardman	●	●	85 A5
2063	Bob's RV Park, Trail	●	●	28 C2
2065	Boiler Bay RV Park, Depoe Bay		●	32 B1
2070	Bridge of the Gods RV Park, Cascade Locks		●	68 C1
2075	Brooke RV and Mobile Home Court, Pendleton		●	86 B1
2080	Bud's Campground, Gearhart	●	●	70 D2
2085	Burns Junction, Jordan Valley	●	●	75 A5
2090	Camp Sundown, Bend	●	●	51 D6
2095	Camper Cove RV Campground, Beaver	●	●	58 B2
2100	Canyon Court & RV Park, Madras	●	●	57 C7
2105	Cape Kiwanda RV Park, Pacific City	●	●	58 C1
2110	Caves Highway RV Park, Cave Junction	●	●	18 C3
2115	Caves Trail Camp, Cave Junction	●	●	18 C4
2120	Charleston Travel Park, Charleston	●	●	33 B6
2125	Chinook Bend Campground, Lincoln City	●	●	52 A1
2130	Circle Creek RV Park & Campground, Seaside	●	●	64 A1
2135	Circle W RV Park, Grants Pass	●	●	19 A7
2140	Columbia River Gorge Resort, Mosier	●	●	69 C6
2145	Condon RV Park, Condon		●	84 D4
2150	Copperfield Park, Oxbow	●	●	88 A4
2155	Corvallis–Albany KOA, Albany	●	●	53 D7
2160	Country Campground, Ontario	●	●	83 D8
2165	Coyote Rock RV Park, Lincoln City	●	●	52 A1
2170	Crater Lake Campground RV Park, Ft. Klamath	●	●	29 B8
2175	Crescent Creek RV Park, Crescent Lake	●	●	44 D1
2180	Crown Point RV Park, Corbett		●	67 D6
2185	Crown Villa RV Park, Bend		●	51 D6
2190	Crystal Corral, Prineville	●	●	80 C2
2195	Cushman Store, RV Park & Marina, Florence		●	32 A4
2200	Darlings Resort, Dunes City	●	●	32 A4
2205	Dewitt's RV Park, Cave Junction	●	●	18 C3
2210	Dexter Shores RV Park, Dexter	●	●	42 A2
2215	Diamond Hill Park, Harrisburg	●	●	47 B8
2220	Diamond Lake RV Park, Diamond Lake		●	37 C7
2225	Driftwood Mobile Home & RV Park, Coos Bay		●	33 B6
2230	Driftwood RV Park, Harbor		●	17 D2
2235	Driftwood Shores RV Park, Bandon		●	33 D5
2240	Elkton RV Park, Elkton	●	●	40 C4
2245	Emigrant Lake Campground, Ashland	●	●	20 C4
2247	Evergreen Terrace Park, Hood River	●	●	68 C4
2250	Far-E-Nuf Travel Trailer Park, LaPine	●	●	44 C4
2255	Fern Ridge Shores, Veneta	●	●	47 D6
2260	The Firs, North Bend	●	●	33 A7
2265	Fish Lake Resort, Medford	●	●	21 A6
2270	Fort Hill RV Park, Willimina	●	●	58 D4
2275	Four Seasons RV Resort, Gold Beach	●	●	17 A2
2280	Ft. Klamath RV Park, Ft. Klamath	●	●	30 C1
2285	Gates Trailer Ranch, Gates	●	●	55 B5
2290	Goebel's RV Park, Wallowa		●	87 B6
2295	Grandma & Grandpa's RV Park, Redmond		●	51 C7
2300	Grants Pass/Redwood Highway KOA, Wilderville	●	●	18 B4
2305	Grants Pass/Sunny Valley KOA, Sunny Valley	●	●	27 C5
2310	Green Acres Mobile Home & RV Park, Prineville	●	●	80 C1
2315	Happy Camp Resort, Netarts		●	58 A1
2320	Harbor Village RV Park, Newport		●	32 C1
2325	Hat Rock Campground, Hermiston	●	●	85 A8
2330	Have-A-Nice-Day Campground, Grants Pass	●	●	19 A7
2335	Hi-Way Haven RV Park, Sutherlin	●	●	35 A6
2340	Highlander Trailer Park, LaPine		●	44 C4
2345	Holiday RV Park, Depoe Bay		●	32 B1
2350	Holiday RV Park, Phoenix		●	20 B2
2355	Honey Bear Campground, Ophir	●	●	25 D5
2360	Howard Prairie Lake Resort, Medford	●	●	21 C5
2365	Huntley Park, Gold Beach	●	●	17 A2
2370	Hyatt Lake Resort, Ashland	●	●	21 C5
2375	J Bar L Guest Ranch, Canyon City	●	●	82 C1
2380	Jackson Hot Springs, Ashland	●	●	20 C2
2385	Jantzen Beach RV Park, Portland		●	66 D3
2390	Jetty Fishery RV Park, Rockaway Beach	●	●	64 C1
2395	Joe Creek Waterfalls Overnighters, Grants Pass	●	●	27 D6
2400	John Day Trailer Park, John Day		●	82 C1
2405	John's RV & Mobile Park, Bend		●	51 D6
2410	Junipers Reservoir RV Resort, Lakeview	●	●	72 D2
2415	KOA Madras, Culver	●	●	57 D7
2417	KOA Salem, Salem	●	●	54 A1
2420	Kah-Nee-Ta Resort, Warm Springs	●	●	57 B7
2425	Kampers West Kampground, Warrenton	●	●	70 C2
2430	Kelley's RV Park, Coos Bay		●	33 A6
2435	Kerby Trailer Park, Kerby	●	●	18 C3
2440	Lake of the Woods Resort, Klamath Falls	●	●	21 A7
2445	Lake's Edge RV Park, Westlake		●	32 A4
2450	Lakeshore Trailer Park, Dune City		●	32 A4
2455	Langlois RV Park, Langlois	●	●	25 A5
2460	Lantern Trailer Park, Chemult		●	38 C2
2465	Lee's Evergreen Park, Rose Lodge	●	●	58 D2
2470	Lemolo Lake Resort, Idleyld Park	●	●	37 B7
2475	Lincoln City KOA Kampground, Lincoln City	●	●	52 A1
2480	Lincoln City Resort, Otis	●	●	58 D1
2485	Lincoln Trailer Park, Depoe Bay		●	32 B1
2490	Loon Lake Lodge, Reedsport	●	●	40 D2
2495	Maple Lane Trailer Park & Marina, Mapleton	●	●	46 D2
2500	Martins Trailer Harbor, Depoe Bay		●	32 B1
2505	McKenzie River Trailer Court, Blue River	●	●	49 C6
2510	Meadowbrook Store & RV Park, Dale	●	●	81 A8
2515	Medford Oaks CamPark, Eagle Point	●	●	20 A3
2520	Mobile Estates, Portland		●	67 D5
2525	Mountain Home Mobile Village, Prospect	●	●	28 C4
2530	Mountain View Holiday Trav-L-Park, Baker	●	●	83 A5
2535	Mt. Hood RV Village, Welches	●	●	62 B1
2537	Mt. Nebo Trailer Park, Roseburg		●	35 C6
2540	Mt. Vernon Motel & Trailer Park, Mt. Vernon		●	81 C8
2545	Mt. View Park, Idanha	●	●	55 C8
2550	Mulkey RV Park, McMinnville	●	●	59 C6
2555	Myrtle Creek RV Park, Myrtle Creek	●	●	35 D6
2560	Neptune Park Resort, Chiloquin	●	●	30 D1
2565	Nesika Beach RV Park, Gold Beach	●	●	25 D5
2570	Nightingale's Fishing Camp, Westlake	●	●	32 A4
2575	North Lake Resort & Marina, Lakeside	●	●	32 D3
2580	Nyssa Trailer Park, Nyssa		●	79 A8
2585	Oasis Cafe & Motel, Juntura	●	●	78 A4
2590	Oregon Cascade RV Co-op, McKenzie Bridge		●	49 C7
2595	Oregon Motel 8 RV Park, Klamath Falls	●	●	22 B2
2600	Oregon Trails West RV Park, Baker	●	●	83 A5
2605	Out Post RV Park, Enterprise	●	●	87 C7
2610	Pacific Campground, Tillamook	●	●	58 A2
2615	Pacific City Trailer Park, Pacific City		●	58 C1
2620	Patio RV Park, Blue River		●	49 C7
2625	R&R RV Park, Christmas Valley	●	●	76 D2
2630	RV Park, Pendleton		●	86 B1
2635	Rainbow Mobile & RV Park, Blue River	●	●	49 C7
2640	Reeder Beach Resort RV Park, Portland	●	●	66 C2
2645	Rhododendron Trailer Park, Florence		●	32 D2
2650	Riverbend Moorage, Newport		●	32 D1
2655	Riverfront RV Trailer Park, Grants Pass	●	●	19 A7
2657	Riverside Lake Resort Park, Seaside	●	●	64 A1
2660	Riverview Trailer Park, LaPine	●	●	45 C5
2665	Riviera Trailer Court, Arlington	●	●	84 B4
2670	Rocky Point Resort, Klamath Falls	●	●	21 A8
2675	Rogue Autel Court, Gold Beach	●	●	17 A1
2680	Rogue Landing, Gold Beach		●	17 A1
2685	Rogue Valley Overniters, Grants Pass	●	●	19 A6
2690	Rolling Hills RV Park, Troutdale	●	●	67 D5
2695	Round-up Trailer Park, LaPine		●	45 C5
2700	The Sands, Hines	●	●	77 B8
2705	Sawyers Landing, Newport		●	32 D1
2710	Scipio's Goble Landing, Goble	●	●	71 B8
2715	Sea Ranch RV Park, Cannon Beach	●	●	64 A1
2720	Sea and Sand RV Park, Lincoln Beach		●	32 B1
2725	Seabird RV Park, Brookings		●	17 D2
2730	Seadrift, Lakeside		●	32 D3
2735	Seal Rocks Trailer Cove, Seal Rock	●	●	32 A2
2740	Seaport RV Park, Charleston		●	33 B6
2743	Shady Acres Mobile Park, Salem		●	60 D1
2745	Shady Acres RV Park, Cave Junction	●	●	18 C3
2750	Shelter Cove Resort, Cascade Summit		●	43 D8
2755	Shorewood Travel Trailer Village, Rockaway		●	64 D1
2760	Silver Lake Trailer Park, Silver Lake		●	39 C8
2763	Sisters KOA Campground, West Bend	●	●	51 B5
2765	Sleepy Hollow, Bridge	●	●	34 D1
2770	Sleepy Hollow RV Park, Lafayette	●	●	59 C8
2775	Smith River Marina, Reedsport	●	●	40 B1
2785	Sportsman's Landing RV Park, Lincoln City	●	●	52 A1
2790	Summer Lake Hot Springs, Summer Lake	●	●	72 B2
2795	Sunset Lake RV & Mobile Park, Warrenton	●	●	70 D2
2800	Sunset RV Park, Hood River		●	68 C4
2805	Surfwood Campground, Winchester Bay	●	●	32 C3
2810	Taylor's Travel Park, Creswell	●	●	41 A8
2815	Taylors Landing, Waldport	●	●	46 A1
2820	Tillamook KOA, Tillamook	●	●	58 B2
2825	Tillamook To The Sea, Tillamook	●	●	58 A1
2830	Tingley Lake Estates, Klamath Falls	●	●	22 D2
2835	Tollgate Mt Chalet, Weston	●	●	86 A4
2840	Town & Country Mobile Estates, Portland		●	60 A4
2845	Trailer Park Village, Salem		●	54 A1
2850	Trailer Park of Portland, Tualatin	●	●	60 A3
2855	Valley Motel RV Park, Clatskanie	●	●	71 D8
2860	Venice RV Park, Seaside		●	70 D2
2865	Vida-Lea Mobile Lodge, Leaburg		●	48 C3
2870	View Point Trailer Court, The Dalles		●	69 D8
2873	Village Estate Mobile Park, Albany		●	53 C8
2875	The Village Green RV Park, Cottage Grove		●	41 B8
2880	Village RV & Trailer Park, Burns	●	●	77 B8
2885	Wagontire RV Park, Riley	●	●	77 C5
2890	Walt's Cozy Camp, Chiloquin	●	●	30 D1
2895	Wandamere Campground, South Beach	●	●	32 D1
2900	The Waterwheel Campground, Chiloquin	●	●	30 D1
2905	Whaleshead Beach Campground, Brookings	●	●	17 C2
2910	Wildlife Safari RV Park, Winston		●	35 C5
2915	Wiseman's RV Park, Klamath Falls		●	22 C3
2920	Woodland Echoes Resort, Cave Junction	●		18 C4
2925	Wright's for Camping, Warrenton	●	●	64 A1

Parks/Forests/ Wilderness Areas

For more information on parks, forests, wilderness areas and other facilities listed in this chart contact: Oregon Parks and Recreation Department, 725 Summer Street NE, Suite C, Salem, OR 97301-1271, (800) 551-6949.

NAME, LOCATION	ACREAGE	CAMPING	FISHING	BOATING	SWIMMING	BEACH	HIKING	PICNICKING	COMMENTS	PAGE & GRID
Agate Beach State Recreation Site, Newport	18		●			●		●	View of Yaquina Head Lighthouse.	32 C1
Ainsworth State Park, 31 mi. E of Portland	156	●					●	●	Connections to Columbia River Gorge *(see Unique Natural Features)* hiking trails.	67 D8
Alderwood State Wayside, 15 mi. SW of Junction City	76		●				●	●	Located along Long Tom River.	47 C5
Alfred A. Loeb State Park, 6 mi. NE of Brookings	320	●	●		●	●	●	●	1-mile trail to redwood grove. Old myrtle trees.	17 D3
Ankeny National Wildlife Refuge, 10 mi. S of Salem	2,796						●		Hunting. Visitor Center. Winter habitat for dusky Canada geese.	53 B8
Arcadia Beach State Recreation Site, Cannon Beach	8		●			●		●	Beach access area.	64 B1
Badger Creek Wilderness, Mt. Hood National Forest	24,000	●	●				●		Glacial features dominate area.	63 B6
Bald Peak State Scenic Viewpoint, 7 mi. NW of Newberg	26							●	View of Willamette Valley and Cascade Range north to Mt. Rainier.	59 A8
Bandon Marsh National Wildlife Refuge, Bandon	712		●				●		All salt marsh. Resting and feeding area for birds. Hunting.	33 C5
Bandon State Natural Area, Bandon	15		●			●	●	●	Coastal dune area.	33 D5
Baskett Slough National Wildlife Refuge, 11 mi. W of Salem	2,492						●		Winter habitat for dusky Canada geese. Visitor Center.	53 A6
Battle Mountain Forest State Scenic Corridor, 9 mi. N of Ukiah	420							●	Commemorates battles fought with Indians in 1878.	86 C1
Beachside State Recreation Site, Waldport	17	●	●			●	●	●	Open year-round. Camping near beach. Hiker–biker camp.	32 A2
Bear Valley National Wildlife Refuge, Worden	4,200								Major nighttime roosting site for wintering bald eagles. Hunting.	22 D1
Ben Hur Lampman State Scenic Corridor, Gold Hill	10		●						Located along Rogue River.	19 A8
Benson State Recreation Area, 27.5 mi. E of Portland	272		●	●	●			●	Motorized boats prohibited on lake.	67 D8
Beverly Beach State Park, 6.5 mi. N of Newport	130	●	●			●	●	●	Heavily vegetated coastal area. Hiker–biker camp. 1-mile hiking trail.	32 C1
Black Canyon Wilderness, Ochoco National Forest	13,400	●	●				●		Old-growth forest, steep canyons, sharp ridges. Hunting.	81 C6
Blue Mountain Forest State Scenic Corridor, 3 mi. S of Meacham	2,152								20-mile-long forest corridor, preserving large evergreen trees.	86 C3
Bob Straub State Park, Pacific City	484		●			●		●	Day-use park.	58 C1
Boiler Bay State Scenic Viewpoint, Depoe Bay	33							●	Scenic ocean viewpoint.	32 B1
Bolon Island Tideways State Scenic Corridor, Reedsport	11		●				●		View of Winchester Bay. Trail to tree-covered island overlook.	32 C4
Bonnie Lure State Recreation Area, Estacada	94		●				●	●	Undeveloped wooded area on Clackamas River. Fishing access only.	61 B5
Booth State Scenic Corridor, 12 mi. W of Lakeview	319							●	Stand of ponderosa pine.	72 D2
Boulder Creek Wilderness, Umpqua National Forest	19,100	●	●				●		Numerous rock monoliths and outcroppings. Stands of ponderosa pine.	36 B4
Bradley State Scenic Viewpoint, 19 mi. E of Astoria	19							●	Scenic viewpoint along lower Columbia River.	71 C6
Bridal Veil Falls State Scenic Viewpoint, 10.5 mi. E of Troutdale	16						●	●	1-mile hiking trail to waterfall. Path to gorge overlook.	67 D7
Bridge Creek Wilderness, Ochoco National Forest	5,400	●	●				●		3.5-mile, unmaintained trail. Steep terrain. Open meadows.	80 C3
Bull of the Woods Wilderness, Mt. Hood/Willamette National Forests	34,900	●	●				●		Steep, mountainous terrain. 75 miles of trails.	55 B8
Bullards Beach State Park, Bandon	1,289	●	●	●		●	●	●	Hiker–biker and horse camps. Hiking, biking and equestrian trails. Lighthouse.	33 C5
Cape Arago State Park, 10 mi. SW of Coos Bay	146		●			●	●	●	High promontory projecting 0.5 mile into ocean.	33 B5
Cape Blanco State Park, Port Orford	1,895	●	●			●	●	●	Hiker–biker and horse camps. 3.5-mile equestrian trail. Scenic views.	24 B4
Cape Kiwanda State Natural Area, Pacific City	185		●	●		●	●		Wave-sculptured sandstone cliffs. Sand dunes. Hang gliding.	58 C1
Cape Lookout State Park, 8.5 mi. SW of Tillamook	2,014	●	●			●	●	●	2.5-mile hiking trail. Headland projecting 1.5 miles into ocean. Hiker–biker camp.	58 B1
Cape Meares National Wildlife Refuge, Cape Meares	139						●		Located along coast. Oregon Coast Trail *(see Hiking)*.	58 A1
Cape Meares State Scenic Viewpoint, 6.5 mi. NW of Tillamook	233						●	●	Lighthouse. Hiker–biker camp. Octopus Tree, multitrunked Sitka spruce.	58 A1
Cape Sebastian State Scenic Corridor, 6 mi. S of Gold Beach	1,401		●			●	●		Oregon Coast Trail *(see Hiking)*. View miles of coastline.	17 B1
Carl G. Washburne Memorial State Park, 14 mi. N of Florence	1,089	●	●			●	●	●	2 miles of ocean beach. Hiker–biker camp. Elk. Tide pools.	32 C2
Cascadia State Park, 12 mi. E of Sweet Home	254	●	●		●		●	●	Waterfall. Soda springs. Group picnic shelters.	49 A5
Casey State Recreation Site, 5.5 mi. E of Trail	80		●	●				●	Located along Rogue River.	28 C3
Catherine Creek State Park, 8 mi. SE of Union	168	●	●				●	●	Forested area at 3,200-foot elevation.	87 D6
Champoeg State Heritage Area, Newberg	616	●	●	●			●	●	10 miles of hiking and biking trails. Museums *(see Historic Sites/Museums)*.	60 B1
Chandler State Wayside, 16 mi. N of Lakeview	85							●	Forested canyon with spring. Elevation 4,475 feet.	72 C3
Clatsop State Forest, Astoria	154,000	●	●	●	●		●	●	Nature Trail. Located on Gnat Creek. Hunting.	70 C3
Clay Myers State Natural Area at Whalen Island, Sandlake	179		●				●		Pristine coastal estuarine ecosystem provides salmon spawning habitat.	58 B1
Cline Falls State Scenic Viewpoint, Redmond	9		●					●	Located on banks of Deschutes River.	51 B6
Clyde Holliday State Recreation Site, 7 mi. W of John Day	40	●	●				●	●	Adjacent to John Day River. Hiker–biker camp.	81 C8
Cold Springs National Wildlife Refuge, 7 mi. E of Hermiston	3,117		●	●			●		Hunting. Boats with electric motors only.	85 A8
Collier Memorial State Park, Chiloquin	537	●	●				●	●	Open-air Logging Museum *(see Historic Sites/Museums)*.	30 C1
Columbia River Gorge National Scenic Area, Hood River	253,500	●	●	●	●	●	●	●	River canyon cutting through volcanic rock of Cascade Mountain Range.	68 C4
Columbia Wilderness, Mt. Hood National Forest	39,000	●	●				●		Basalt cliffs. Broad plateaus. 125 miles of trails.	68 D1
Conde B. McCullough State Recreation Site, North Bend	23			●				●	Primarily boating area.	33 A7
Coquille Myrtle Grove State Natural Site, Gaylord	7		●		●			●	Myrtle grove on banks of Coquille River.	25 A8
The Cove Palisades State Park, 9.5 mi. SW of Madras	4,430	●	●	●	●		●	●	Massive formations and colorful pinnacles rise from canyon walls.	57 D6
Crater Lake National Park, 16 mi. NW of Fort Klamath	183,180	●	●		●		●	●	Deepest U.S. lake *(see Unique Natural Features)*. Boat tours.	29 A7
Crissey Field State Recreation Site, Brookings	40		●	●	●	●	●		Primitive park. First beach access north of Oregon–California border. Wildlife viewing.	17 D3
Crooked River National Grassland, Madras	106,000	●	●	●	●			●	Scenic canyon bottom with cliff-like walls. Rugged terrain.	57 D7
Crown Point State Scenic Corridor, 20 mi. E of Portland	307						●	●	Columbia River Gorge. Vista House *(see Historic Sites/Museums)*.	67 D6
Cummins Creek Wilderness, Siuslaw National Forest	9,173	●	●				●		Old-growth Sitka spruce. Spotted owl and red-legged frog habitat.	32 B2
"D" River State Recreation Site, Lincoln City	4		●			●			Beach access site adjacent to "D" River (said to be world's shortest).	32 A1
Dabney State Recreation Area, 15 mi. E of Portland on Sandy River	135		●	●	●		●	●	1.5-mile hiking trail along Sandy River.	67 D6
Darlingtonia State Natural Site, Florence	18						●	●	Unusual carnivorous plants, including Darlingtonia. Viewing deck.	32 D2
Del Rey Beach State Recreation Site, Gearhart	19					●			Coastal wayside with access to ocean beach.	70 D2
Deschutes National Forest, Bend	1,605,297	●	●	●	●	●	●	●	Lava casts and caves *(see Unique Natural Features)*. Hunting.	51 D5
Deschutes River State Recreation Area, 13 mi. E of The Dalles	783	●	●	●			●	●	Oregon Trail exhibit.	84 B1
Detroit Lake State Recreation Area, Detroit	104	●	●	●	●			●	Moorage and fishing docks. Paved boat ramp.	55 C7
Devil's Lake State Park, Lincoln City	109	●	●	●	●			●	2 areas on shores of Devil's Lake. Hiker–biker camp.	32 A1
Devil's Punch Bowl State Natural Area, 7.5 mi. N of Newport	8					●	●	●	Devil's Punchbowl *(see Unique Natural Features)*.	32 C1
Dexter State Recreation Site, Dexter	94		●	●	●			●	Access to Dexter Reservoir. Hiking, biking and equestrian trail. Disc golf course.	42 A2
Diamond Peak Wilderness, Willamette/Deschutes National Forests	54,185	●	●				●		125 miles of trails including Pacific Crest National Scenic Trail *(see Hiking)*.	43 D8
Drift Creek Wilderness, Siuslaw National Forest	5,798	●	●				●		One of largest stands of old-growth forest in Coast Range Mountains.	46 A1
Driftwood Beach State Recreation Site, Waldport	8		●			●		●	Located on sand bluff.	32 A2
Dyer State Wayside, 7.5 mi. S of Condon	0.53							●	Day-use park.	84 D4
Eagle Cap Wilderness, Wallowa–Whitman National Forest	358,461	●	●				●		480 miles of trails. 3 peaks over 9,000 feet.	87 C7
Ecola State Park, Cannon Beach	1,304		●			●	●	●	Near end of Lewis and Clark Trail. 6 miles of shore frontage. Whale-watching.	64 A1
Elijah Bristow State Park, Dexter	848		●				●	●	16 miles of hiking, biking and equestrian trails.	42 A2
Elliott R. Corbett II Memorial State Recreation Site, 14 mi. W of Sisters	63						●	●	Access to park on 0.5-mile trail. Located at south end of Blue Lake.	50 A2
Elliott State Forest, 5.5 mi. E of Reedsport	90,000	●	●		●		●		Primitive camping only. Hunting.	40 C1
Ellmaker State Wayside, Burnt Woods	63							●	Located along Tum Tum Creek.	52 D3
Elmer Feldenheimer Forest Preserve, Cannon Beach	1,476						●		Preserve for native wildlife. Trails. No motor vehicle access. Whale-watching.	64 A1
Emigrant Springs State Heritage Area, Meacham	23	●					●	●	Oregon Trail exhibit. Near summit of Blue Mountains.	86 B3
Erratic Rock State Natural Site, 5.5 mi. NE of Sheridan	4						●		Iceberg carried rock from Washington during Ice Age. Trail to rock.	59 C6
Face Rock State Scenic Viewpoint, Bandon	879		●			●	●	●	Tall, slender rocks offshore, said to resemble human and animal faces.	33 D5
Fall Creek State Recreation Area, Unity	167	●	●	●	●			●	Located on Fall Creek Reservoir. Primitive camping only.	42 A2
Farewell Bend State Recreation Area, Huntington	77	●	●	●	●			●	Where pioneer wagon trains left Snake River in trek westward. Exhibit.	83 C8
Fogarty Creek State Recreation Area, Depoe Bay	165		●			●	●	●	Coastal beach area with adjoining sheltered creek.	32 B1
Fort Rock State Natural Area, Fort Rock	210						●	●	Ancient volcanic crater *(see Unique Natural Features)*. 0.5-mile trail.	39 B8
Fort Stevens State Park, 7 mi. W of Astoria	3,810	●	●	●	●	●	●	●	13 miles of biking and hiking trails. Visitor Center. Hiker–biker camp.	70 C2
Fremont National Forest, 13 mi. W of Lakeview	1,201,194	●	●	●			●	●	Abert Rim and Big Hole *(see Unique Natural Features)*. Hunting.	72 D2
Frenchglen Hotel State Heritage Site, Frenchglen	33							●	Entrance to Steens Mountain *(see Unique Natural Features)*.	74 A1
Gearhart Mountain Wilderness, Fremont National Forest	22,809	●	●				●		8,634-foot (2,632-meter) Gearhart Mountain. 16 miles of trails.	72 C1
Geisel Monument State Heritage Site, 5.5 mi. N of Gold Beach	3							●	Named after John Geisel and sons, killed 1856 during Indian battle.	17 A1
Gleneden Beach State Recreation Site, 6 mi. S of Lincoln City	13		●			●		●	Coastal beach access site.	32 A1
Golden and Silver Falls State Natural Area, 20 mi. NE of Coos Bay	157		●				●	●	2 waterfalls over 100 feet tall. Old-growth myrtle trees.	34 A1
Goose Lake State Recreation Area, 13 mi. S of Lakeview	64	●	●	●				●	Located at Oregon–California border.	72 D3
Government Island State Recreation Area, 7 mi. NE of Portland	1,578	●	●	●	●	●	●	●	Columbia River island with 15-mile shoreline. Boat access only. Primitive camping only.	66 D4
Governor Patterson Memorial State Recreation Site, Waldport	10		●			●	●	●	Landscaped seashore park.	32 A2
Grassy Knob Wilderness, Siskiyou National Forest	17,200	●	●				●		Steep, rugged terrain. Rainforest-covered canyons and ridges.	25 C5
Guy W. Talbot State Park, 21 mi. E of Portland	378						●	●	3.4-mile hiking trail to 250-foot Latourell Falls.	67 D7
H.B. Van Duzer Forest State Scenic Corridor, 8.5 mi. W of Grande Ronde	1,525		●					●	Hiker–biker camp. Old-growth forest of spruce, hemlock and fir.	58 D2
Harris Beach State Recreation Area, Brookings	174	●	●			●	●	●	Hiker–biker camp. Rock cliffs along ocean. Year-round camping.	17 D2
Hart Mountain National Antelope Refuge, 17 mi. NE of Plush	241,104	●	●				●	●	4,500–8,000 feet. Primitive camping only. Antelope. Hunting.	73 B6
Hat Rock State Park, 8 mi. E of Umatilla	756		●	●	●		●	●	Located on banks of Lake Wallula formed by McNary Dam.	85 A8
Heceta Head Lighthouse State Scenic Viewpoint, 11 mi. N of Florence	549		●			●	●	●	Trail to Heceta Head Lighthouse. Scenic views.	32 C2

PARKS/FORESTS/ WILDERNESS AREAS, *continued*

NAME, LOCATION	ACREAGE	CAMPING	FISHING	BOATING	SWIMMING	BEACH	HIKING	PICNICKING	COMMENTS	PAGE & GRID
Hells Canyon National Recreation Area, Imnaha	541,336	●	●	●	●		●	●	900 miles of trails. *(See Unique Natural Features.)*	88 B1
Hells Canyon Wilderness, Wallowa–Whitman National Forest	130,095	●	●				●		Canyons, benchland, ridgetops. *(See Unique Natural Features.)*	88 C2
Hilgard Junction State Recreation Area, 7 mi. W of La Grande	269	●	●					●	Oregon Trail exhibit. River rafting access point. Tent camping only.	86 C4
Hoffman Memorial State Wayside, 10.5 mi. S of Coquille	4		●					●	Wooded wayside on South Fork of Coquille River.	33 D8
Holman State Wayside, Salem	10							●	Located in Willamette Valley. Day-use park.	53 A8
Hug Point State Recreation Site, Cannon Beach	42		●			●		●	Sheltered ocean beach.	64 B1
Humbug Mountain State Park, Port Orford	1,842	●	●			●	●	●	Hiker–biker camp. 3-mile trail to 1,750 foot (533-meter) summit.	25 C5
Illinois River Forks State Park, Cave Junction	368		●					●	Located at confluence of East and West Forks of Illinois River.	18 C3
Jackson F. Kimball State Recreation Site, Fort Klamath	19	●	●				●	●	Located at headwaters of Wood River. 0.5-mile hiking trail.	30 C1
Jasper State Recreation Site, 12 mi. SE of Eugene	66		●				●	●	Along Middle Fork of the Willamette River. Group picnic shelters. Wildlife viewing.	42 A1
Jessie M. Honeyman Memorial State Park, Florence	522	●	●	●	●		●	●	Hiker–biker camp. 500-foot-high sand dunes. 3 lakes.	32 A4
John B. Yeon State Scenic Corridor, 24 mi. W of Hood River	284						●		1.8 miles of hiking trails to waterfall and scenic viewpoints.	68 D1
Joseph H. Stewart State Recreation Area, 9.5 mi. E of Trail	911	●	●	●	●		●	●	11 miles of hiking and biking trails. Marina. Open year-round.	28 C3
Kalmiopsis Wilderness, Siskiyou National Forest	179,700	●	●				●		Rocky, brushy, low elevation canyons. Rare plants. Hunting.	18 B2
Klamath Marsh National Wildlife Refuge, 22 mi. N of Chiloquin	40,646		●						Large marsh. Nesting area for cranes and waterfowl. Waterfowl hunting.	30 A3
Koberg Beach State Recreation Site, Hood River	75		●			●		●	Roadside area bordering Columbia River with access to small beach.	69 C5
Lake Owyhee State Park, 15 mi. SW of Owyhee	730	●	●	●				●	52-mile-long lake formed by Owyhee Dam.	79 B8
LaPine State Park, 7 mi. N of LaPine	2,333	●	●	●	●		●	●	Big Tree, 162-foot ponderosa pine said to be Oregon's largest.	44 B4
Lewis and Clark National Wildlife Refuge, Astoria	35,000		●	●			●		Several islands clustered in Columbia River. Boat access only. Hunting.	70 C4
Lewis and Clark State Recreation Site, 14 mi. E of Portland	54		●	●	●		●	●	Lewis and Clark camped here in 1805.	67 D6
Lost Creek State Recreation Site, 6 mi. S of Newport	34		●			●		●	Beach access area. Picnic tables.	32 D1
Lowell State Recreation Site, 17 mi. SE of Eugene	55		●	●	●		●	●	Located on Dexter Reservoir. Marina. Group shelter.	42 A2
Lower Klamath National Wildlife Refuge, 24 mi. S of Klamath Falls	50,912						●		Bicycling. Auto tour. Bald eagles. Waterfowl hunting.	22 D2
Malheur National Forest, 8 mi. S of John Day	1,465,396	●	●	●	●		●	●	Winter sports. Unusual rock formations. Fossil beds. Hunting.	82 C1
Malheur National Wildlife Refuge, 30 mi. SE of Burns	187,000		●	●			●		Visitor Center. Auto tour. Environmental study area. Hunting.	78 C1
Manhattan Beach State Recreation Site, Rockaway	41		●			●		●	Access to beach.	64 C1
Mary S. Young State Recreation Area, Lake Oswego	133		●				●	●	2.5 miles of hiking and biking trails. Scenic viewpoint.	60 A3
Maud Williamson State Recreation Site, 8 mi. S of Dayton	24							●	Heavily shaded by second-growth Douglas fir and scattered oaks.	59 D8
Mayer State Park, 8 mi. W of The Dalles	637		●	●	●	●		●	2 sections with views of Columbia River Gorge and Columbia River.	69 C6
McDonald State Forest, 5 mi. N of Corvallis	7,000		●				●		Motor vehicle access by permit only. 8 miles of trails. Hunting.	53 C7
McKay Creek National Wildlife Refuge, 5 mi. S of Pendleton	1,837		●	●			●		Open water, marsh and grasslands. Canada geese and ducks. Hunting.	86 B1
McVay Rock State Recreation Site, 3 mi. S of Brookings	19		●		●	●	●	●	Beach access area. Surf fishing and clamming. Whale-watching.	17 D2
Memaloose State Park, [illegible]0 mi. W of The Dalles	355	●							Named for Columbia River island used by Indians for burial ground.	69 C6
Menagerie Wilderness, Willamette National Forest	4,800	●	●				●		Popular technical climbing area. 4 miles of trails.	49 A6
Middle Santiam Wilderness, Willamette National Forest	7,500	●	●				●		Steep slopes, high peaks, ridges and river bottoms. 7 miles of trails.	55 D7
Mill Creek Wilderness, Ochoco National Forest	17,400	●	●				●		Twin Pillars *(see Unique Natural Features and Hiking).*	80 C2
Milo McIver State Park, Estacada	952	●	●	●			●	●	4.5-mile equestrian trail. Fish hatchery. Views of Mt. Hood.	61 B5
Minam State Recreation Area, 10 mi. NE of Elgin	602	●	●					●	Forested park on Minam River. Primitive camping only.	87 B6
Molalla River State Park, Canby	567		●	●			●	●	Great blue heron rookery. 1.5-mile hiking trail.	60 B3
Monument Rock Wilderness, Malheur/Wallowa–Whitman National Forests	19,650	●	●				●		Three prominent rock formations. 12 miles of trails.	82 C3
Mountain Lakes Wilderness, Winema National Forest	23,071	●	●				●		Several lakes formed during extensive glacial gouging.	21 A8
Mt. Hood National Forest, Zigzag	1,067,043	●	●	●	●	●	●	●	Multnomah Falls *(see Unique Natural Features).* Hot springs. Hunting.	62 B1
Mt. Hood Wilderness, Mt. Hood National Forest	46,520	●	●				●		Mt. Hood *(see Unique Natural Features).* Alpine meadows.	62 B2
Mt. Jefferson Wilderness, Willamette/Deschutes/Mt.Hood National Forests	107,008	●	●				●		193 miles of trails and 150 lakes. Alpine meadows and steep slopes.	50 A1
Mt. Thielsen Wilderness, Umpqua/Winema/Deschutes National Forests	54,267	●	●				●		Mt. Thielsen *(see Unique Natural Features).*	37 D8
Mt. Washington Wilderness, Willamette/Deschutes National Forests	52,738	●	●				●		Mt. Washington rises above lava-strewn plains.	50 B2
Munson Creek Falls State Natural Site, 7 mi. S of Tillamook	62						●	●	319-foot waterfall, highest in Coast Range. Ancient western red cedar and Sitka spruce.	58 B2
Muriel O. Ponsler Memorial State Scenic Viewpoint, 14.5 mi. N of Florence	2		●			●		●	Ocean wayside providing access to beach and interesting sea panorama.	32 C2
Nehalem Bay State Park, Manzanita	895	●	●	●		●	●	●	Horse camp, corrals, 7.5-mile equestrian trail. 1.5 mi. bike trail. Hiker–biker camp.	64 C1
Neptune State Scenic Viewpoint, Yachats	302		●			●	●	●	Harbor seal community on rocks below Strawberry Hill.	32 B2
Neskowin Beach State Recreation Site, Neskowin	8		●			●			Beach access area.	58 D1
Newberry National Volcanic Monument, 14 mi. E of LaPine	54,822	●	●	●	●	●	●	●	Newberry Crater *(see Unique Natural Features).* Volcanically formed lakes.	45 C7
North Fork John Day Wilderness, Umatilla/Wallowa–Whitman National Forests	121,352	●	●				●		130 miles of trails. Granitic outcroppings and gorge.	86 D2
North Fork Umatilla Wilderness, Umatilla National Forest	20,435	●	●				●		Gently sloping plateaus. Canyons. 18 miles of trails. Hunting.	86 B4
North Santiam State Recreation Area, Mill City	120		●				●	●	Forested area along North Santiam River.	54 B4
Oceanside Beach State Recreation Site, 6 mi. W of Tillamook	7		●			●			Excellent view of three arch rocks. Beach access area.	58 A1
Ochoco National Forest, 13 mi. NE of Prineville	847,898	●	●				●	●	Rockhounding. Wild horses. Hunting.	80 C2
Ochoco State Scenic Viewpoint, Prineville	251						●		Viewpoint of Prineville, Crooked River Valley and Ochoco Mountains.	80 C1
Ona Beach State Park, 9 mi. S of Newport	220		●	●	●	●		●	On Beaver Creek with access to ocean beach. Boat ramp.	32 D1
Ontario State Recreation Site, Ontario	78		●	●				●	Day-use area located along Snake River.	88 D4
Oregon Dunes National Recreation Area, Florence	31,566	●	●	●	●	●	●	●	38 miles of ocean beach. Sand dunes *(see Unique Natural Features).*	32 A4
Oswald West State Park, Manzanita	2,474	●	●			●	●	●	Rain forest with massive trees. Primitive camping only.	64 B1
Otter Crest State Scenic Viewpoint, 10 mi. N of Newport	1								Headland viewpoint overlooking shoreline south to Yaquina Head. Whale-watching.	32 B1
Otter Point State Recreation Site, Gold Beach	86					●	●	●	Coastal wayside with ocean views. Trail to beach.	17 A1
Paradise Point State Recreation Site, Port Orford	12					●			Beach access area.	24 B4
Peter Skene Ogden State Scenic Viewpoint, 9 mi. N of Redmond	86							●	View of Crooked River Gorge *(see Unique Natural Features).*	51 A7
Pilot Butte State Scenic Viewpoint, Bend	96						●		511-foot, lone volcanic cinder cone. Views of Cascade Mountain Range.	51 D6
Pistol River State Scenic Viewpoint, 10 mi. S of Gold Beach	448		●			●	●		Large sand dunes adjacent to wide sandy beach.	17 B1
Port Orford Heads State Park, Port Orford	102		●				●	●	Day-use park.	24 C4
Portland Women's Forum State Scenic Viewpoint, 9 mi. E of Troutdale	7								Clifftop views of Columbia River Gorge and Vista House.	67 D6
Prineville Reservoir State Park, 10.5 mi. SE of Prineville	385	●	●	●	●		●	●	Outdoor theater.	80 D2
Prospect State Scenic Viewpoint, Prospect	11						●	●	Picnic area located on Rogue River. Waterfall. Scenic viewpoints.	29 C5
Red Bridge State Wayside, 12.5 mi. W of La Grande	37	●	●					●	Forested area along Grande Ronde River.	86 C3
Red Buttes Wilderness, Siskiyou National Forest	3,750	●	●				●		Rocky buttes, forested ridges and meadows. Several hiking trails.	19 D5
Roads End State Recreation Site, Lincoln City	5					●		●	Coastal area with ocean beach access.	58 D1
Rock Creek Wilderness, Siuslaw National Forest	7,486	●	●				●		Steep and brushy terrain.	32 C2
Rocky Creek State Scenic Viewpoint, Depoe Bay	58		●					●	Adjacent to ocean, along rugged coastline. Viewpoint.	32 B1
Rogue River National Forest, Prospect	575,445	●	●	●	●	●	●	●	40 campgrounds. 400 miles of trails. Skiing. Hunting.	29 B5
Rogue–Umpqua Divide Wilderness, Umpqua/Rogue River National Forests	33,200	●	●				●		High meadows and forested valleys. Extensive trail system.	37 D5
Rooster Rock State Park, 20 mi. E of Portland	873		●	●	●	●	●	●	3.2 miles of hiking trails. Named for unusual rock formations.	67 D7
Saddle Mountain State Natural Area, 11 mi. E of Seaside	2,911	●					●	●	2.5-mile trail to summit. Rare plants. Tent camping only.	64 A3
Salmon–Huckleberry Wilderness, Mt. Hood National Forest	44,560	●	●				●		Volcanic plugs, pinnacles and cliffs. 70 miles of trails. Hunting.	62 B1
Samuel H. Boardman State Scenic Corridor, 7 mi. N of Brookings	1,471		●			●	●	●	Scenic views of rugged Oregon coast.	17 C2
Santiam State Forest, Mill City	47,721	●	●	●	●		●	●	Composed of different sections along Santiam River. Hunting.	55 C5
Sarah Helmick State Recreation Site, Monmouth	82		●					●	Grove of yew trees.	53 B7
Seal Rock State Recreation Site, Waldport	5		●			●	●	●	Located along rugged Oregon coastline.	32 A2
Seneca Fouts Memorial State Natural Area, Hood River	426						●		Viewpoint. Eastbound access only.	68 C4
Seven Devils State Recreation Site, 8 mi. N of Bandon	54		●			●		●	Coastal area with ocean beach access.	33 C5
Shelton State Wayside, [illegible]0 mi. SE of Fossil	180	●					●	●	Yellow pine forest with 2-mile hiking trail. Primitive camping only.	80 A4
Shepperd's Dell State Natural Area, 24.5 mi. E of Portland	521						●		Overlooks Columbia River. Short trail to waterfall viewpoint.	67 D7
Shore Acres State Park, [illegible] mi. SW of Coos Bay	745					●	●	●	7-acre botanical garden includes plants from around world.	33 B5
Silver Falls State Park, 20 mi. E of Salem	8,706	●	●		●		●	●	10 waterfalls. 25 miles of biking, jogging and equestrian trails.	54 A3
Siskiyou National Forest, 15 mi. SW of Grants Pass	1,061,395	●	●	●	●	●	●	●	Rafting. Special botanical areas. Hunting.	18 B4
Siuslaw National Forest, Mapleton	630,257	●	●	●	●	●	●	●	Miles of Pacific Ocean coastline, including Cape Perpetua. Sand dunes.	46 D2
Sky Lakes Wilderness, Rogue River/Winema National Forests	116,300	●	●				●		Mt. McLoughlin and Pacific Crest National Scenic trails *(see Hiking).*	29 C6
Smelt Sands State Recreation Site, Yachats	9		●			●	●		Access to rugged coastline. Traditional smelt-dipping area.	32 B2
Smith Rock State Park, [illegible] mi. N of Redmond on Crooked River	651	●	●				●	●	7 miles of trails. Rock formations. Rock-climbing. Hiker–biker camp.	51 B7
South Beach State Park, Newport	499	●	●			●	●	●	Hiker–biker camp. High sand dunes.	32 D1
Starvation Creek State Park, 8 mi. W of Hood River	153						●	●	0.25-mile hiking trail to waterfall.	68 C3
Stonefield Beach State Recreation Site, 5.5 mi. S of Yachats	19		●			●			Rockhounding for agates and other semiprecious stones.	32 C2
Strawberry Mountain Wilderness, Malheur National Forest	68,700	●	●				●		Extensive trail system. 7 mountain lakes.	82 C1
Succor Creek State Natural Area, 20 mi. SW of Owyhee	1,910	●					●	●	Colorful rock formations. Thundereggs *(see Unique Natural Features).*	79 C8
Sumpter Valley Dredge State Heritage Area, Sumpter	84		●						Historic gold mining dredge.	82 A4
Sun Pass State Forest, Fort Klamath	20,031	●	●				●		Oregon's smallest state forest. Primitive camping only.	30 C1

continued on next page

PARKS/FORESTS/ WILDERNESS AREAS, *continued*

For more information on parks, forests, wilderness areas and other facilities listed in this chart contact: Oregon Parks and Recreation Department, 725 Summer Street NE, Suite C, Salem, OR 97301-1271, (800) 551-6949.

NAME, LOCATION	ACREAGE	CAMPING	FISHING	BOATING	SWIMMING	BEACH	HIKING	PICNICKING	COMMENTS	PAGE & GRID
Sunset Bay State Park, 8 mi. SW of Coos Bay	395	●	●	●	●	●	●	●	Hiker–biker camp. Wind-protected bay area. Views of rocky coast.	33 B6
Table Rock Wilderness, 19 mi. SW of Molalla	5,500	●	●				●		Steep, rugged terrain. 17 miles of trails.	55 A5
Three Sisters Wilderness, Willamette/Deschutes National Forests	286,708	●	●				●		Alpine meadows, waterfalls, lakes and lava fields. 433 miles of trails.	50 B3
Tillamook State Forest, 5.5 mi. E of Tillamook	364,000	●	●	●	●		●	●	25 miles of trails. Hunting.	58 A3
Tokatee Klootchman State Natural Site, 7 mi. S of Yachats	7					●			Elevated ocean views. Whale-watching.	32 C2
Tolovana Beach State Recreation Site, Cannon Beach	3		●			●		●	Beach access site.	64 A1
Tou Velle State Recreation Site, 8 mi. N of Medford on Rogue River	57		●	●			●	●	Group picnic shelter.	20 A1
Tryon Creek State Natural Area, Portland	643						●		Park located in urban zone. 14 miles of hiking, biking and equestrian trails.	60 A3
Tubb Springs State Wayside, 18 mi. E of Ashland	40							●	Forested area with unique roadside fountain.	21 D5
Tumalo State Park, Bend	327	●	●	●			●	●	Hiker–biker camp. Group picnic shelter.	51 C6
Ukiah–Dale Forest State Scenic Corridor, Ukiah	2,987	●	●						Canyon along Camas Creek and John Day River. Tent camping only.	86 D1
Umatilla National Forest, 10 mi. S of Ukiah	1,094,981	●	●	●	●	●	●	●	Winter sports. Rafting. Lava outflows. Hunting.	82 A1
Umatilla National Wildlife Refuge, 11 mi. W of Umatilla	29,370		●	●			●		On Columbia River. Horseback riding. Waterfowl area. Hunting.	85 A6
Umpqua Lighthouse State Park, Reedsport	450	●	●	●		●	●	●	High sand dunes. Lighthouse.	32 C3
Umpqua National Forest, 12 mi. E of Glide	984,602	●	●	●	●	●	●	●	Winter sports. Geologic formations. Hunting.	36 B2
Umpqua State Scenic corridor, 7 mi. E of Reedsport	111		●	●				●	Roadside area. Access to Umpqua River.	40 C1
Unity Lake State Recreation Site, Unity	39	●	●	●	●		●	●	Hiker–biker camp. Elevation 3,866 feet.	82 C4
Upper Klamath National Wildlife Refuge, 24 mi. NW of Klamath Falls	14,966		●	●					Marsh and open water. Boat access only. Waterfowl hunting.	21 A8
Valley of the Rogue State Recreation Area, 10 mi. E of Grants Pass	278	●	●	●			●	●	Group picnic shelter. Access to Rogue River.	19 A8
Viento State Park, 6.5 mi. W of Hood River	248	●	●				●	●	Forested area on Viento Creek.	68 C3
Vinzenz Lausmann Memorial State Natural Area, Hood River	126						●		Scenic area located within Columbia River Gorge *(see Unique Natural Features).*	68 C4
W.B. Nelson State Recreation Site, Waldport	2		●				●	●	Shaded area bordering Eckman Slough.	32 A2
Waldo Lake Wilderness, Willamette National Forest	39,200	●	●				●		Meadows, slopes and rock outcroppings. 84 miles of trails.	43 B8
Wallowa Lake Highway Forest State Scenic Corridor, Wallowa	284		●					●	Located along highway.	87 B6
Wallowa Lake State Recreation Area, Joseph	216	●	●	●	●		●	●	Marina. 1 mile nature trail. Elevation 4,427 feet.	87 C8
Wallowa–Whitman National Forest, 10 mi. SW of Baker	2,261,147	●	●	●	●	●	●	●	Combines 2 national forests. Winter sports. Hunting.	82 A3
Washburne State Wayside, Junction City	37						●	●	Forested area.	47 B7
Wenaha–Tucannon Wilderness, Umatilla National Forest	66,375	●	●				●		Canyons, lava mesas and plateaus. Large elk population.	87 A5
White River Falls State Park, Tygh Valley	299		●				●	●	Located on White River. Scenic waterfalls. Old electric power station.	63 C8
Wild Rogue Wilderness, Siskiyou National Forest	25,658	●	●	●			●		Rafting *(see Oar/Paddle Trips).* Lodging along river.	26 C1
Willamette Mission State Park, 8 mi. N of Salem	1,686		●	●			●	●	Hiking and equestrian trails. 155-foot-tall black cottonwood tree.	59 D8
Willamette National Forest, Blue River	1,686,418	●	●	●	●	●	●	●	Along western slopes of Cascade Mountain Range. Winter sports. Hunting.	49 C6
William L. Finley National Wildlife Refuge, 10 mi. S of Corvallis	5,325		●				●		Winter habitat for dusky Canada geese. Visitor Center. Hunting.	47 A6
William M. Tugman State Park, 9 mi. S of Reedsport	560	●	●	●	●		●	●	Located in scenic coastal lake region. Hiker–biker camp.	32 D3
Winchuck State Recreation Site, 4 mi. S of Brookings	7		●	●	●	●			Day-use park. Winchuck River access.	17 D3
Winema National Forest, Chiloquin	1,040,437	●	●	●			●	●	Pacific Crest National Scenic Trail *(see Hiking).* Winter sports. Hunting.	30 D1
Wygant State Natural Area, Hood River	667						●		6-mile hiking trail.	68 C3
Yachats Ocean Road State Natural Site, Yachats	79					●		●	Along rocky shoreline. Spruce and fir trees.	32 B2
Yachats State Recreation Area, Yachats	93		●			●		●	Borders Yachats River. Saltwater fishing.	32 B2
Yaquina Bay State Recreation Site, Newport	33		●			●	●	●	Coast resort since 1865. Historic lighthouse with exhibits.	32 D1

Oar/Paddle Trips

The river and lake trips described here offer a sampling of the boating opportunities Oregon has to offer. Many rivers are seasonal—level and flow are dependent on snowmelt or rain. Other waterways are dam-controlled. To obtain Oregon stream flow information, call the River Forecast Center in Portland at (503) 261-9246.

Many public agencies offer maps and guides to streams. Check with the appropriate district of the Bureau of Land Management or national forest. There are also several whitewater boating organizations offering guidance and information. Some trips are through parks and forests—see Parks/Forests/ Wilderness Areas.

This category was compiled with the assistance of the North West Rafters Association, P.O. Box 19008, Portland, OR 97240.

RIVER CLASSIFICATION

The International River Classification System used here indicates the various difficulties encountered on whitewater rivers. While this system is an established guide for planning a safe trip, always remember that experience, sound judgement and precautionary safety measures are very important.

Class I: Very easy. Waves small, regular; passages clear; sandbanks, artificial difficulties like bridge piers; riffles.

Class II: Easy. Rapids of medium difficulty, with passages clear and wide; low ledges.

Class III: Medium. Waves numerous, high; irregular rocks, eddies; rapids with passages that are clear but narrow, requiring expertise in maneuvering; inspection usually needed.

Class IV: Difficult. Long rapids; waves powerful, irregular; dangerous rocks; boiling eddies; passages difficult to reconnoiter; inspection mandatory first time; powerful and precise maneuvering required.

Water beyond Class IV: Generally considered unrunnable except with covered or specially equipped boats.

CLACKAMAS RIVER – Milo McIver State Park – Page 61 B6 – 8-mile route Popular river with rafters and kayakers because of scenic beauty and close proximity to Portland. Partially within Mt. Hood National Forest. Runnable year-round due to dam-controlled flow. Many runs with varying difficulties, Class II–VI. Popular raft trip: Put-in at Milo McIver State Park, take-out at Barton County Park. Mostly Class II with one Class III rapid near put-in.

GRANDE RONDE RIVER – Elgin – Page 87 B5 – 13-mile route National Wild and Scenic River. Most stretches of river suitable for novice rafters and intermediate canoeists and kayakers. Suggested raft trip: Put-in at Elgin, take-out at Palmer Junction. Andy's Rapids, Class III; other class II rapids and riffles. Some flatwater. Open agricultural land and rangeland first several miles, changing to canyonland valley for remainder.

JOHN DAY RIVER – Clarno – Page 80 A3 – 44-mile route National Wild and Scenic River with headwaters in forested mountain area of north-central Oregon, changing to rugged canyonland with towering rock formations in lower sections. Slow, calm water, good for canoeists, drift boaters, and novice kayakers and rafters. Popular with fishermen—noted for bass and winter steelhead. Flow dependent on snowmelt/precipitation. Suggested trip: Put-in off State Route 218 at Clarno Bridge, take-out off State Route 206, at Cottonwood Bridge. Two Class III–IV rapids near beginning. Beware of gusty winds in canyon.

KLAMATH RIVER – 10 mi. SE of King Cole – Page 21 D8 – 11-mile route Challenging whitewater for experienced rafters and kayakers. Numerous rapids include Caldera, Hell's Corner and Satan's Gate. Flow dependent upon dam releases. Route through scenic, steep-cliffed, basalt canyons. Suggested trip: Put-in off State Route 66 on road lead-ing to John Boyle Power Plant, take-out at state-line access off Topsy Grade Road at Oregon–California border.

LOWER DESCHUTES RIVER – Maupin – Page 63 C8 – 10-mile route Popular recreation river because of close proximity to Portland metropolitan area. Flows northerly to Columbia River, paralleling Cascade Mountain Range. National Wild and Scenic River. Boater pass required for use on Lower Deschutes from Pelton Dam to Columbia River. Noted for exceptional steelhead, wild trout and salmon fishing. Popular intermediate whitewater trip: Put-in at Harpham Flat launch area, take-out before Sherars Falls at Sandy Beach access. Two Class IV rapids. Travels through canyon. Beware of gusty winds and summer thunderstorms. Dam-controlled flow.

McKENZIE RIVER – Finn Rock – Page 49 C5 – 10-mile route Scenic river, popular for rafters, kayakers, canoeists and drift boating on flatwater. Terrain varies from agricultural areas to old-growth forests with rocky outcroppings. Good wildlife viewing areas. Suggested trip for rafts and kayaks: Put-in at Finn Rock Rest Area, take-out at Helfrich Landing. Some flatwater with two difficult spots—Brown's Hole and Martin Rapids.

NEHALEM RIVER – Elsie – Page 64 B4 – 17-mile route Travels through rugged forestland from Coast Range Mountains to Pacific Ocean. Dependent upon rainy season for adequate flow. Suggested trip: Put-in at Spruce Run Recreation Site in Clatsop State Forest, take-out below Nehalem Falls at Beaver Slide access, or just above falls at Nehalem Falls Recreation Site in Tillamook State Forest. Mainly Class III trip with several rapids up to Class IV. Adequate flow needed to run Nehalem Falls—use caution.

NEW RIVER – Denmark – Page 24 A4 – 8-mile route Shallow estuary paralleling Pacific Ocean. Seasonal canoeing dependent on rainfall. Nesting and feeding area for migrating waterfowl and shorebirds including snowy plover and Aleutian Canada goose. Good fishing. Put-in at Boise–Cope County Park on Floras Lake, through Floras Outlet to New River; take-out at confluence of New River and Fourmile Creek.

NORTH SANTIAM RIVER – Minto – Page 55 B6 – 14-mile route Popular river close to Salem for drift boaters, kayakers, rafters and whitewater canoeists. Several good sections between Detroit Lake and just south of Salem. Dam-controlled flow. Suggested Class III–IV trip: Put-in at Packsaddle County Park, take-out at Mehama Bridge. Beware of Spencer's Hole rapids and Mill City Falls.

NORTH UMPQUA RIVER – Umpqua National Forest – Page 36 B4 – 15-mile route Popular river for rafters, kayakers and whitewater canoeists. Designated National Wild and Scenic River. Contains some flatwater, such as near confluence with South Umpqua River, but known for whitewater. Most widely used section located within Umpqua National Forest. Renowned steelhead fishing area—boating restrictions may apply, check ahead with North Umpqua Ranger District. Suggested raft trip: Put-in at Boulder Flat Campground, take-out 15 miles downstream at Gravel Bin access. Class III–IV. Passes through steep, heavily forested canyon area. Dam-controlled river, but waterflow still heavily dependent on precipitation.

OWYHEE RIVER – Rome – Page 75 A6 – 63-mile route River runs within towering canyons, passing many outstanding geologic and historic features including caves, rock pinnacles and petroglyphs. Portion from Oregon–Idaho border to Lake Owyhee designated National Wild and Scenic River. Season dependent on precipitation; usually runnable only in spring. Middle section of river from Three Forks to Rome, recommended only for expert rafters and kayakers. Suggested trip: Put-in at Rome, to Leslie Gulch take-out on Lake Owyhee. Suitable for rafters, kayakers and canoeists with experience. Numerous Class II–III rapids. Boulder gardens. Isolated stretches with no access.

ROGUE RIVER – Merlin – Page 26 D4 – 14-mile route Popular river for rafters, drift boaters and kayakers. 84 miles designated National Wild and Scenic River. Surrounded by towering cliffs, canyons and heavily wooded forest. Many rapids, riffles and falls. Some mandatory scouting and portaging. Jet boat traffic—use caution. Float permits required for section between Grave Creek and Watson Creek during summer months. Popular trip: Through Hellgate Recreation Section from Hog Creek Landing to Grave Creek. Some Class I–II rapids. For more information contact:

Bureau of Land Management, 3040 Biddle Road, Medford, OR 97504.

SANDY RIVER – Bull Run – Page 61 A6 – 6-mile route National Wild and Scenic River with headwaters on Mt. Hood and terminus at Columbia River. Portions suitable for kayak, raft or whitewater canoe. Some Class III–IV sections. Flow dependent on precipitation. Suggested trip for intermediate rafters: Put-in at Dodge Park access, take-out at Oxbow County Park. Boulder gardens—use caution. Route through scenic forested gorge.

SIUSLAW RIVER – Austa – Page 40 A3 – 17-mile route Located in central coast area, with terminus at Pacific Ocean near Florence. Mosaic vegetative cover—new, old and clearcut areas. Trout, steelhead and salmon fishing. Flatwater popular with drift boaters. Suggested canoe or drift boat trip: Put-in at Whittaker Creek Recreation Area south of Austa, take-out at Swisshome access. Additional access points along route.

SNAKE RIVER – Hells Canyon National Recreation Area – Page 88 C2 – 32-mile route Challenging whitewater for rafters, kayakers, drift boaters and whitewater canoeists. Many rapids up to Class V. Scenic area within Hells Canyon *(see Unique Natural Features)*. National Wild and Scenic River. Permit required during summer season. Jet boat traffic. Numerous landing sites with facilities along river. Popular raft/kayak trip from Hells Canyon Creek Recreation Site to Pittsburg Landing. For more information contact: Hells Canyon National Recreation Area, 88401 Highway 82, Enterprise, OR 97828.

UPPER DESCHUTES RIVER – 11 mi. S of Bend – Page 45 A5 – 2-mile route Short, scenic canoe trip between two Class VI waterfalls within Deschutes National Forest. Flat, slow water meanders through ponderosa pine forest. Good wildlife viewing area with possible sightings of elk, deer and eagles. Best paddled in spring or fall. Put-in at Slough Camp Campground, take-out at Dillon Falls Campground.

UPPER KLAMATH CANOE TRAIL – Upper Klamath National Wildlife Refuge – Page 21 A8 – 6-mile route Route traverses small segment of refuge marsh. Variety of wildlife includes white pelican, sandhill crane, bald eagle, river otter and beaver. Loop route begins at Rocky Point, heading north on Recreation Creek. At junction, head south on Crystal Creek to Pelican Bay, back to beginning.

WALLOWA–GRANDE RONDE RIVER – Minam – Page 87 B6 – 38-mile route Portions appropriate for canoeists, rafters or kayakers. Scenic route through canyonlands, passing forest and grasslands. Suggested novice raft trip: Put-in on Wallowa River at Minam State Recreation Area, continuing north to junction with Grande Ronde River; take-out at Mud Creek access site. Many riffles and rapids up to Class III.

WARNER WETLANDS – 34 mi. N of Adel – Page 73 B6 – 8-mile route Series of interconnected lakes and channels within Warner Valley desert area suitable for canoeists. Cyclical drainage—adequate water levels in lakes and channels will be followed by several years of drought. When abundant levels prevail, complex channel system offers up to 300 miles of routes. Abundant wildlife including raptors, waterfowl and bighorn sheep. Bordered on east by mountain ridge including Hart Mountain (7,648 feet/2,331 meters). Suggested canoe route: Winding channel between Turpin and Campbell lakes.

WHITE RIVER – Mt. Hood National Forest – Page 62 C4 – 18-mile route Scenic river running from Mt. Hood to confluence with Deschutes River, passing through both canyonlands and flatland. Drops and frequent log jams. Flow dependent on snowmelt. Suggested Class III–IV day trip: Put-in at Barlow Crossing Campground, take-out at Victor Road bridge.

WILLAMETTE RIVER – Springfield – Page 47 D8 – 10-mile route Popular river for boating because of proximity to large metropolitan centers including Eugene, Salem and Portland. Tends to be slow-moving, with some riffles and rapids, good for canoeists. Suggested day trip through Eugene–Springfield: Put-in at Island Park access, take-out at Whitely Landing County Park. Some rapids—I-5 rapids can be portaged or maneuvered around.

WILSON RIVER – Lees Camp – Page 64 D4 – 8-mile route Coast range stream flowing into Tillamook Bay. Noted for steelhead and salmon fishing with drift boaters. Flow dependent on rain—can increase from Class II–IV depending on runoff. Rapids and drops. Suggested day trip: Put-in at Jones Creek Recreation Site in Tillamook State Forest, take-out at Milepost 15.

Bicycle Routes

Many of the trips listed here are in parks and forests—see Parks/Forests/Wilderness Areas.

TOURING

CHAMPOEG BIKE PATH – Champoeg State Heritage Area – Page 60 B1 – 3.5-mile route Bike path follows Willamette River, connecting Champoeg State Heritage Area with Butteville. Passes through both forest and field.

CORVALLIS–PHILOMATH BIKE PATH – Corvallis – Page 53 D6 – 6-mile route Developed bike path runs along Willamette River, Mary's River, then continues west to Philomath. Begin in downtown Corvallis at 2nd Street and Tyler Avenue and follow south along river.

EUGENE BIKE PATH – Eugene – Page 47 D8 – distances vary Bike path runs 11.25 miles along Willamette River on both banks. Bridges connect banks in five places. Possible to travel from Valley River Center to Springfield on north bank and from River Road to University of Oregon campus on south bank. Suggested route: Start in Eugene at Baker Park and follow path east to Island Park in Springfield.

FORT STEVENS BICYCLE TRAILS – Fort Stevens State Park – Page 70 C2 – distances vary 8 miles of paved paths wind through historic areas, rain forest and near beach. Easy terrain. Several access points. *(See Historic Sites/Museums.)*

THE GREENWAY – Central Point – Page 20 B1 – 26-mile route Paved bike path goes from Central Point to 3 miles north of Ashland, passing through several parks. Parallel to Interstate 5, path runs partly on old State Route 99. Starts at Railroad Park.

LOLO PASS LOOP – Mt. Hood National Forest – Page 62 B1 – 22-mile loop Views of Mt. Hood. 2,000-foot elevation gain. ROUTE: Begin at Zigzag Ranger Station • Take U.S. Route 26 one block • Right on Forest Route 18/Lolo Pass Road • After 4 miles, right on NFD 1825 • After 1 mile, left on NFD 1828 • At Lolo Pass Road, left and follow back to Ranger Station.

MARINE DRIVE TRAIL – Portland – Page 66 D4 – 12-mile route 12-foot-wide paved trail parallels Marine Drive and Columbia River. Views of Mt. Hood, Government Island and river landscape. Route connects M. James Gleason boat ramp with Blue Lake Park and Troutdale.

MINTO–BROWNS ISLAND BIKEWAY – Salem – Page 53 A8 – 5-mile route Path loops around Minto Island and through Browns Island. Begin route in Salem at intersection of River and Minto Island roads. All of ride within Minto–Browns Island Park except for short jog on Homestead Road.

OREGON COAST BIKE ROUTE – Astoria – Page 70 C3 – 370-mile route Signed, scenic route along coast comprises Oregon's portion of 1,830-mile Pacific Coast Bicycle Route, which begins in Vancouver, British Columbia, and ends in Imperial Beach, California. Follow U.S. Route 101 and smaller side roads along coast through Cannon Beach, Tillamook, Lincoln City, Newport, Florence, North Bend, Gold Beach, Brookings to California border. Two side loops offer additional views of lighthouses, wildlife and monoliths. For more information about Pacific Coast Bicycle Route contact: Adventure Cycling Association, P.O. Box 8308, Missoula, MT 59807.

SAUVIE ISLAND LOOP – 12 mi. N of Portland – Page 66 C2 – 12-mile loop Popular, scenic route through rural area with flat terrain. Island at mouth of Willamette River. ROUTE: Begin at east end of Sauvie Island Bridge. Follow Gillihan Loop Road north • South on Reeder Road • Left on Sauvie Island Road back to bridge.

SHEVLIN–TUMALO LOOP – Bend – Page 51 D6 – 14-mile loop Loop through two parks. Moderate hills. ROUTE: Begin in downtown Bend heading west on Newport Avenue • Continue on Shevlin Park Market Road to Johnson Road • Cross Deschutes River into Tumalo State Park • Climb hill and follow O.B. Riley Road to end • Right on State Route 97 • Follow signs back to downtown.

TRANSAMERICA BICYCLE TRAIL – Astoria – Page 70 C3 – 625-mile route Trail begins in Astoria and ends in York, Virginia, covering 4,300 miles. ROUTE: Follow U.S. Route 101 almost to Lincoln City • Head inland on State Route 18 • South on State Route 22 • Trail continues through Eugene, Sisters, John Day, Baker, Half.com (Halfway), into Idaho and on to Virginia. For more information contact: Adventure Cycling Association, P.O. Box 8308, Missoula, MT 59807.

WILLAMETTE VALLEY BICYCLE LOOP – 7 mi. N of Eugene – Page 47 D7 – 195-mile loop Loop winds through some of Willamette Valley's most scenic areas, skirting river. ROUTE: Begin at Mahlon Sweet Airport • North through Junction City, Corvallis, Salem and Wheatland • Then south back through Salem, to Albany, and Eugene.

MOUNTAIN BIKING

COPPLE BUTTE TRAIL – Umatilla National Forest – Page 85 D7 – 6-mile route Trail #3052. Good views of three buttes. 180-foot elevation gain. Trail mostly follows ridgetop. Trailhead at wooden gate on Porcupine Ridge Road. Ends at Madison Butte.

CRATER LAKE RIM LOOP – Crater Lake National Park – Page 29 A7 – 33-mile loop Narrow road with no shoulder circling Crater Lake, subject to tourist traffic. Part one-way. Begin at Rim Village. Possible side trip on dirt road: 8-mile Grayback Motor Nature Road, one-way. *(See Scenic Drives and Unique Natural Features.)*

CRESCENT LAKE LOOP – Deschutes National Forest – Page 44 D1 – 14-mile loop Easy ride around Crescent Lake with 250-foot elevation gain. ROUTE: Begin at Crescent Lake Snowpark (junction of Forest Route 60 and NFD 6015) • West on paved Forest Route 60 to Tandy Bay • Next 9 miles gravel to NFD 6015 • Left on NFD 6015 to complete loop.

DIAMOND LAKE BICYCLE PATH – Umpqua National Forest – Page 37 C7 – 11-mile route Paved and gravel route winds around scenic Diamond Lake. Begin route across from Visitor Center at Diamond Lake Campground. Information on path available at Visitor Center.

GREEN RIDGE TRAIL – Deschutes National Forest – Page 56 D4 – 30-mile route Ridgetop riding, with views of Cascade Mountain Range. Moderate to difficult. Elevation gain 1,700 feet. To reach trailhead take U.S. Route 20 to Forest Route 14 north and follow to NFD 1490. Park at Pioneer Ford Campground. ROUTE: Climb up NFD 1490, 5 miles • Take NFD 1140 south, following signs to Green Ridge Lookout • South from lookout on NFD 600 • Follow yellow diamonds on north side of trail • Trail ends at road leading to Riverside Campground on Forest Route 14 • Follow Metolius River downstream on Forest Route 14 back to car.

GUANO CREEK LOOP – Hart Mountain National Antelope Refuge – Page 73 B6 – 23-mile loop Good views of refuge wildlife habitats. ROUTE: Begin at Hot Springs Campground • North 2.8 miles • Right to begin gradual climb • Continue south passing Robinson Draw and Deer Creek • Road swings to west, entering Guano Creek Valley, continuing along Upper Guano Creek, back to campground.

LEIF ERIKSON DRIVE – Portland – Page 66 D3 – 11-mile route Closed to motor vehicles, partially paved road runs length of Forest Park. Views of downtown Portland, Willamette River, Columbia River and Mt. Hood. Begin route at locked gate at western end of Thurman Street in northwest Portland. Ends at Germantown Road southwest of St. John's Bridge.

LITHIA LOOP – Ashland – Page 20 C3 – 28-mile loop Popular ride looping through Rogue River National Forest, starting and ending in Lithia Park. Steep 6-mile uphill in beginning, steep 7-mile descent at end. Strenuous. Elevation gain 3,000 feet. ROUTE: Follow Ashland Creek south on Granite Street for about 1 mile • At fork, left onto Glenview Drive for 0.5 mile to Ashland Loop Road/NFD 2060 • Follow for about 25 miles back to Granite Street and Lithia Park.

LOWER ROGUE RIVER TRAIL – Siskiyou National Forest – Page 17 A3 – 35-mile route Trail #1168. Remnant of 19th-century road linking area to inland Rogue River Valley. To reach trailhead follow Jerrys Flat Road from Gold Beach. After crossing Lobster Creek Bridge, turn right onto NFD 3533. After 5 miles turn right onto NFD 340 ending at trailhead. ROUTE: Follow trail to Agness • Return same trail or on South Bank Road.

NEWBERRY CRATER RIM LOOP – Deschutes National Forest – Page 45 C6 – 14-mile loop Loop around Newberry Crater *(see Unique Natural Features)*. Steep hills. Strenuous ride. ROUTE: Begin loop at Paulina Lake Lodge and follow Trail 57 around crater • Trail goes north along western rim of Paulina Lake • At fork take either Trail 57 or 58 • Trail 58 easier and shorter • On Trail 57 just southeast of North Paulina Peak, take right fork.

RYE SPUR TRAIL – Winema National Forest – Page 21 A7 – 10-mile route Trail #3771. Views of Upper Klamath Lake and Pelican Butte. Scenic rock outcroppings. Moderate difficulty. Elevation gain 750 feet. Trail begins at Milepost 36 along State Route 140 northwest of Klamath Falls (trail access unmarked on north side of highway).

SALT CREEK SUMMIT LOOP – Joseph – Page 87 C8 – 50-mile loop Contrasting route along paved and dirt roads, through grassland, streams and forest. Little traffic. ROUTE: Head east on State Route 350 towards Imnaha • After 8 miles, right onto Forest Route 39 south along Little Sheep Creek • Follow to Salt Creek Summit • Right onto NFD 3920 • Continue north out of hills until State Route 350 • Turn west for last 5 miles back to Joseph.

STEENS MOUNTAIN LOOP – Frenchglen – Page 74 A1 – 64-mile loop Strenuous ride through scenic, high-mountain area. Washboard, gravel roads. ROUTE: Begin and end at either Page Springs Campground or Frenchglen Hotel • Ride east past Fish Lake near top of Mountain • Continue past Whorehouse Meadows and Jackman Park to Kiger Gorge • Continue past East Rim Viewpoint and downhill to Blitzen Crossing • Follow road to State Route 205, taking right on pavement back to Frenchglen. *(See Scenic Drives and Unique Natural Features.)*

Hiking

Oregon offers numerous trails to the hiker, from short paths to long, involved climbs. Diverse topography provides ocean, mountain and desert scenery throughout various state and federal lands (see Parks/Forests/Wilderness Areas). Check with the appropriate agency to obtain trail guides and additional information.

CAPE PERPETUA TRAILS – Siuslaw National Forest – Page 32 B2 – 22-mile network Series of trails through wooded areas, open meadows and along ocean. Most offer scenic ocean overlooks. Some paved trails. Varying difficulties. Trailhead and trail map available at Cape Perpetua Visitor Center.

CHERRY CREEK TRAIL – Winema National Forest – Page 29 D8 – 5.3-mile route Trail #3708. Strenuous climb leading to Sky Lakes Area within Sky Lakes Wilderness. Path follows Cherry Creek drainage. Passes through Cherry Creek Natural Research Area. Outstanding scenery. Trailhead at end of Forest Route 3450.

CLEETWOOD TRAIL – Crater Lake National Park – Page 29 A8 – 1-mile route Strenuous trail leading down to only access to Crater Lake. Steep path descends 760 feet in elevation to Cleetwood Cove, where boat service is available to Wizard Island. Island trail to summit cone crater. Trailhead located along Rim Drive (see *Unique Natural Features, Scenic Drives and Bicycle Routes—Mountain Biking*).

CRANE MOUNTAIN TRAIL – Fremont National Forest – Page 72 D4 – 9-mile route Trail #106. Begins near summit of Crane Mountain (8,456 feet/2,577 meters). Rugged trail follows ridgeline offering scenic viewpoints of surrounding forest lands. Ends 1 mile across border in California's Modoc National Forest (see *DeLorme's Northern California Atlas & Gazetteer*). Strenuous. National Recreation Trail. Trailhead near end of Forest Road 015, continuation of Forest Route 4011.

EAGLE CREEK TRAIL – Mt. Hood National Forest – Page 68 C1 – 13-mile route Trail #440. Within Colombia River Gorge National Scenic Area. Trail follows high cliffs along Eagle Creek passing waterfalls, scenic viewpoints and seasonal wildflower displays. Trail ends at Wahtum Lake and connection with Pacific Crest National Scenic Trail (see *this section*). Trailhead at end of Forest Road 241 next to Eagle Creek Campground.

40-MILE LOOP – Portland – Page 66 D3 – 65-mile network Series of singular and multiuse trails connecting 35 state, city and county parks in and around Portland. Originally intended as 40-mile trail circling city, presently planned to form trail network 140 miles long when complete, for hikers, bikers and canoeists. Trailhead near World Forestry Center (see *Historic Sites/Museums*) in Washington Park. For more information contact: City of Portland, Parks and Recreation, 1120 SW 5th Avenue, Suite 1302, Portland, OR 97204.

GARFIELD PEAK TRAIL – Crater Lake National Park – Page 29 A7 – 1.7-mile route Trail to summit of 8,054-foot (2,455-meter) Garfield Peak. Outstanding views of Crater Lake (see *Unique Natural Features*) and surrounding area. Wildflower displays. Good vantage point for viewing hawks and eagles. Moderately strenuous. Trailhead east of Crater Lake Lodge.

HUMBUG MOUNTAIN TRAIL – Humbug Mountain State Park – Page 25 C5 – 3-mile route Winding trail up side of mountain offers view of Coast Range Mountains. Summit overlooks southern Oregon coast and, on clear day, California. Wildflowers. Moderately strenuous trail. Trailhead at parking area off U.S. Route 101.

LARCH MOUNTAIN TRAIL – Mt. Hood National Forest – Page 67 D8 – 6.8-mile route Trail #441. Within Columbia River Gorge National Scenic Area. Trail to summit of Larch Mountain (4,056 feet/1,236 meters). Passes several waterfalls including Multnomah Falls (see *Unique Natural Features*). Mountaintop offers panoramic views of Columbia River Gorge and Mt. Hood. Trailhead at Multnomah Falls Lodge.

LAVA CAST FOREST – Deschutes National Forest – Page 45 B6 – 1-mile route Interpretive trail through volcanic landscape illustrates natural reclamation from volcanic eruption more than 6,000 years ago (see *Unique Natural Features*). Flat-surfaced path. Detailed trail guide available.

LOST CREEK TRAIL – Mt. Hood National Forest – Page 62 A2 – 0.5 mile-route Trail #776. Handicapped-accessible, paved trail offering views of Mt. Hood. Passes old beaver pond. Wilderness setting. Trailhead at Lost Creek Picnic Area.

McCLELLAN MOUNTAIN TRAIL - Malheur National Forest - Page 81 C8 - 10-mile route Trail #216. Travels through open, high-mountain country. Many scenic views. Semiprimitive area. Big game wildlife. Within Aldrich Mountains. Strenuous. Connect to trail via Riley Creek Trail (#216A), at end of Forest Route 2190.

McDONALD STATE FOREST TRAILS – Lewisburg – Page 53 C7 – 8-mile route Six trails located within one of Oregon State University's Research forests. Interpretive trails illustrate various aspects of forest management, ecology and research. Highlights include Peavy Arboretum, views of Cascade Mountain Range and coastal mountains, and historic powder house site. Trails vary from 0.5 to 3 miles. Trailhead for most trails located at Peavy Arboretum.

MIRROR LAKE TRAIL – Mt. Hood National Forest – Page 62 B2 – 4-mile route Trail #664. Popular trail leading to Mirror Lake and 5,066-foot (1,544-meter) Tom, Dick and Harry Mountain. Views of Mt. Hood and Mt. Hood Corridor. Easy day hike. Trailhead located at parking area on south side of U.S. Route 26, 1 mile west of Government Camp.

MT. McLOUGHLIN TRAIL – Winema/Rogue River National Forests – Page 21 A6 – 5-mile route Trail #3716. Winding trail leading to summit of 9,495-foot (2,894-meter) Mt. McLoughlin. Follows portion of Pacific Crest National Scenic Trail (see *this section*). Trail sometimes difficult to see and follow. Rocky terrain. Very strenuous. Trailhead off Forest Route 3650, south of Fourmile Lake.

MT. SCOTT TRAIL – Crater Lake National Park – Page 29 A8 – 2.5-mile route Trail leading to 8,929-foot (2,722-meter) summit of Mt. Scott (highest point in park). Fire lookout tower at peak. Panoramic views of region. Strenuous. Trailhead at parking area off Rim Drive (see *Scenic Drives and Bicycle Routes—Mountain Biking*) near Cloudcap Junction.

MT. THIELSEN TRAIL – Umpqua National Forest – Page 37 C8 – 4-mile route Trail #1456. Leads to 9,182-foot (2,799-meter) Mt. Thielsen (see *Unique Natural Feaures*). Trail begins as wooded path, becoming loose, rocky slope. Outstanding views of Cascade Mountain Range. Optional technical climb to summit pinnacle. Strenuous. Trailhead on east side of State Route 138, north of intersection with State Route 230 near Diamond Lake.

NEE-ME-POO TRAIL – Hells Canyon National Recreation Area – Page 88 A2 – 5-mile route Trail #1721. Difficult trail following historic route of Nez Perce tribe led by Chief Joseph during forced exodus of 1877. Traverses Lone Pine Saddle and Big Canyon before ending on bank of Snake River at Dug Bar. Trailhead located off Forest Road 4260 approximately 15 miles north of Imnaha. National Recreation Trail.

NORTH UMPQUA TRAIL – Umpqua National Forest – Page 37 B7 – 77-mile route Multiuse trail paralleling North Umpqua River. Passes through Boulder Creek and Mt. Thielsen wilderness areas and Oregon Cascades Recreation Area. Numerous access points and recreation sites along route. Good fishing. For more information contact: Umpqua National Forest, 2900 NW Stewart Parkway, Roseburg, OR 97470.

OLD WILSON RIVER WAGON ROAD – Tillamook State Forest – Page 65 D5 – 9-mile route Route begins by following former toll road opened in 1893. Path then leads to University Falls and on to Camp Brown; alternate can lead to Wilson River Highway/State Route 6 and Rogers Camp. Easy trail. Trailhead at Elk Creek Park Campground. For more information contact: Tillamook District Office, 5005 E Third Street, Tillamook, OR 97141.

OREGON COAST TRAIL – Hammond – Page 70 C1 – 360-mile route Hiking trail hugs coastline from Columbia River south to California border. Follows both beach and inland routes, sometimes along U.S. Route 101. Passes many state parks, waysides and points of interest. Signed with tall cedar trail markers. Trailhead at south jetty of Columbia River, north of Fort Stevens State Park. For more information contact: Oregon Parks and Recreation Department, 725 Summer Street NE, Suite C, Salem, OR 97301-1271.

OREGON DESERT TRAIL – 18 mi. S of Fields – Page 74 D2 – 150-mile route Oregon section of proposed National Scenic Desert Trail to extend from Canada to Mexico when complete. Located in southeastern section of state, trail presently extends from Nevada border, through Pueblo Mountains, Steens Mountain and Diamond Craters (see *Unique Natural Features*) to State Route 78. No constructed trailbed—marked by rock cairns along former roads, animal paths and pack trails. For more information contact: Desert Trail Association, P.O. Box 34, Madras, OR 97741.

PACIFIC CREST NATIONAL SCENIC TRAIL – Cascade Locks – Page 68 C1 – 441-mile route Trail #2000. High-mountain trail extending from Canada to Mexico, totaling 2,638 miles. Within Oregon, trail follows Cascade Mountain Range, traversing numerous national forests, wilderness areas and Crater Lake National Park. Open to hikers and equestrians. *(Trail marked in this Atlas, see Legend for symbol.)* For more information contact: Pacific Crest Trail Association, 5325 Elkhorn Boulevard, PMB #256, Sacramento, CA 95842-2526.

RIM ROCK SPRINGS TRAIL – Ochoco National Forest – Page 51 A8 – 1.3-mile route Trail #850. Interpretive trail within Crooked River National Grassland. Crosses flat terrain through high-desert environments. Viewing decks overlook rock formations and riparian areas. Wildlife. Within Rim Rock Springs Wildlife Management Area, 18 miles northwest of Prineville.

ROGUE RIVER TRAIL – Rand – Page 26 C4 – 40-mile route Follows north bank of Rogue River, officially designated National Wild and Scenic River. Passes many historic and unique areas including former mining sites, waterfalls and geologic features. Wildlife sightings. Strenuous. Trailhead at Grave Creek boat landing near confluence of Grave Creek and Rogue River. Ends at Foster Bar boat landing. For more information contact: Siskiyou National Forest, P.O. Box 440, Grants Pass, OR 97526.

SADDLE MOUNTAIN TRAIL – Saddle Mountain State Natural Area – Page 64 A3 – 2.5-mile route Route leads to summit of 3,283-foot (1,001-meter) Saddle Mountain with views of Cascade Mountain Range, Columbia River and Pacific Ocean. Strenuous trail traverses forest, meadow and rock ledges. Nearing summit, some areas steep and treacherous. Many species of wildflowers, some unique to area. Trailhead near parking lot.

SILVER CREEK CANYON TRAIL – Silver Falls State Park – Page 54 A3 – 7-mile route Route through scenic canyon, passing 10 waterfalls ranging from 27 to 178 feet. Trail leads behind several falls. Additional shorter loops and trails. Some portions paved and handicapped-accessible. Trailhead at South Falls near parking area.

SQUAW ROCK TRAIL – Malheur National Forest – Page 82 A2 – 11-mile route Forest Trail #251. Travels through heart of Vinegar Hill–Indian Rock Scenic Area offering scenic vistas of North Fork John Day and Strawberry Mountain wilderness areas. Alpine wildflowers. Remnants of former mining operations. Moderately strenuous. Trailhead on Forest Route 45 just south of Umatilla National Forest border. Trail ends at Dupratt Springs.

TAHKENITCH DUNES/THREEMILE LAKE LOOP – Oregon Dunes National Recreation Area – Page 32 B3 – 6.5-mile loop Separate trails begin together, then split. Tahkenitch Dunes Trail heads west, traveling through conifer forest and open dunes, ending on beach near confluence of Tahkenitch Creek and ocean. Threemile Lake Trail travels south through forest to lake located next to beach. Trails connect and become loop by hiking section of beach in between. Trailhead located at Tahkenitch Campground parking area.

TIMBERLINE TRAIL – Mt. Hood National Forest – Page 62 B3 – 40-mile route Trail #600. Route encircles Mt. Hood (see *Unique Natural Features*) providing outstanding views of mountain and meadows. Primarily within Mt. Hood Wilderness. Shares path with Pacific Crest National Scenic Trail (see *this section*) on south and west sides of mountain. Passes waterfalls, glaciers and wildflowers. Many stream crossings. Numerous trail junctions provide additional accesses. Trailhead located 200 yards north of Timberline Lodge (see *Historic Sites/Museums*).

TOKETEE FALLS TRAIL – Umpqua National Forest – Page 37 B5 – 0.4-mile route Trail #1495. Easy trail follows North Umpqua River through old-growth forest to falls. Double falls flows through basalt columns, dropping 40 feet, then 80, into river canyon below. Viewing platform. Trailhead at end of Forest Road 34 off State Route 138.

TRYON CREEK STATE NATURAL AREA – Portland – Page 60 A3 – 8-mile network Trail system with routes of varying lengths, ranging from approximately 0.25 to 2 miles. Explores Tryon Creek Canyon, area formerly logged in 1880s to provide fuel for nearby iron smelter. Three Nature Center trails provide views of canyon, while others lead down into it. Trail access begins at park entrance. Trail guide available at Nature House.

TWIN PILLARS TRAIL – Ochoco National Forest – Page 80 B2 – 10-mile route Trail #832. Scenic trail traversing Mill Creek Wilderness. Route begins in meadow, leading to dense stands of lodgepole pine. Passes Twin Pillars (see *Unique Natural Features*). Trail continues through large ponderosa pine stands, then follows East Fork Mill Creek, ending at Wildcat Campground. Trailhead at Bingham Prairie, off Forest Road 27.

Hunting

This chart includes all state and federal hunting areas. Information on hunting, including rules, regulations and boundaries, may be obtained from any of the Oregon Department of Fish & Wildlife offices listed below.

STATE HUNTING AREAS

	Pronghorn	Black-Tailed Deer	Mule Deer	White-Tailed Deer	Elk	Bighorn Sheep	Black Bear	Cougar	Rabbit	Turkey	Forest Grouse	Sage Grouse	Partridge	Pheasant	Quail	Dove	Pigeon	Waterfowl	Page Location
Alsea Unit 18		•			•		•	•	•	•	•			•	•	•	•	•	32, 46–47, 52–53
Applegate Unit 28		•			•		•	•	•	•	•			•	•	•	•	•	18–20
Beatys Butte Unit 70	•		•		•	•	•	•	•		•	•	•	•	•			•	73–74
Beulah Unit 65 (including Snake River Island WMA)	•		•	•	•	•	•	•	•	•	•		•	•	•			•	78–79, 82–83
Biggs Unit 43 (including Lower Deschutes WMA)	•		•	•	•	•	•	•	•	•			•	•	•			•	63, 69, 80, 84
Catherine Creek Unit 58		•	•	•	•		•	•	•	•	•		•	•	•			•	83, 86–87
Chesnimus Unit 58		•	•	•	•	•	•	•	•	•	•		•	•	•			•	87–88
Chetco Unit 27		•			•		•	•	•		•			•	•	•	•	•	17–18, 25–26
Columbia Basin Unit 44 (including Irrigon and Willow Creek WMA's)		•	•	•	•		•	•	•	•			•	•	•			•	84–86
Desolation Unit 50		•	•	•	•		•	•	•	•	•		•	•	•			•	82
Dixon Unit 22		•			•		•	•	•	•	•			•	•	•	•	•	28–29, 36–37
Evans Creek Unit 29 (including Denman WMA)		•			•		•	•	•		•			•	•	•	•	•	18–20, 26–28
Fort Rock Unit 77	•		•		•		•	•	•		•	•	•	•	•			•	30, 37–39, 43
Fossil Unit 45		•	•		•		•	•	•	•	•		•	•	•			•	80–81, 84–85
Grizzly Unit 38 (including Rimrock Springs WMA)	•	•	•		•		•	•	•	•	•		•	•	•			•	51, 57, 80
Heppner Unit 48		•	•		•		•	•	•	•	•		•	•	•			•	81, 85
Hood Unit 42	•	•	•		•		•	•	•	•	•		•	•	•	•	•	•	62, 68
Imnaha Unit 61		•	•	•	•	•	•	•	•	•	•		•	•	•			•	87–88
Indigo Unit 21		•			•		•	•	•	•	•			•	•	•	•	•	35–37, 41–43
Interstate Unit 75	•		•		•	•	•	•	•		•	•	•	•	•			•	23, 31, 72
Juniper Unit 71	•		•		•		•	•	•		•	•	•	•	•			•	73, 77
Keating Unit 63	•		•		•		•	•	•	•	•		•	•	•			•	83, 87
Keno Unit 31 (including Klamath WMA)		•	•		•		•	•	•	•	•		•	•	•			•	21–22, 29–30
Klamath Falls Unit 32		•	•		•		•	•	•	•	•		•	•	•			•	22–23, 30
Lookout Mountain Unit 64	•		•		•		•	•	•	•	•	•	•	•	•			•	83
Malheur River Unit 66	•		•	•	•	•	•	•	•	•	•		•	•	•			•	78–79, 82
Maupin Unit 40	•		•		•		•	•	•	•	•		•	•	•			•	57, 63, 80, 84
Maury Unit 36	•		•		•		•	•	•	•	•		•	•	•			•	76–77, 80–81
McKenzie Unit 19		•	•		•		•	•	•	•	•			•	•	•	•	•	42–44, 47–49, 54
Melrose Unit 23		•			•		•	•	•		•		•	•	•	•	•	•	26–27, 34–35, 40–41
Metolius Unit 39		•	•		•		•	•	•	•	•		•	•	•			•	50–51, 56–57
Minam Unit 60		•	•	•	•		•	•	•	•	•		•	•	•			•	87
Mt. Emily Unit 54		•	•	•	•		•	•	•	•	•		•	•	•			•	86
Murderers Creek Unit 45 (including Murderers Creek WMA)	•		•	•	•	•	•	•	•	•	•		•	•	•			•	77, 81–82
Northside Unit 47		•	•		•		•	•	•	•	•		•	•	•			•	81–82
Ochoco Unit 37	•		•		•		•	•	•	•	•		•	•	•			•	80–81
Owyhee Unit 67	•		•		•		•	•	•	•	•	•	•	•	•			•	75, 79
Paulina Unit 35	•		•		•		•	•	•	•	•		•	•	•			•	39, 44–45, 76
Pine Creek Unit 62		•	•	•	•		•	•	•	•	•		•	•	•			•	83, 87–88
Powers Unit 26		•			•		•	•	•		•			•	•	•	•	•	25–27, 33–34
Rogue Unit 30		•			•		•	•	•	•	•			•	•	•	•	•	20–21, 28–29
Saddle Mountain Unit 12 (including Jewell WMA)		•			•		•	•	•		•			•	•	•	•	•	64–65, 70–71
Santiam Unit 16		•			•		•	•	•	•	•			•	•	•	•	•	48–50, 54–56, 60–62, 67–68
Scappoose Unit 11 (including Sauvie Island WMA)		•			•		•	•	•		•			•	•	•	•	•	65–66, 71
Silver Lake Unit 76	•		•		•		•	•	•	•	•		•	•	•			•	31, 39, 72, 76
Silvies Unit 72	•		•		•		•	•	•	•	•	•	•	•	•			•	76–77, 81
Siuslaw Unit 20		•			•		•	•	•		•			•	•	•	•	•	32, 40–41, 46–47
Sixes Unit 25		•			•		•	•	•		•			•	•	•	•	•	24–25, 33
Sled Springs Unit 57		•	•	•	•		•	•	•	•	•		•	•	•			•	87–88
Snake River Unit 59		•	•	•	•		•	•	•	•	•		•	•	•			•	88
Sprague Unit 33		•	•		•		•	•	•	•	•		•	•	•			•	23, 29–31
Starkey Unit 52 (including Ladd Marsh and Elkhorn WMA's)		•	•	•	•		•	•	•	•	•		•	•	•			•	82, 86
Steens Mountain Unit 69	•		•		•	•	•	•	•	•	•		•	•	•			•	73–74, 77–78
Stott Mountain Unit 17		•			•		•	•	•		•			•	•	•	•	•	52–53, 58–59
Sumpter Unit 51 (including Elkhorn WMA)	•		•		•		•	•	•	•	•		•	•	•			•	82–83
Tioga Unit 24		•			•		•	•	•		•			•	•	•	•	•	32–34, 40
Trask Unit 14		•			•		•	•	•		•			•	•	•	•	•	58–59, 64–65
Ukiah Unit 49 (including Bridge Creek WMA)		•	•	•	•		•	•	•	•	•		•	•	•			•	82, 86
Upper Deschutes Unit 34		•	•		•		•	•	•	•	•		•	•	•			•	38, 43–45, 50–51
Wagontire Unit 73 (including Summer Lake WMA)	•		•		•		•	•	•	•	•		•	•	•			•	72, 76–77
Walla Walla Unit 55		•	•	•	•		•	•	•	•	•		•	•	•			•	86
Warner Unit 74	•		•		•		•	•	•	•	•		•	•	•			•	72–73
Wenaha Unit 56 (including Wenaha WMA)		•	•	•	•	•	•	•	•	•	•		•	•	•			•	86–87
White River Unit 41 (including White River WMA)	•		•		•		•	•	•	•	•		•	•	•			•	62–63, 69
Whitehorse Unit 68	•		•		•		•	•	•	•	•		•	•	•			•	74–75, 78
Willamette Unit 15 (including E.E. Wilson and Fern Ridge WMA's)		•			•		•	•	•	•	•			•	•	•	•	•	47, 53–54, 59–61, 65–66
Wilson Unit 12		•			•		•	•	•		•			•	•	•	•	•	52, 58–59, 64

NATIONAL WILDLIFE REFUGES

	Pronghorn	Black-Tailed Deer	Mule Deer	White-Tailed Deer	Elk	Bighorn Sheep	Black Bear	Cougar	Rabbit	Turkey	Forest Grouse	Sage Grouse	Partridge	Pheasant	Quail	Dove	Pigeon	Waterfowl	Page Location
Ankeny NWR																•	•		53
Bandon Marsh NWR																•	•	•	33
Bear Valley NWR			•																22
Cold Springs NWR								•					•	•	•			•	85
Deer Flat NWR			•																88
Hart Mountain National Antelope Refuge	•	•			•						•			•					73
Klamath Forest NWR																		•	30
Lewis and Clark NWR																		•	70–71
Lower Klamath NWR																	•		22
Malheur NWR	•		•					•					•	•	•	•			74, 78
McKay Creek NWR																		•	86
Sheldon NWR	•		•									•	•		•				73
Umatilla NWR								•					•	•	•			•	85
Upper Klamath NWR																		•	29
Wm. L. Finley NWR		•														•	•		47

OREGON DEPARTMENT OF FISH & WILDLIFE OFFICES

Headquarters, 3406 Cherry Avenue NE, Salem 97303, (503) 947-6000 .... Page 53 A8
High Desert Region (Central & Southeast Oregon), 61374 Parrell Road, Bend 97702, (541) 388-6363 ... Page 51 D6
Marine Resources Program, 2040 SE Marine Science Drive, Newport 97365, (541) 867-4741 .. Page 32 D1
Northeast Region, 107 20th Street, La Grande 97850, (541) 963-2138 .... Page 86 C4
Northwest Region, 17330 SE Evelyn Street, Clackamas 97015, (503) 657-2000 .... Page 60 A4
Southwest Region, 4192 North Umpqua Highway, Roseburg 97470, (541) 440-3353 .... Page 35 C6

Historic Sites/Museums

A.C. GILBERT'S DISCOVERY VILLAGE – Salem – Page 53 A8 Hands-on exhibits include health, shapes, math and trains. Classes.

THE AMERICAN ADVERTISING MUSEUM – Portland – Page 66 D3 One of only museums in U.S. completely dedicated to advertising history. Collection includes print, radio and television ads from 1683 to present.

ASTORIA COLUMN – Astoria – Page 70 C3 125-foot tower built in 1926, patterned after Trojan's Column in Rome. Mural spirals up outside depicting history of Northwest Territory. Scenic views of Columbia River, Mount St. Helens and Pacific Ocean from top.

BENTON COUNTY HISTORICAL MUSEUM – Philomath – Page 53 D6 Located in original Philomath College building. Exhibits include household items, quilts, dollhouses, artifacts of Kalapuya tribe, and printing and logging equipment.

BOWMAN MUSEUM – Prineville – Page 80 C1 Historical exhibits relating to Crook County. Housed in century-old stone building.

BURROWS HOUSE MUSEUM – Newport – Page 32 C1 Lincoln County history. Located in 1895 house including furnishings and clothing.

CANBY DEPOT MUSEUM – Canby – Page 60 B3 More than century old, one of oldest remaining railroad stations in Oregon. Mementoes from early area residents, pioneer homes and farms.

CAPE PERPETUA INTERPRETIVE CENTER – Yachats – Page 32 B2 Exhibits depict area history and prehistory for last 5,000 years. Artifacts and photographs of early American Indians, logging, Civilian Conservation Corps activities and U.S. Forest Service management practices.

CHAMPOEG VISITOR CENTER – Champoeg State Heritage Area – Page 60 B1 Exhibits on Champoeg, site of Oregon's first government. Displays on Kalapuya tribe, explorers, fur trappers and settlers of Willamette Valley. *(See Parks, Forests/Wilderness Areas.)*

CHILDREN'S MUSEUM – Portland – Page 66 D3 Hands-on exploration allows children to learn while having fun. Detailed exhibits investigate properties of various materials including water, fabrics and food. Classes and workshops.

COLUMBIA RIVER MARITIME MUSEUM – Astoria – Page 70 C3 Museum contains one of most complete maritime collections in Northwest. Exhibits include fishing, rescue boats, lighthouses, navigation and naval history. Self-guided tour of lightship *Columbia.*

COOS ART MUSEUM – Coos Bay – Page 33 B7 Print collection of nationally known contemporary artists. Also community-oriented exhibits.

THE CORVALLIS ARTS CENTER – Corvallis – Page 53 D6 Exhibits of national and local artists changing monthly. Guild Gallery includes pottery, photographs, furniture, marquetry and spinning.

THE CRATER ROCK MUSEUM – Central Point – Page 20 A1 Large collection of fossils, geodes, artifacts, crystals, minerals, faceted gems and petrified wood.

DES CHUTES HISTORICAL CENTER – Bend – Page 51 D6 Located in old Reid School building, on National Register of Historic Places. Exhibits include relics and artifacts of Deschutes County early history.

DOUGLAS COUNTY MUSEUM OF HISTORY AND NATURAL HISTORY – Roseburg – Page 35 C6 Exhibits of pioneer and American Indian life, as well as animals native to area including one-million-year-old saber-toothed tiger. Extensive photograph collection and 1882 Dillard Oregon and California Railroad Depot.

EAST LINN MUSEUM – Sweet Home – Page 48 A3 Pioneer museum containing artifacts, documents and photographs depicting history and life of Linn County from 1850s to early 1900s.

END OF THE OREGON TRAIL INTERPRETIVE CENTER – Oregon City – Page 60 B4 Museum interprets 2,000-mile journey undertaken by over 300,000 19th-century pioneers.

ERMATINGER HOUSE – Oregon City – Page 60 B4 One of Oregon's oldest houses, owned by chief trader for Hudson's Bay Company, Francis Ermatinger. Two-story Federal-style house, restored to include original flat roof.

FAVELL MUSEUM OF WESTERN ART AND INDIAN ARTIFACTS – Klamath Falls – Page 22 C2 American Indian artifacts from West, British Columbia and Mexico. Exhibits include over 60,000 arrowheads, basketry, pottery, carvings, bead and shell work, and miniature firearms. Contemporary Western art representing over 300 artists in various media.

FLAVEL HOUSE – Astoria – Page 70 C3 Example of Queen Anne–style architecture built in 1885 by river pilot and entrepren-eur, Captain George Flavel. Period furnishings and paintings. Carriage house.

FORT CLATSOP NATIONAL MEMORIAL – 5 mi. SW of Astoria – Page 70 C2 Winter shelter for Lewis and Clark Expedition, 1805–1806. Fort reconstructed from original plans drawn by Clark. Fort buildings, natural spring, site of original canoe landing, exhibitions and self-guided trails.

FORT DALLES MUSEUM – The Dalles – Page 69 D7 Museum details history of strategically important army post. Located in 1857 surgeon's quarters, only remaining fort building. Artifacts of early fort life including guns, saddles and furniture.

FORT STEVENS – Hammond – Page 70 C2 Constructed during Civil War. Remained active through World War II, fort attacked in 1942 by Japanese submarine. Self-guided and narrated tours. Museum includes historical displays and artifacts.

HERITAGE MUSEUM – Astoria – Page 70 C3 Located in Astoria's former city hall, exhibits include natural history, geology, American Indian artifacts, nautical history, logging and fishing. Ethnic exhibits represent heritage of 22 pioneer groups.

THE HIGH DESERT MUSEUM – 6 mi. S of Bend – Page 45 A6 Unique living museum of cultural and natural history with variety of indoor and outdoor exhibits. Nature trails, galleries, walk-through pioneer and American Indian scenes, live animals and pioneer presentations.

THE HOOVER–MINTHORN HOUSE – Newberg – Page 60 B1 Boyhood home of Herbert Hoover, 31st U.S. president. Oldest standing house in Newberg. Contains many original furnishings and memorabilia of late 1800s.

JACKSONVILLE MUSEUM OF SOUTHERN OREGON HISTORY – Jacksonville – Page 20 B1 Exhibits include Rogue River Valley railroading, pioneer potters and photographs.

JENKINS ESTATE – Beaverton – Page 60 A1 Early 1900s estate. 68 acres include original farmhouse, country farmhouse, stable, tea house, carriage house, pump house, greenhouse, water tower and English-style gardens.

KAM WAH CHUNG & CO. MUSEUM – John Day – Page 82 C1 Building built 1886–1887 as trading post, served as center for Chinese community until 1940s. Thousands of artifacts and relics illustrating structure's many uses—home, general store, temple, doctor's office and pharmacy.

KLAMATH COUNTY MUSEUM – Klamath Falls – Page 22 C2 Exhibits include area geology, history, anthropology and wildlife. Pioneer and agricultural artifacts.

LANE COUNTY HISTORICAL MUSEUM – Eugene – Page 47 D8 Displays, demonstrations and slide presentations depict county history and settlement. Logging, agriculture and occupational artifacts.

LAVA LANDS VISITOR CENTER – 10 mi. S of Bend – Page 45 A6 Exhibits centered around volcanic sites and scenic area of central Oregon. Displays include prehistoric toolmaking process, tools found locally and drawings of early American Indian life. Guided walks, slide presentations and interpretive trails.

LINN COUNTY HISTORICAL MUSEUM – Brownsville – Page 48 A1 Located in late 1880s railroad depot. Collection of pioneer artifacts. Old boxcars and caboose. Museum also includes 1881 furnished home, Moyer House.

LOG CABIN MUSEUM – Newport – Page 32 C1 Artifacts from Siletz Indian Reservation. Also logging, farming and maritime displays.

LOGGING MUSEUM AND PIONEER VILLAGE – Collier Memorial State Park – Page 30 C1 Outdoor museum depicts development of logging equipment. Various hand- and steam-powered tools, logger's homestead, blacksmith shed, donkey engines, railroad equipment and authentic pioneer cabins filled with artifacts. *(See Parks/Forests/Wilderness Areas.)*

MAUDE KERNS ART CENTER – Eugene – Page 47 D8 Museum features contemporary art and hosts national, regional and local exhibits.

McLOUGHLIN HOUSE – Oregon City – Page 60 B4 Restored 1845 home of John McLoughlin, superintendent of trade for Hudson's Bay Company. Called "Father of Oregon" for accomplishments in establishing Oregon Territory. Original and period furnishings. National Historic Site.

MISSION MILL VILLAGE – Salem – Page 53 A8 Pioneer village includes restored Thomas Kay Woolen Mill, historic houses of Methodist mission and Marion Museum of History with exhibits of American Indian canoes and photographs. Water-powered turbine still in use. Guided and self-guided tours.

MORROW COUNTY MUSEUM – Heppner – Page 85 C6 Pioneer artifacts, documents, photographs, medical equipment. American Indian collection. Contemporary local art.

NATIONAL HISTORIC OREGON TRAIL INTERPRETIVE CENTER – Baker City – Page 83 A6 Permanent and changing exhibits, multimedia displays and living-history presentations illustrate pioneer life on Oregon Trail. 4.2-mile interpretive trail system. Re-created lode mine site.

OLD AURORA COLONY MUSEUM – Aurora – Page 60 C2 Five-building museum with exhibits depicting life in 19th-century religious communal settlement.

OREGON ART INSTITUTE – Portland – Page 66 D3 Museum and film center. Collection of European, American, American Indian, African and Asian art. Works from ancient times to present.

OREGON HISTORICAL CENTER – Portland – Page 66 D3 History of entire state. Exhibits include photographs, documents, artifacts, art and models. Murals depict historic scenes. Permanent and rotating exhibits.

OREGON MUSEUM OF SCIENCE AND INDUSTRY – Portland – Page 66 D3 Hands-on exhibits of science and industry. Demonstrations, planetarium and laser light show.

OREGON TRAIL REGIONAL MUSEUM – Baker City – Page 83 A5 Exhibits include collection of rocks, minerals and semiprecious stones; period clothing; school, mining, farm, agriculture and logging artifacts; and American Indian artifacts. Extensive collection of sea shells, corals and dried sea life.

PAUL JENSEN ARCTIC MUSEUM – Monmouth – Page 53 B7 Collection of art and artifacts representing various Arctic regions.

PIONEER MOTHERS MEMORIAL LOG CABIN MUSEUM – Champoeg State Heritage Area – Page 60 B1 Enlarged replica of typical early pioneer log cabin. Many articles and home furnishings brought across plains by pioneer women. Cabin dedicated to all pioneer women who braved trip on Oregon Trail to establish new homes. *(See Parks/Forests/Wilderness Areas.)*

ROBERT NEWELL HOUSE MUSEUM – Champoeg State Heritage Area – Page 60 C1 Complete restoration of house of Robert Newell, one of men who established first Oregon Territory laws in 1843. Period furniture, American Indian artifacts, inaugural gowns, handwork and Masonic items. Old jail and typical pioneer, one-room schoolhouse on grounds. *(See Parks/Forests/Wilderness Areas.)*

SEASIDE MUSEUM – Seaside – Page 64 A1 Exhibits of Seaside history including artifacts from 230 A.D.; Clatsop Indian display; photographs and memorabilia of early 1900s beach life; and fire, logging and printing equipment.

THE SIUSLAW PIONEER MUSEUM – Florence – Page 32 A4 Museum housed in former Lutheran church. American Indian artifacts including baskets and canoes. Pioneer artifacts including furniture, clothing, quilts, tools and 1877 pump organ. Reconstructed rooms.

SPRINGFIELD MUSEUM – Springfield – Page 47 D8 Located in 1908 Pacific Power and Light building. Collection contains photographs and artifacts important to city's pioneer heritage including exhibits on industry, logging and agriculture.

STEVENS–CRAWFORD MUSEUM – Oregon City – Page 60 B4 1908 Georgian Revival–style house, built by one of Oregon's earliest families. Period furniture. Tours with costumed guides.

TILLAMOOK COUNTY PIONEER MUSEUM – Tillamook – Page 58 A2 Located in old courthouse. Cultural and natural history exhibits include pioneer home, guns, clothing, pump organs, animals and birds, stagecoach and firefighting equipment.

TIMBERLINE LODGE – Government Camp – Page 62 B3 Large stone and timber mountain inn at 6,000-foot-level of Mt. Hood. Built with local materials during Depression in 1930s as WPA project. Ski resort. National Historic Landmark.

UNIVERSITY OF OREGON MUSEUM OF ART – Eugene – Page 47 D8 Collection includes Oriental and European art and African crafts. Contemporary American art including Pacific Northwest artists.

UNIVERSITY OF OREGON MUSEUM OF NATURAL HISTORY – Eugene – Page 47 D8 Exhibits include geology, fossils, plants, and anthropology and archaeology materials. Zoology collection includes birds, eggs and mounted specimens.

UPPERTOWN FIRE FIGHTERS MUSEUM – Astoria – Page 70 C3 Houses collection of firefighting equipment and machinery from 1887 to 1921.

VISTA HOUSE – Crown Point State Scenic Corridor – Page 67 D6 Circular stone building constructed in 1918 to honor Oregon pioneers. On top of 720-foot-high Crown Point, picturesque views of Columbia River Gorge. Information Center. *(See Parks/Forests/Wilderness Areas.)*

WILLAMETTE SCIENCE & TECHNOLOGY CENTER – Eugene – Page 47 D8 Hands-on exhibits about technology and science, including creating laser art, programming a computer and learning about human body. Planetarium.

WISEMAN GALLERY – Grants Pass – Page 19 A5 On Rogue Community College campus. Wide variety of works in different styles, including oil, watercolor, mixed media, sculpture and ceramics. Ten exhibits per year.

WOODVILLE MUSEUM – Rogue River – Page 19 A7 Located in turn-of-20th-century house, museum displays clothing, furniture, documents and other artifacts depicting early pioneer life in area.

WORLD FORESTRY CENTER – Portland – Page 66 D3 Center concentrates on beauty and usefulness of forests. Exhibits include multi-image presentation and 70-foot talking tree. Demonstration forest and Magness Memorial Tree Farm showing various woodland management techniques.

Scenic Drives

AUFDERHEIDE MEMORIAL DRIVE – Westfir – Page 43 B5 – 85-mile route National Scenic Byway within Willamette National Forest *(see Parks/Forests/Wilderness Areas)*. ROUTE: Follows Forest Route 19 north from Westfir to junction with State Route 126/McKenzie Highway, near Rainbow.

BENTON COUNTY SCENIC LOOP – Monroe – Page 47 B6 – 78-mile loop Signed route includes parks, recreation areas, historic sites and wineries. Many short side trips. ROUTE: Begin junction State Route 99W and Alpine Road, just north of Monroe • Follow Alpine Road to Alpine • In Alpine continue on Bellfountain Road heading north to Philomath • Left on Chapel Drive, then right on 19th Street • Follow U.S. Route 20 north toward Wren • In Wren, take Kings Valley Highway north to Maxfield Creek Road • Right onto Maxfield Creek Road • Continue on Airlie Road • At junction of State Route 99W, follow route south through Corvallis, back to Monroe.

CASCADE LAKES TOUR – Bend – Page 51 D6 – 89-mile route Signed route offering views of Cascade Mountain Range, lakes and forests. Two connecting tours: Cascade Lakes Highway (designated National Scenic Byway) and Corridor 97 Route. ROUTE: Follow Colorado Street to Century Drive Highway • Century Drive Highway becomes Cascade Lakes Highway • Cascade Lakes Highway becomes Lava Lake Road and finally Odell Road • Take Forest Route 42 to South Century Drive to Sun River to U.S. Route 97, back to Bend. For more information contact: Bend Chamber of Commerce, 777 Northwest Wall Steet, Bend, OR 97701.

COLUMBIA RIVER SCENIC HIGHWAY – Troutdale – Page 67 D5 – 31-mile route Two separate, original sections of scenic highway built 1914, currently being restored. Includes parks, waterfalls, historic sites and panoramic views. First section begins in Troutdale, following Crown Point Highway to Ainsworth State Park *(see Parks/Forests/Wilderness Areas)*. Second section begins at Mosier and follows U.S. Route 30/Mosier–The Dalles Highway. Includes Rowena Loop to natural wildflower area.

COVE PALISADES TOUR – Madras – Page 57 C7 – 31-mile route Canyons, rivers, Cascade Mountain Range and The Cove Palisades State Park *(see Parks/Forests/Wilderness Areas)*. Many scenic views. ROUTE: Begin in Madras at corner of Culver Highway and Belmont Lane • Follow Belmont Lane • Left on Mountain View Drive • Right on Peck Road then right on Jordan Road • Follow to turnaround in The Cove Palisades State Park • Backtrack to Peck Road • Right on Frazier Drive, left on Fisch Lane • Right on Feather Drive, then left on Huber Lane • May return to Madras on Culver Highway heading north.

DIAMOND CRATERS AUTO TOUR – 10 mi. W of Diamond – Page 78 D1 – 40-mile route Drive through diverse volcanic area *(see Unique Natural Features)*. For more information contact: Bureau of Land Management, Burns District Office, 28910 Highway 20 West, Hines, OR 97738.

ELKHORN DRIVE – Baker – Page 83 A5 – 103-mile route Signed route through historic, scenic, gold mining areas and Wallowa–Whitman National Forest *(see Parks/Forests/Wilderness Areas)*. Short side trips to various points of interest. ROUTE: Begin in Baker at Post Office Square, on State Route 7/Whitney Highway, traveling south and west to Sumpter • Continue west on Granite Hill Road to Bull Run Road • At Granite, follow Forest Route 73 north • Continue following signs to Haines • Finish on U.S. Route 30, south back to Baker.

FRENCH PRAIRIE LOOP – Champoeg State Heritage Area – Page 60 C1 – 41-mile loop Signed route through lush farmlands, Willamette River Valley and historic areas (also bike route). ROUTE: Begin at Champoeg State Heritage Area entrance • West on Champoeg Road • Continue to Riverside Drive, turning left • Outside St. Paul, left on Blanchet Avenue, then right on River Road • Follow to State Route 219/French Prairie Road, turning left • Continue for 1 mile, turning right on St. Louis Road • At State Route 99E turn left • Follow to Woodburn, turning left on Cleveland Road • Right on Settlemeier Avenue • Continue to State Routes 214 and 211, turning right, crossing Pudding River • Left on Meridian Road • Follow to Lone Elder Road, turn left • Continue to Ehlen Road, then Yergen Road • Right on Case Road, then left on Champoeg Road. *(See Parks/Forest/Wilderness Areas.)*

HIGHWAY 101 – Astoria – Page 70 C3 – 350-mile route Route traveling length of coast. Passes through state parks, national forest, waysides and beach towns. Whales, sea lions, wildflowers, historic areas and lighthouses. Trip driven from north or south. Follow U.S. Route 101/Oregon Coast Highway, watching for markers for scenic side trips. *(See Bicycle Routes—Touring.)*

HIGHWAY 26 PRINEVILLE TOUR LOOP A – Prineville – Page 80 C1 – 50-mile loop Views of desert, grassland and forest areas. ROUTE: Begin at U.S. Route 26/Madras–Prineville Highway • Follow U.S. Route 26 north to Madras • From Madras, take U.S. Route 97/The Dalles–California Highway south to Terrebonne • Left on Smith Rock Market Road • Continue on Elkins Road • Right on Lone Pine Road to O'Neil Highway • Continue on O'Neil Highway back to Prineville.

McKENZIE–SANTIAM TOUR ROUTE – Redmond – Page 51 B7 – 130-mile route Route showcases high desert, Cascade Mountain Range, glacial lakes and waterfalls. ROUTE: Head west on State Route 126/McKenzie Highway to Sisters where road joins U.S. Route 20/Santiam Highway • Continue to State Route 126/Belknap Springs Highway west of Santiam Junc-tion • South to Belknap Springs • Follow State Route 242/McKenzie Highway east returning to Sisters and Redmond.

THE MT. HOOD/COLUMBIA GORGE LOOP – Gresham – Page 61 A5 – 160-mile loop Signed route includes forests, meadows, waterfalls, historic and recreation sites and many scenic views. Possible side trips along Lolo Pass Road and Columbia River Scenic Highway *(see this section)*. ROUTE: From Gresham, follow U.S. Route 26/Mt. Hood Highway • East of Government Camp, pick up State Route 35 • Follow State Route 35 north to Hood River • At Hood River, take Interstate 84 west, returning to Portland metropolitan area. For more information contact: Mt. Hood Area Chamber of Commerce, P.O. Box 819, Welches, OR 97067.

99W SCENIC ROUTE – Eugene – Page 47 D8 – 145-mile route Signed route with views of rolling hills, vineyards and orchards, historic sites and homes. ROUTE: Begin in Eugene at corner of State Route 99/6th Avenue and Jefferson Street heading north • State Route 99 becomes State Route 99W north of Junction City • Follow State Route 99W north to Portland.

BACK COUNTRY BYWAYS

The Bureau of Land Management (BLM) of the U.S. Department of the Interior has developed the Byways Program to provide travelers access to a diversity of landscapes and attractions in lesser-known and out-of-the way areas.

While most roads are well-maintained, road surfaces and conditions may vary and some may require high-clearance vehicles. Check ahead with the regional BLM office before beginning a trip. For brochures detailing each Byway listed here, contact: BLM, Oregon State Office, P.O. Box 2965, Portland, OR 97208, (503) 808-6002.

CHRISTMAS VALLEY BYWAY – Fort Rock – Page 39 B7 – 102-mile loop Loop drive through high-desert landscape of south-central Oregon.

GALICE–HELLGATE BYWAY – Merlin – Page 19 A6 – 39-mile route Route through Rogue River country, including scenic canyon vistas from Siskiyou Mountains. Old mining operations.

GRAVE CREEK TO MARIAL BYWAY – 6 mi. N of Galice – Page 26 C4 – 33-mile route Route through scenic and rugged mountains of Rogue River Canyon.

LAKEVIEW TO STEENS BYWAY – 6 mi. N Lakeview – Page 72 C3 – 90-mile route Through Warner Mountains, Warner Valley, Hart Mountain National Antelope Refuge and large section of high desert.

LESLIE GULCH–SUCCOR CREEK BYWAY – Nyssa – Page 79 D8 – 52-mile route Route through scenic and rugged landscape of eastern Oregon.

LOWER CROOKED RIVER BYWAY – 40 mi. SE of Bend – Page 76 A2 – 43-mile route Views of wildlife, steep-walled canyons, Arthur R. Bowman Dam and high desert.

LOWER DESCHUTES RIVER BYWAY – Maupin – Page 63 C8 – 36-mile route Trip through Columbia River Basalt Plateau, historic areas and along whitewater.

NESTUCCA RIVER BYWAY – 6 mi. E of Blaine – Page 58 B4 – 12-mile route Follows Nestucca River through typical coastal forest region.

SOUTH FORK ALSEA RIVER BYWAY – Alsea – Page 46 B4 – 11-mile route Scenic, leisurely connection between Oregon Coast and Willamette Valley. Typical coastal forest.

SOUTH FORK JOHN DAY RIVER BYWAY – Dayville – Page 81 C6 – 50-mile route Wildlife, fishing, camping and Murderer's Creek Wildhorse Management Area.

STEENS MOUNTAIN BYWAY – Frenchglen – Page 74 A1 – 66-mile loop High-desert country of southeastern Oregon. *(See Unique Natural Features and Bicycle Routes—Mountain Biking.)*

OLD RIVER ROAD SCENIC DRIVE – Pendleton – Page 86 B1 – 21-mile route Lush farmland, geologic formations, forests and Umatilla River. ROUTE: Begin in Pendleton at corner of Old Pendleton River Road and U.S. Route 30 • Follow Old Pendleton River Road west to Echo.

RIM DRIVE – Crater Lake National Park – Page 29 A7 – 33-mile loop Loop drive circling Crater Lake. Scenic overlooks and side trip to The Pinnacles. Start from north entrance road, crossing Pumice Desert or from south entrance road, crossing Annie Creek Canyon. Park Headquarters near south entrance. *(See Unique Natural Features, Bicycle Routes—Mountain Biking and Parks/Forest/Wilderness Areas.)*

THE SISKIYOU LOOP – Medford – Page 20 B1 – 85-mile loop Views of Siskiyou Mountains, Rogue River Valley, forests, meadows and wildlife. ROUTE: Begin at corner of West Main Street and Oakdale Avenue • West on Jacksonville Highway to Jacksonville • Continue on State Route 238/Jacksonville Highway to Ruch • South to Applegate Road • Left after McKee Bridge to Forest Route 20 • Follow to Siskiyou and Interstate 5 • Take Interstate 5 north through Ashland back to Medford.

THREE CAPES LOOP – Tillamook – Page 58 A2 – 38-mile loop Scenic oceanfront drive off U.S. Route 101. Lighthouses, state parks, beaches and wildlife. ROUTE: Take 3rd Street exit west from U.S. Route 101/Oregon Coast Highway • Follow Netarts Highway to Bayocean Road to Cape Meares Loop Road to Netarts Bay Drive • South along Whiskey Creek Road to Cape Lookout Road • South on Sand Lake Road • South to Cape Drive • East into Pacific City on Pacific Avenue • South on Brotten Road back to U.S. Route 101.

UPPER KLAMATH LAKE LOOP TOUR – Klamath Falls – Page 22 C2 – 93-mile loop Signed route offering views of Cascade Mountain Range. Passes through Winema National Forest, Upper Klamath National Wildlife Refuge and Crater Lake National Park *(see Parks/Forests/Wilderness Areas)*. ROUTE: Take Lakeshore Drive west from Klamath Falls to State Route 140/Lake of the Woods Highway • North on State Route 140 to Harriman Lodge • North on West Side Road to Sevenmile Road heading east • North on Weed Road to Fort Klamath • North on State Route 62/Crater Lake Highway • East on Dixon Road to Sun Mountain Road • South to Fort Klamath Junction • South on State Route 62/Crater Lake Highway • East on Chiloquin Highway to U.S. Route 97/The Dalles–California Highway • South back to Klamath Falls.

WASHINGTON COUNTY SCENIC LOOP – Tigard – Page 60 A2 – 100-mile loop Signed tour through picturesque countryside including wineries, historic museums and homes, parks and wildlife areas. ROUTE: Begin corner Beef Bend Road and Scholls Ferry Road • Follow State Route 210/Scholls Ferry Road east to State Route 217 • Continue north on State Route 217 to U.S. Route 26/Sunset Highway • Turn left on State Route 6/Wilson River Highway, following west • South on State Route 8/Gales Creek Road to Forest Grove • Follow signs to State Route 47, going south • Right on Scoggins Valley Road, looping around Henry Hagg Lake and continuing south on State Route 47 • In Gaston, left onto Gaston Road, then right on Spring Hill Road • Left on Laurelwood Road, left on Bald Peak Road • Then follow Laurel Road West straight • Continue to State Route 219, turning right • Left on State Route 210, returning to starting point.

Boat Ramps/Fishing

To locate boat ramps in this Atlas, look on the appropriate map for the boat ramp symbol and corresponding number. The fish type category includes the most popular species. For more information contact: Oregon Department of Fish & Wildlife, Headquarters, 3406 Cherry Avenue NE, Salem, OR 97303, (503) 947-6000.

Abbreviations

Ramp Types

- A–Asphalt
- C–Concrete
- E–Earth/Sand
- G–Gravel
- H–Hoist
- P–Pole Slide
- O–Other

Fish Types

- A–Sturgeon
- B–Salmon
- C–Crab
- D–Striped Bass
- M–Marine Sport Fish
- S–Steelhead
- T–Trout
- W–Warmwater Fishes

BODY OF WATER	FACILITY	FISH TYPE	RAMP TYPE	PARKING	FEES	RESTROOMS	PAGE & GRID
3000 Agate Lake	Agate Lake	TW	C	●	●	●	20 A2
3003 Agency Lake	Henzel Park	T	C	●		●	30 D1
3006 Agency Lake	Neptune Park Resort	T	G	●	●	●	30 D1
3009 Agency Lake	Petric Park	T	C	●		●	30 D1
3012 Alsea Bay	McKinleys Marina	BCMT	A	●	●	●	32 A2
3015 Alsea Bay	Port of Alsea	BCMT	C	●		●	32 A2
3018 Alsea River	Barkleys	BST	E	●			46 A2
3021 Alsea River	Blackberry Park	BST	C	●		●	46 B2
3024 Alsea River	Campbell Park	BST	C	●		●	46 B3
3027 Alsea River	County Launch	BST	G	●			46 B2
3030 Alsea River	Drift Creek Landing	BST	C	●	●	●	32 A2
3033 Alsea River	Fishin Hole Trailer Park	BST	C	●	●	●	32 A2
3036 Alsea River	Happy Landing	BST	C	●	●	●	46 A1
3039 Alsea River	Hellion Rapids	BST	G	●			46 A2
3042 Alsea River	King Silver	BST	G	●	●	●	32 A2
3045 Alsea River	Kozy Kove	BST	A	●	●	●	46 A1
3048 Alsea River	Launching Forest Camp	BST	C	●		●	46 B2
3051 Alsea River	Mike Bauer Wayside	BST	E	●		●	46 A2
3054 Alsea River	Mill Creek Park	BST	C	●		●	46 A3
3057 Alsea River	Missouri Bend	BST	P	●		●	46 B3
3060 Alsea River	Oaklands Marina	BST	C	●	●	●	32 A2
3063 Alsea River	Quarry Hole	BST	E	●			46 A2
3066 Alsea River	Salmonberry Park	BST	C	●		●	46 B3
3069 Alsea River	Stoney Point	BST	E	●		●	46 B2
3072 Alsea River	Taylors Landing	BST	A	●	●	●	46 A1
3075 Ana Reservoir	Ana Reservoir Landing	TW	C	●		●	72 A1
3078 Antelope Flat Reservoir	Antelope Flat Reservoir	T	A	●		●	80 D3
3081 Antelope Res	Antelope Reservoir	T	G	●		●	75 A8
3084 Anthony Lake	Anthony Lake Ramp	T	C	●		●	82 A4
3087 Applegate Lake	Copper Ramp	T	G	●		●	19 D7
3090 Applegate Lake	French Gulch Ramp	T	A	●		●	19 D8
3093 Applegate Lake	Hart–Tish Boat Ramp	TW	C	●	●	●	19 D7
3096 Balm Creek Reservoir	Balm Creek Campground	T	G	●		●	83 A7
3099 Ben Irving Reservoir	Ben Irving Reservoir	TW	C	●		●	34 D4
3102 Beulah Reservoir	Beulah Reservoir Ramp	T	A	●		●	78 A4
3105 Big Cliff Reservoir	Detroit Dam Road	T	O	●			55 C7
3108 Big Lake	Big Lake	T	A	●		●	50 A2
3111 Blue Lake	Blue Lake	T	E	●	●	●	50 A2
3114 Blue Lake	Blue Lake Lodge	T	C	●	●	●	50 A2
3117 Blue Lake	Blue Lake Park	W	C	●	●	●	67 D5
3120 Blue River Lake	Lookout	T	C	●		●	49 C6
3123 Blue River Lake	Mona Campground	T	E	●		●	49 C6
3126 Blue River Lake	Saddle Dam	T	G	●		●	49 C6
3129 Bolan Lake	Bolan Lake Campground	T	E	●		●	19 D5
3132 Bradley Lake	Bradley Lake Park	TW	G	●		●	33 D5
3135 Brownlee Reservoir	Farewell Bend	TW	C	●		●	83 C8
3138 Brownlee Reservoir	Hewitt Park Campground	TW	C	●		●	83 A8
3141 Brownlee Reservoir	Hewitt Park Day Use	TW	C	●		●	83 A8
3142 Brownlee Reservoir	Noble Holcomb	TW	C	●			83 A8
3144 Brownlee Reservoir	Spring Recreation Site	TW	C	●		●	83 C8
3147 Brownlee Reservoir	Swedes Landing	TW	G			●	83 B8
3150 Bully Creek Reservoir	Bully Creek Campground	TW	C	●		●	83 D7
3153 Campbell Lake	Campbell Lake Campgd	T	C	●		●	72 B1
3156 Canyons Meadows L	West Side Campground	T	G	●		●	82 D1
3159 Cape Meares Lake	Cape Meares Lake	TW	G	●			64 D1
3162 Carmen Reservoir	Ice Cap Creek	T	G	●			50 B1
3165 Carter Lake	East Carter	TW	A	●		●	32 B4
3168 Chetco River	Ice Box Hole	BS	G	●			17 D2
3171 Chetco River	Alfred A. Loeb SP	BS	G	●		●	17 D3
3174 Chetco River	Miller Bar	BS	G	●			17 C3
3177 Chetco River	Nook Bar	BS	G	●			17 C3
3180 Chetco River	Port of Brookings Harbor	BCS	C	●	●	●	17 D2
3183 Chetco River	Redwood Bar	BS	G	●			17 C3
3186 Chetco River	Social Security Bar	BS	C	●			17 D2
3189 Chetco River	South Fork	BS	G	●			17 C3
3190 Clackamas River	Barton Park	BST	A	●	●	●	61 A5
3191 Clackamas River	Carver Ramp	BST	C	●		●	61 A5
3193 Clackamas River	Dam Ramp	BST	A	●		●	61 B6
3195 Clackamas River	Feldheimer Ramp	BST	G	●		●	61 B5
3196 Clackamas River	Milo McIver State Park	BST	G	●	●	●	61 B6
3198 Clackamas River	Milo McIver State Park	BST	G	●	●	●	61 B5
3207 Clackamas River	Riverside Park	BST	C	●		●	60 A4
3210 Clatskanie River	Beaver Landing	BS	C	●		●	71 D8
3213 Clear Lake	Clear Lake Campground	T	G	●		●	62 C3
3216 Clear Lake	Clear Lake Day Use Area	T	A	●		●	50 B1
3219 Clear Lake	South Shore Access	T	A	●		●	80 B1
3222 Cleawox Lake	J.M. Honeyman Mem SP	T	G	●		●	32 A4
3225 Clusters Lake	Chickahominy Landing	T	C	●		●	77 B6
3231 Coffenbury Lake	Coffenbury Lake	TW	A	●			70 C2
3234 Cold Springs Res	South Point	W	G	●		●	85 A8
3237 Columbia River	Aldrich Point	ABCM	C	●		●	71 C5
3240 Columbia River	Boardman Park	ABSW	C	●		●	85 A6
3243 Columbia River	Celilo Park	ABSW	A	●		●	84 B1
3244 Columbia River	Chinook Landing	ABS	C	●	●	●	67 D5
3246 Columbia River	Coverts Landing	ABS	C	●	●	●	67 D8
3249 Columbia River	Dalton Point	ABS	A	●		●	67 D7
3252 Columbia River	East Mooring Basin	ABCM	C	●		●	70 C3
3255 Columbia River	Giles French Park	ABS	C	●		●	84 B2
3258 Columbia River	Hammond Mooring Basin	ABCM	A	●	●	●	70 C2
3261 Columbia River	Harbor 1	ABSW	H	●	●	●	66 D4
3264 Columbia River	Hood River Marina	ABS	C	●		●	68 C4
3267 Columbia River	Irrigon Marina Park	SW	C	●		●	85 A7
3268 Columbia River	Jantzen Beach Moorage	ABSW	A	●		●	66 D3
3270 Columbia River	M. James Gleason Ramp	ABSW	C	●	●	●	66 D4
3273 Columbia River	Mayer State Park	ABSW	C	●		●	69 C6
3274 Columbia River	Paterson Ferry	SW	C	●			85 A6
3276 Columbia River	Pier 99 Marine Center	ABSW	H	●	●		66 D3
3279 Columbia River	Port of Arlington	ABS	C	●		●	84 B4
3282 Columbia River	Port of Cascade Locks	ABSW	A	●		●	68 C1
3285 Columbia River	Port of the Dalles	ABS	C	●		●	69 D7
3288 Columbia River	Quesnel Park	ABS	C	●		●	85 A5
3291 Columbia River	Rainier Marina	ABS	A	●	●	●	71 B8
3294 Columbia River	Rooster Rock State Park	ABS	A	●	●	●	67 D7
3297 Columbia River	Scipios Goble Landing	ABS	C	●	●	●	71 B9
3300 Columbia River	St Helens Marina	ABS	A	●	●	●	66 B2
3303 Columbia River	Sundance Moorage	ABSW	H	●	●		66 D3
3306 Columbia River	Sundial	ABS	A	●	●	●	67 D5
3309 Columbia River	Umatilla Marina	SW	C	●		●	85 A7
3312 Columbia River	Westport Ramp	ABCM	C	●			71 C5
3315 Cooper Creek Res	Cooper Cr Res—E End	TW	C	●		●	35 A6
3318 Cooper Creek Res	Cooper Cr Res—W End	TW	C	●		●	35 A6
3321 Coos Bay	Charleston Boat Basin	BCDM	C	●		●	33 B6
3324 Coos Bay	Conde McCullough	BCDM	G				33 A7
3327 Coos Bay	Empire Boat Ramp	BCDM	C	●		●	33 A6
3328 Coos Bay	North Spit	BCDM	C	●		●	33 A6
3330 Coos Bay	Pony Point	BCDM	C	●		●	33 A7
3331 Coos River, S Fk	Myrtle Tree Boat Ramp	ABDST	C	●	●	●	33 B8
3333 Coquille River	Arago	BS	C	●		●	33 D7
3336 Coquille River	Bryant Ramp	BS	A	●			33 D7
3337 Coquille River	Bullards Beach SP	BCS	C	●		●	33 C5
3339 Coquille River	Coquille	BS	C	●		●	33 C7
3342 Coquille River	Port of Bandon	BS	C	●		●	33 D5
3345 Coquille River	Riverton Boat Ramp	BDS	C	●		●	33 C6
3348 Coquille River	Rocky Point	BCS	C	●		●	33 C6
3351 Coquille River	Sturdivant Park	BCM	C	●	●	●	33 C7
3352 Coquille River, S Fk	Baker Creek	BS	G	●			25 A8
3353 Coquille River, S Fk	Beaver Creek	BS	P	●			25 A8
3354 Coquille River, S Fk	Orchard Park	BS	G	●			25 B8
3357 Cottage Grove Lake	Lakeside Park	TW	A	●		●	41 C8
3360 Cottage Grove Lake	Wilson Creek Park	TW	A	●		●	41 C8
3363 Cottonwood Meadow L	Cottonwood Meadow	T	C	●		●	72 C2
3366 Cottonwood Res	Cottonwood Reservoir	T	A	●		●	72 C2
3369 Cougar Reservoir	Echo	T	A	●		●	49 D7
3372 Cougar Reservoir	Slide Creek	T	A	●		●	49 D7
3375 Cow Lake, Upper	Lake Outlet	W	E	●			79 D7
3378 Crabapple Lake	Crabapple Lake	W	G	●		●	70 C2
3381 Crane Prairie Res	Browns Mtn Boating	TW	C	●		●	44 B2
3384 Crane Prairie Res	Cow Meadow	TW	E			●	44 B2
3387 Crane Prairie Res	Crane Prairie Campgd	TW	C			●	44 B2
3390 Crane Prairie Res	Crane Prairie Resort	TW	C	●	●	●	44 B2
3393 Crane Prairie Res	Quinn River	TW	C	●		●	44 B2
3396 Crane Prairie Res	Rock Creek Campgd	TW	A	●		●	44 B2
3399 Crescent Lake	Crescent Lake	T	C	●		●	38 A1
3402 Crescent Lake	Spring Campground	T	C	●		●	37 A8
3405 Crump Lake	Crump Lake Landing	W	E	●			73 C5
3408 Crystal Creek	Malone Springs	TW	G	●		●	29 D8
3411 Cullaby Lake	Carnahan Park	TW	C	●		●	70 D2
3414 Cullaby Lake	Cullaby Lake Park	TW	C	●		●	70 D2
3417 Cultus Lake	Cultus Lake Campgd	T	C	●		●	44 B2
3420 Cultus Lake	Cultus Lake Lodge	T	E	●		●	44 B2
3423 Davis Lake	Lava Flow Campground	T	C	●		●	44 D2
3426 Davis Lake	West Davis L Campgd	T	E	●		●	44 D2
3429 Deadhorse Lake	Deadhorse L Campgd	T	C	●		●	72 B1
3432 Delintment Lake	Delintment Lake	T	G	●		●	77 A6
3435 Depoe Bay	Port of Depoe Bay	B	C	●		●	32 B1
3438 Deschutes River	Beavertail Campground	BST	G	●		●	84 C1
3441 Deschutes River	Benham Falls	T	C	●		●	45 A5
3444 Deschutes River	Besson Boating Beach	T	C	●		●	45 A5
3447 Deschutes River	Big River Campground	T	C	●		●	45 B5
3450 Deschutes River	Buckhollow	ST	E				63 B8
3453 Deschutes River	Bull Bend Campground	T	C	●		●	44 C3
3456 Deschutes River	Dillon Falls	T	C	●		●	45 A5
3459 Deschutes River	Harpham Flat	BST	G	●		●	63 C8
3462 Deschutes River	Deschutes River SRA	ABSTW	C	●	●	●	84 B1
3465 Deschutes River	Macks Canyon Campgd	BST	C	●		●	84 C1
3468 Deschutes River	Maupin City Park	BST	G	●	●	●	63 C8
3469 Deschutes River	Nena Creek Camp	BST	E			●	63 D7
3471 Deschutes River	Pine Tree	ST	E				63 B8
3472 Deschutes River	Sandy Beach	BST	G	●		●	63 C8
3474 Deschutes River	Slough Camp	T	C	●		●	45 A5
3477 Deschutes River	Tenino Boating Site	T	C	●			44 C3
3480 Deschutes River	Trout Creek Campgd	T	E	●		●	57 B8
3483 Deschutes River	Wapinitia Campsite	BST	G	●		●	63 C8
3486 Deschutes River	Warm Springs	T	E	●		●	57 C7
3489 Deschutes River	Wyeth	T	C	●		●	44 C4
3490 Detroit Lake	Cove Creek	T	C	●		●	55 C7
3492 Detroit Lake	Detroit L SRA—D Loop	T	A	●	●	●	55 C7
3495 Detroit Lake	Detroit L SRA—G Loop	T	A	●	●	●	55 C7
3498 Detroit Lake	Hoover	T	C	●			55 C8
3504 Detroit Lake	Mongold Day Use Area	T	C	●	●	●	55 C7
3507 Detroit Lake	Southshore	T	G	●		●	55 C4
3510 Devils Lake	Devils Lake Landing	TW	G	●			32 A1
3513 Devils Lake	East Devils Lake	TW	C	●		●	52 A1
3516 Devils Lake	Holmes Road Park	TW	A	●		●	52 A1
3519 Devils Lake	Regatta Grounds Park	TW	A	●		●	52 A1
3522 Devils Lake	Sand Point	TW	G				52 A1
3525 Devils Lake	West Side Park	TW	G	●			32 A1
3528 Dexter Reservoir	Dexter State Rec Site	TW	A	●		●	42 A2
3531 Dexter Reservoir	Lowell State Rec Site	BS	A	●		●	42 A2
3534 Diamond Lake	North End Boat Site	T	C	●		●	37 C7
3537 Diamond Lake	S Diamond Lk Campgd	T	C	●		●	37 C7
3540 Diamond Lake	South Shore	T	G	●		●	37 C7
3543 Diamond Lake	Thielsen View	T	C	●		●	37 C7
3546 Dog Lake	Dog Lake	W	C	●		●	72 D2
3549 Dorena Lake	Baker Bay	TW	A	●	●	●	42 B1
3552 Dorena Lake	Harms Park	TW	G	●		●	42 B1
3555 Drews Reservoir	Drews Reservoir Access	W	O	●		●	72 D2
3558 Duncan Reservoir	Duncan Reservoir Access	T	E	●			76 D1
3561 East Lake	Cinder Hill Campground	T	O	●		●	45 C7
3564 East Lake	East Lake Campground	T	C	●		●	45 C7
3567 East Lake	East Lake Resort		C			●	45 C7
3570 East Lake	Hot Springs Boating	T	C	●		●	45 C7
3573 Eel Lake	William M. Tugman SP	TW	A	●		●	32 D3
3576 Elbow Lake	Elbow Lake Rec Area	TW	E	●			32 B4
3579 Elk Lake	Elk Lake Campground	T	E	●		●	44 A2
3582 Elk Lake	Elk Lake Campground	T	E	●		●	55 B8
3585 Elk Lake	Elk Lake Lodge	T	C	●		●	44 A2
3588 Elk Lake	Little Fawn Boating	T	C	●		●	44 A2
3591 Elk Lake	Point Campground	T	E	●		●	44 A2
3594 Elk River	Fish Hatchery	BS	G	●			25 C5
3597 Elk River	Iron Head	BS	E	●			25 B5
3600 Emigrant Lake	Emigrant Lake Rec Area	TW	C	●	●	●	20 C4
3603 Emigrant Lake	Songer Wayside	TW	E	●	●	●	20 C4
3606 Empire Lakes	Lower Lake	TW	E	●			33 A6
3609 Empire Lakes	Upper Lake	TW	G	●			33 A6
3615 Fall Creek Reservoir	North Shore	T	A	●		●	42 A2
3618 Fall Creek Reservoir	Upper End Campground	T	G	●		●	42 A3
3621 Fall Creek Reservoir	Fall Creek SRA	T	C	●	●	●	42 A3
3624 Fern Ridge Lake	Mega Resort	W	A	●	●	●	47 D6
3627 Fern Ridge Lake	Orchard Point Park	W	C	●	●	●	46 D6
3630 Fern Ridge Lake	Perkins Peninsula Park	W	A	●		●	47 D6
3633 Fern Ridge Lake	Richardson Park	W	C	●	●	●	47 D6
3636 Fish Lake	Fish Lake Boat Launch	T	A	●		●	21 A6
3639 Fish Lake	Fish Lake Campground	T	E	●		●	87 D8
3642 Fish Lake	Fish Lake Rec Area	T	A	●			74 B2
3645 Fish Lake	Fish Lake Resort	T	E	●		●	21 A6
3648 Floras Lake	Boise–Cope Park	TW	C	●		●	24 A4
3651 Foster Reservoir	Calkins Park	TW	E	●		●	48 A3
3654 Foster Reservoir	Gedney Creek	TW	A	●		●	48 A3
3657 Foster Reservoir	Sunnyside Park	TW	C	●		●	48 A4
3660 Fourmile Lake	Fourmile Lake	T	E	●		●	21 A7
3663 Freeway Lakes	Freeway Lakes #1	TW	G	●		●	53 D8
3666 Freeway Lakes	Freeway Lakes #2	TW	G	●		●	53 D8
3669 Frog Lake	Frog Lake	T	A	●		●	62 C3
3672 Galesville Reservoir	Chief Miwaleta Park	TW	C	●		●	27 B7
3675 Galesville Reservoir	Upper Ramp	TW	A	●		●	27 B7
3678 Garrison Lake	City Ramp	TW	C	●		●	24 B4
3681 Garrison Lake	County Ramp	TW	G	●			24 B4
3687 Gerber Reservoir	Gerber Recreation Area	TW	C	●		●	23 C7
3690 Gerber Reservoir	Gerber Reservoir	TW	G	●		●	23 C8
3693 Gold Lake	Gold Lake	T	A	●		●	43 C8
3696 Goose Lake	Goose Lake SRA	T	E	●			72 D3
3699 Grand Ronde River	Mud Creek	ST	E	●			87 A7
3702 Grand Ronde River	Palmer	ST	E	●			87 B5
3703 Grand Ronde River	Powwatka Bridge	ST	E	●			87 A7
3705 Grand Ronde River	Troy Access #1	ST	E	●			87 A7
3708 Grand Ronde River	Troy Access #2	ST	E	●			87 A7
3714 Grande Ronde Lake	Grande Ronde Camp	T	E	●		●	82 A4
3717 Green Peter Res	Thistle Creek	TW	C	●		●	48 A4
3720 Green Peter Res	Whitcomb Creek	TW	C	●		●	48 A4
3721 Green Point Upper Res	Kingsley Campground	T	A	●		●	68 C3
3723 Harriet Lake	Harriet Lake	T	G			●	62 D1
3726 Hart Lake	Hart Lake Landing	W	E	●		●	73 C5
3729 Haystack Reservoir	Haystack West	TW	C	●			51 A7
3732 Haystack Reservoir	USFS Campground	TW	C	●		●	51 A7
3735 Heart Lake	Heart Lake Landing	T	G	●			72 C1
3738 Hemlock Lake	Hemlock Lake	T	G	●		●	36 C3
3741 Henry Hagg Lake	Henry Hagg L—Ramp A	TW	C	●	●	●	59 A7
3744 Henry Hagg Lake	Henry Hagg L—Ramp C	TW	C	●	●	●	59 A7
3747 Hills Creek Reservoir	Bingham	TW	A	●		●	43 C5
3750 Hills Creek Reservoir	CT Beach	TW	A	●		●	43 C5
3753 Hills Creek Reservoir	Packard Creek	TW	A	●		●	43 C5
3756 Holbrook Reservoir	Holbrook	T	C	●			72 C1
3759 Hoquarton Slough	Marine Park	BT	C	●			58 A2

BOAT RAMPS/FISHING, *continued*

Abbreviations

Ramp Types		*Fish Types*	
A–Asphalt	*H–Hoist*	*A–Sturgeon*	*M–Marine Sport Fish*
C–Concrete	*P–Pole Slide*	*B–Salmon*	*S–Steelhead*
E–Earth/Sand	*O–Other*	*C–Crab*	*T–Trout*
G–Gravel		*D–Striped Bass*	*W–Warmwater Fishes*

BODY OF WATER	FACILITY	FISH TYPE	RAMP TYPE	PARKING	FEES	RESTROOMS	PAGE & GRID
3762 Hosmer Lake	South Campground	T	C	●		●	44 A2
3765 Howard Prairie Lake	Grizzly Creek	T	C	●	●	●	21 B5
3768 Howard Prairie Lake	Howard Prairie L Resort	T	C	●		●	21 C5
3771 Howard Prairie Lake	Klum Landing	T	C	●	●	●	21 C5
3774 Howard Prairie Lake	Willow Point	T	C	●	●	●	21 C5
3780 Hyatt Lake	Campers Cove	TW	E	●	●	●	21 C5
3783 Hyatt Lake	Hyatt Lake Rec Site	TW	A	●		●	21 C5
3784 Hyatt Lake	Hyatt Lake Resort	TW	E	●	●	●	21 C5
3786 Illinois River	Miami Bar	S	G	●			18 B2
3789 John Boyle Reservoir	Pioneer Park	TW	C	●		●	21 C8
3792 John Boyle Reservoir	Topsy	TW	A	●		●	21 C8
3794 John Day River	Clarno Bridge Launch Site	BSW	E	●			80 A3
3795 John Day River	Cottonwood Park	BSW	G	●		●	84 C3
3798 John Day River	John Day	ABT	C	●		●	70 C3
3804 John Day River	Kimberly	SW	G				81 A6
3807 John Day River	Le Page Park	BSW	C	●	●	●	84 B2
3810 John Day River	Mule Shoe	BSTW	G	●		●	81 A5
3813 John Day River	Service Creek Access	TW	G	●			81 A5
3816 John Day River	Spray	SW	E				81 A5
3819 John Day River	Twickenham	SW	E				80 B4
3822 Jubilee Reservoir	Jubilee Lake	T	C	●		●	87 A5
3825 Kilchis River	County Park	BST	G	●			64 D2
3828 Kilchis River	Mapes Creek	BST	G	●			64 D2
3831 Kilchis River	Parks Landing	BST	C	●			58 A2
3837 Klamath River	Keno Park	TW	C	●		●	22 C1
3840 Klamath River	Klamath Mgmt Area	TW	G	●		●	22 C2
3843 Klamath River	Klamath River Put-in	T	G	●		●	21 D8
3846 Klaskanine River	Klaskanine Park	BST	G	●			70 D3
3849 Krumbo Reservoir	Malheur NWR	T	C	●		●	74 A1
3852 Lake Billy Chinook	The Cove Palisades SP	TW	C	●		●	57 D6
3855 Lake Billy Chinook	The Cove Palisades SP	TW	A	●			57 D6
3858 Lake Billy Chinook	The Cove Palisades SP	TW	A	●		●	57 D6
3861 Lake Billy Chinook	Perry South Boating	TW	C	●		●	57 D5
3864 Lake Creek	Camp Indiola	BST	E	●		●	46 D2
3867 Lake Creek	Deadwood Ramp	ST	G	●			46 D2
3870 Lake Creek	Greenleaf Creek	ST	P	●			46 C4
3873 Lake Creek	Indiola Landing	BST	E	●		●	46 D2
3876 Lake Creek	Ronnie Fishing Access	ST	C	●		●	46 D2
3879 Lake Ewauna	Veterans Park	TW	C	●		●	22 C2
3882 Lake Lytle	Lake Lytle Public Access	TW	G	●		●	64 C1
3885 Lake Owyhee	Lake Owyhee SP	W	A	●		●	79 B8
3888 Lake Owyhee	Lake Owyhee SP	W	A	●		●	79 B7
3891 Lake Owyhee	Leslie Gulch	W	C	●		●	79 C7
3894 Lake Owyhee	Owyhee Dam Ramp	W	C	●		●	79 B8
3897 Lake Owyhee	Owyhee Lake Resort	W	C	●		●	79 B7
3900 Lake Penland	Lake Penland	T	G	●		●	85 D7
3903 Lake Selmac	Lake Selmac	TW	C	●		●	18 B4
3906 Lake Selmac	Reeves Creek	TW	C	●		●	18 B4
3909 Lake Simtustus	Pelton Park	T	E	●		●	57 C7
3912 Lake Wallula	Gold Springs Rec Area	W	E	●			85 A8
3915 Lake Wallula	Hat Rock State Park	SW	A	●		●	85 A8
3918 Lake Wallula	McNary Dam	W	C	●	●	●	85 A7
3921 Lake of the Woods	Aspen	TW	C	●		●	21 A7
3924 Lake of the Woods	Lake of the Woods Resort	TW	C	●		●	21 A7
3927 Lake of the Woods	Sunset Beach	TW	C	●		●	21 B7
3930 Lava Lake	Lava Lake Campgd	T	C	●		●	44 A2
3933 Lawrance Lake	Lawrance Lake	T	G	●		●	62 A3
3936 Lemolo Reservoir	Lemolo Lake Resort	T	G	●	●	●	37 B7
3939 Lemolo Reservoir	Poole Creek	T	A	●		●	37 B7
3942 Little Cultus Lake	Little Cultus Lake	T	C	●		●	44 B2
3945 Little Lava Lake	Little Lava L Campgd	T	C	●		●	44 A2
3948 Little Nestucca River	Little Nestucca Ramp	BCT	C	●		●	58 C1
3951 Lofton Reservoir	Lofton Campground	T	C	●		●	72 C1
3957 Lookout Point Res	Black Canyon	T	A	●		●	42 B4
3960 Lookout Point Res	Hampton	T	A	●		●	42 B4
3963 Lookout Point Res	Ivan Oakes	T	G	●		●	42 B3
3964 Lookout Point Res	North Shore Boat Ramp	T	A	●		●	42 A3
3965 Lookout Point Res	Signal Point	T	C	●			42 A3
3966 Loon Lake	Loon Lake	TW	C	●	●	●	41 D2
3969 Loon Lake	Loon Lake Lodge Resorts	TW	C	●	●	●	41 D2
3972 Lost Creek Lake	Joseph H. Stewart SRA	TW	C	●		●	28 C3
3975 Lost Creek Lake	Lost Creek Dam	TW	C	●		●	28 C3
3978 Lost Lake	Lost Lake	T	G	●		●	62 A2
3981 Lost Lake	Lost Lake Campground	T	G	●		●	50 A1
3984 Lost River	Crystal Springs	W	C	●		●	22 C3
3987 Luce Reservoir	Luce Reservoir Access	T	E	●		●	72 C4
3990 Lucky Reservoir	Lucky Reservoir Access	T	E	●			73 D5
3993 Magone Lake	Magone Lake Camp	T	C	●		●	82 B1
3996 Malheur Reservoir	New Reservoir Ramp	T	C	●		●	83 C6
3999 Malheur Reservoir	Old Reservoir Ramp	T	E	●		●	83 C6
4002 Mann Lake	East Mann Lake Access	T	G	●		●	74 A3
4003 Mann Lake	West Mann Lake Access	T	G	●		●	74 A3
4005 McKay Reservoir	McKay Ramp North	TW	C	●		●	86 B1
4008 McKay Reservoir	McKay Ramp South	TW	E	●			86 B1
4011 McKenzie River	Armitage Park	BST	A	●	●	●	47 D8
4014 McKenzie River	Bellinger Landing	BST	C	●		●	48 D1
4020 McKenzie River	Deerhorn	BST	G	●			48 D3
4023 McKenzie River	Ben and Kay Dorris SP	BST	A	●		●	48 C4

BODY OF WATER	FACILITY	FISH TYPE	RAMP TYPE	PARKING	FEES	RESTROOMS	PAGE & GRID
4026 McKenzie River	Emmerich Landing	BST	P	●			48 D2
4029 McKenzie River	Eweb Slip	BST	P	●			48 C4
4032 McKenzie River	Finn Rock Landing	BST	G	●			49 C5
4035 McKenzie River	Forest Glen Landing	BST	G	●		●	49 C6
4038 McKenzie River	Frissell	BST	E	●			49 C8
4041 McKenzie River	Greenwood Dr	BST	A	●			48 D3
4044 McKenzie River	Hamlin	BST	G	●			49 C6
4047 McKenzie River	Harvest Lane	BST	C	●		●	47 D8
4050 McKenzie River	Hayden Bridge	BST	P	●			48 D1
4053 McKenzie River	Helfrich	BST	G	●			48 C4
4056 McKenzie River	Hendricks Bridge Wayside	BST	A	●		●	48 D2
4062 McKenzie River	Leaburg Landing	BST	G	●			48 D3
4065 McKenzie River	McKenzie Bridge	BST	G	●		●	49 C7
4068 McKenzie River	McMullens Landing	BST	P				49 C5
4071 McKenzie River	Olallie Creek Campgd	T	P	●			49 B8
4074 McKenzie River	Paradise Campground	BST	G	●		●	49 C8
4077 McKenzie River	Power Canal	BST	G	●			48 D2
4080 McKenzie River	Rennie Landing	BST	G	●			49 C5
4083 McKenzie River	Shepards Landing	BST	P				49 C5
4086 McKenzie River	Silver Creek Landing	BST	A	●			49 D5
4089 Mercer Lake	Mercer Lake Landing	TW	A	●		●	32 D2
4092 Mercer Lake	Mercer Lake Resort	TW	A	●	●	●	32 D2
4095 Miller Lake	Digit Point	T	C	●		●	38 C1
4098 Millicoma River	Doras Place Boat Ramp	BDST	C	●		●	33 A8
4101 Millicoma River	Rooke/Higgins Co Pk	BDST	C	●		●	33 A8
4102 Millicoma River, W Fk	Stonehouse Bridge	S	P	●			33 A8
4104 Minam River	Minam Rec Area	T	G	●		●	87 B6
4107 Mission Lake	Mission Lake	W	A	●		●	59 D8
4110 Molalla River	Knights Bridge	S	C	●			60 B3
4113 Molalla River	Meadowbrook Bridge	S	P	●			60 C4
4116 Molalla River	Wagon Wheel	S	G	●			60 C4
4119 Monon Lake	Monon Lake	T	G	●			56 B2
4122 Moon Reservoir	Moon Reservoir Landing	W	E	●		●	77 C7
4125 Morgan Lake	Morgan Lake Campgd	TW	E	●		●	86 C4
4128 Mud Lake	Mud Lake Access	T	G	●			73 D6
4131 Mule Lake	Mule Lake Access	T	E	●			72 B4
4134 Multnomah Channel	Browns Landing	BSW	A	●	●		66 C2
4140 Multnomah Channel	Casidy/Marina Way	ABSW	C	●	●	●	66 D2
4143 Multnomah Channel	Freds Marina	ABSW	A	●	●	●	66 D2
4146 Multnomah Channel	Gilbert River Ramp	ABSW	C	●		●	66 B2
4149 Multnomah Channel	Larsons Moorage	ABSW	A		●	●	66 C2
4152 Multnomah Channel	Sauvie Island Ramp	ABSW	C	●		●	66 C2
4155 Munsel Lake	Munsel Landing	TW	A	●		●	32 D2
4158 Necanicum River	Cartwright Park	BST	C	●		●	64 A1
4161 Necanicum River	Johnson Const Company	BST	G	●	●		64 A1
4164 Necanicum River	Klootchie Creek Park	BST	G	●			64 A1
4167 Necanicum River	Quatat Marine Park	BST	C	●	●	●	64 A1
4170 Necanicum River	Sef Johnson Tract	BST	G	●			64 A1
4173 Nehalem Bay	Brighton Moorage	BCMT	A	●	●	●	64 C1
4176 Nehalem Bay	Jetty Fishery	BCMT	C	●	●	●	64 C1
4179 Nehalem Bay	Nehalem Bay Ramp	BCMT	C	●		●	64 C1
4182 Nehalem Bay	Nehalem Bay State Park	BCMT	C	●		●	64 C1
4185 Nehalem Bay	Paradise Cove Resort	BCMT	A	●	●	●	64 C1
4188 Nehalem Bay	Wheeler Ramp	BCMT	C	●		●	64 C1
4191 Nehalem River	Beaver Slide	BST	C				64 C2
4194 Nehalem River	Big Eddy	BST	C			●	65 A7
4197 Nehalem River	Mohler Sand and Gravel	BST	G		●		64 C2
4200 Nehalem River	Pope–Meeker Access	BST	G	●			64 B4
4203 Nehalem River	Roy Creek Park	BST	G	●		●	64 C2
4204 Nehalem River, N Fk	Aldervale Ramp	BST	C	●			64 B2
4205 Nehalem River, N Fk	N Fk Nehalem Hatchery	BST	G	●		●	64 B2
4206 Nestucca Bay	Fisher Tract	BCT	G	●		●	58 C1
4209 Nestucca River	Bixby	BST	G	●			58 B2
4212 Nestucca River	Cloverdale	BST	C	●			58 C1
4215 Nestucca River	Farmer Creek	BST	A	●			58 B2
4218 Nestucca River	First Bridge Ramp	BST	A	●			58 B2
4221 Nestucca River	Fourth Bridge	BST	G	●			58 B2
4224 Nestucca River	Pacific City Ramp	BCST	A	●		●	58 C1
4227 Nestucca River	Three Rivers	BST	G	●		●	58 C2
4230 Netarts Bay	Netarts Landing	CM	C	●		●	58 A1
4233 Newanna Creek	Broadway Park	T	C	●		●	64 A1
4242 North Fork Reservoir	North Shore	ST	G	●		●	61 C6
4245 North Fork Reservoir	Promontory Park	ST	C	●		●	61 C6
4257 North Santiam River	Buell Miller	BST	C	●		●	54 B2
4260 North Santiam River	Fishermans Bend	BST	G	●		●	54 B4
4263 North Santiam River	Greens Bridge	BST	G	●		●	54 C1
4266 North Santiam River	John Neal Memorial Park	BST	A	●		●	54 B4
4269 North Santiam River	Mehama Bridge	BST	A	●		●	54 B4
4272 North Santiam River	Packsaddle Park	BST	E	●		●	55 B6
4275 North Santiam River	Stayton Bridge	BST	C	●		●	54 B2
4278 North Twin Lake	N Twin Lake Campgrd	T	E	●		●	44 C2
4281 North Umpqua River	Amacher Park	BST	A	●		●	35 B6
4284 North Umpqua River	Apple Creek	S	G	●		●	36 B3
4287 North Umpqua River	Bogus Creek	S	G	●		●	36 B2
4290 North Umpqua River	Boulder Flat	S	G	●		●	36 B4
4293 North Umpqua River	Colliding Rivers	BS	C	●		●	35 B8
4296 North Umpqua River	Dry Creek	S	G	●			36 B4
4299 North Umpqua River	Gravel Bin	ST	G	●		●	36 B3

BODY OF WATER	FACILITY	FISH TYPE	RAMP TYPE	PARKING	FEES	RESTROOMS	PAGE & GRID
4302 North Umpqua River	Hestnes Landing	BS	C	●		●	35 B5
4305 North Umpqua River	Horseshoe	ST	G	●		●	36 B4
4308 North Umpqua River	Lone Rock	BS	P	●		●	35 B8
4311 North Umpqua River	Susan Creek	ST	E	●		●	36 B1
4314 North Umpqua River	Weeping Rocks	S	G	●			36 B4
4317 North Umpqua River	Whistlers Bend Park	BST	C	●		●	35 B7
4318 North Umpqua River	Winchester	BS	P				35 B6
4320 North Umpqua River	Wright Creek	ST	G	●		●	36 B2
4323 Ochoco Reservoir	Ochoco Lake Campgd	T	A	●		●	80 C2
4326 Odell Lake	Odell Lake Lodge	T	C	●	●	●	44 D1
4329 Odell Lake	Princess	T	C	●		●	43 D8
4332 Odell Lake	Shelter Cove Resort	T	C	●	●	●	43 D8
4335 Odell Lake	Sunset Cove Campgd	T	C	●		●	44 D1
4338 Odell Lake	Trapper Creek Campgd	T	C	●		●	43 D8
4341 Olallie Lake	Olallie Lake Campgd	T	E	●		●	56 B2
4344 Olive Lake	Olive Lake	T	C	●		●	82 A2
4347 Owyhee River	Rome Access	W	G	●		●	75 A6
4350 Owyhee River	Three Forks Access	W	E	●			75 B8
4353 Oxbow Pool	Oxbow Pool	W	G	●			88 A4
4356 Pacific Ocean	Cape Kiwanda	BM	E	●		●	58 C1
4359 Pacific Ocean	Dory Launch	BM	E	●		●	64 B1
4362 Pacific Ocean	Port of Port Orford	BM	H	●	●	●	25 C5
4365 Paulina Lake	Little Crater Campgd	T	C	●		●	45 C7
4368 Paulina Lake	Paulina Lake Campgd	T	C	●		●	45 C6
4371 Paulina Lake	Paulina Lake Resort		C				45 C6
4374 Phillips Lake	Mason Ramp	TW	A	●		●	82 B4
4377 Phillips Lake	South West Shore Launch	TW	G	●		●	82 B4
4380 Phillips Lake	Union Creek Camp	TW	A	●		●	82 B4
4383 Pilcher Creek Res	Pilcher Creek Reservoir	T	C	●		●	86 D4
4386 Pinehollow Reservoir	Cascade Hyland Resort	TW	C	●		●	63 C6
4389 Pinehollow Reservoir	Cascade Hyland Resort	TW	C	●		●	63 C6
4392 Powers Park Pond	Powers Park	TW	A	●		●	25 A8
4395 Priday Reservoir	Priday Reservoir Access	T	E	●			73 C5
4398 Prineville Reservoir	County Ramp #1	TW	A	●		●	80 D2
4401 Prineville Reservoir	Jasper Point	TW	A	●		●	80 D2
4404 Prineville Reservoir	Powder Cove	TW	G	●		●	80 D1
4407 Prineville Reservoir	Prineville Res SP	TW	A	●		●	80 D2
4410 Prineville Reservoir	Prineville Resort	TW	G	●	●	●	80 D2
4413 Prineville Reservoir	Roberts Bay East	TW	E	●			80 D2
4416 Rock Creek Reservoir	Rock Creek Reservoir	TW	E	●		●	63 C5
4419 Rogue River	Almeda Bar	BST	C	●		●	26 D4
4420 Rogue River	Baker Park	BST	C	●		●	19 A6
4422 Rogue River	Casey State Rec Site	BST	C	●		●	28 C3
4425 Rogue River	Chinook Park	BST	C	●		●	19 A7
4431 Rogue River	Cougar Lane Store	BS	G	●		●	25 D8
4434 Rogue River	Coyote Evans Wayside	BST	C	●		●	19 A7
4437 Rogue River	Dodge Bridge	BST	C	●	●	●	28 D2
4440 Rogue River	Ennis Riffle	BST	C	●		●	26 D4
4443 Rogue River	Ferry Hole	BST	C	●		●	19 A5
4446 Rogue River	Ferry Ramp	BS	C	●			17 A2
4449 Rogue River	Fishers Ferry	BST	C				19 A8
4452 Rogue River	Foster Bar	BS	C	●		●	25 C8
4455 Rogue River	Galice Boat Landing	BST	C	●		●	26 D4
4458 Rogue River	Gold Hill	BST	C	●		●	19 A8
4461 Rogue River	Grave Creek Landing	BST	A	●		●	26 C4
4464 Rogue River	Griffin Park	BST	C	●		●	19 A5
4467 Rogue River	Hog Creek Landing	BST	C	●		●	26 D4
4470 Rogue River	Huntley Park	BS	G	●		●	17 A2
4473 Rogue River	Indian Mary	BST	C	●		●	26 D4
4476 Rogue River	Lathrop Landing	BST	C	●			19 A5
4479 Rogue River	Lobster Creek	BS	C	●		●	25 D6
4482 Rogue River	Lucas Beach	BS	E	●			25 D8
4485 Rogue River	Matson Park	BST	E	●		●	19 A5
4488 Rogue River	McGregor Park	BST	C	●		●	28 C3
4491 Rogue River	Pierce Riffle	BST	C	●		●	19 A7
4494 Rogue River	Quosatana Campground	BS	C	●		●	17 A3
4497 Rogue River	Rand Access	BST	G	●			26 D4
4500 Rogue River	Riverside Park	BST	C	●		●	19 A6
4503 Rogue River	Robertson Bridge	BST	C	●		●	19 A5
4506 Rogue River	Rogue Elk	BST	C	●	●	●	28 C3
4509 Rogue River	Savage Rapids	BST	C	●		●	19 A7
4512 Rogue River	Schroeder Park	BST	C	●		●	19 A5
4515 Rogue River	Shady Cove	BST	C	●	●	●	28 D2
4518 Rogue River	Takelma	BST	A	●	●	●	28 D2
4521 Rogue River	Tou Velle State Park	BST	C	●		●	20 A1
4524 Rogue River	Valley of the Rogue SRA	BST	C	●		●	19 A8
4527 Rogue River	Whitehorse Park	BST	C	●		●	19 A5
4530 Rogue River Bay	Jots Resort	BS	A			●	17 A1
4533 Rogue River Bay	Port of Gold Beach	BS	C	●	●	●	17 A1
4536 Row River	Schwarz Pk Hand Launch	BS	E	●		●	42 B1
4539 Salmon River	Knight Park	BMT	C	●		●	58 D1
4542 Sand Lake	Whalen Island County Pk	CMT	G	●		●	58 B1
4545 Sandy River	Dabney State Rec Area	BS	E	●		●	67 D6
4548 Sandy River	Lewis and Clark SRS	BS	C	●		●	67 D5
4551 Sandy River	Oxbow Park	BS	C	●	●	●	61 A6
4554 Santiam River	Jefferson Junction	BST	C	●		●	53 C8
4557 Santiam River	Jefferson Site	BST	A	●			53 C8
4560 Saunders Lake	Jack Ripper–Saunders L	TW	G	●		●	32 D3

continued on next page

BOAT RAMPS/FISHING, *continued*

To locate boat ramps in this Atlas, look on the appropriate map for the boat ramp symbol and corresponding number. The fish type category includes the most popular species. For more information contact: Oregon Department of Fish & Wildlife, Headquarters, 3406 Cherry Avenue NE, Salem, OR 97303, (503) 947-6000.

Abbreviations

Ramp Types

A–Asphalt
C–Concrete
E–Earth/Sand
G–Gravel
H–Hoist
P–Pole Slide
O–Other

Fish Types

A–Sturgeon
B–Salmon
C–Crab
D–Striped Bass
M–Marine Sport Fish
S–Steelhead
T–Trout
W–Warmwater Fishes

BODY OF WATER	FACILITY	FISH TYPE	RAMP TYPE	PARKING	FEES	RESTROOMS	PAGE & GRID
4563 Scappoose Bay	Scappoose Bay Marina	BW	C	●		●	66 B2
4569 Siletz River	Coyote Rock RV Park	BST	A	●	●	●	52 A1
4572 Siletz River	Hee Hee Illahee	BST	A	●		●	52 C1
4573 Siletz River	Mill Park	BST	A	●			52 C1
4575 Siletz River	Moonshine Park	BST	C	●		●	52 B2
4576 Siletz River	Morgan Park	BST	A	●		●	52 B1
4578 Siletz River	Ojalla Park	BST	E	●			52 B1
4581 Siletz River	Sam Creek	BST	A	●		●	52 C2
4584 Siletz River	Siletz Moorage	BST	A	●	●	●	32 A1
4587 Siletz River	Sportsmans Landing	BST	H	●	●	●	52 A1
4590 Siletz River	Stroms Landing	BST	A	●		●	52 B1
4593 Siletz River	Sunset Landing	BST	H	●	●	●	52 A1
4596 Siltcoos Lake	Ada County Park	BTW	C			●	32 B4
4599 Siltcoos Lake	Ada Resort	BTW	C	●	●	●	32 B4
4602 Siltcoos Lake	Darlings Resort	BTW	C	●	●	●	32 A4
4605 Siltcoos Lake	Fishmill Lodges	BTW	E	●			32 A4
4608 Siltcoos Lake	Nightengales Resort	BTW	G	●		●	32 A4
4611 Siltcoos Lake	Siltcoos Lake Resort	BTW	G			●	32 A4
4614 Siltcoos Lake	West Lake	BTW	A	●		●	32 A4
4617 Siltcoos River	Tyee Campground	BST	A	●		●	32 A4
4623 Silverton Reservoir	Silverton Reservoir	T	A	●		●	54 A3
4626 Siuslaw River	Austa Boat Ramp	BDST	E	●			46 D3
4629 Siuslaw River	C and D Dock	BST	H	●	●	●	46 D1
4632 Siuslaw River	Cushman RV and Marina	BST	G	●	●	●	32 A4
4635 Siuslaw River	Farnham Landing	BST	P	●		●	46 D1
4638 Siuslaw River	Florence Public Ramp	BST	C	●	●	●	32 A4
4641 Siuslaw River	Ford Access	BDST	E	●			40 A3
4644 Siuslaw River	Linslaw Park	BS	E	●		●	40 A3
4647 Siuslaw River	Mapleton Landing	BST	C	●			46 D2
4650 Siuslaw River	Midway Dock	BST	H	●	●	●	46 D1
4653 Siuslaw River	Richardsons Pole Slide	BST	P	●			46 D3
4656 Siuslaw River	Siuslaw Marina	BST	G	●	●	●	32 A4
4659 Siuslaw River	Tide Wayside	BST	A	●		●	46 D2
4662 Siuslaw River	Tiernan Boat Ramp	BST	C	●			46 D1
4665 Siuslaw River	Whittaker Creek	BDST	P	●		●	40 A3
4668 Siuslaw River	Wolf Creek Boat Ramp	BDST	E	●			40 A4
4669 Siuslaw River, N Fk	Bender Landing	BST	A	●		●	32 D2
4670 Siuslaw River, N Fk	Houghton Landing	BST	E	●			46 D1
4671 Sixes River	Cape Blanco State Park	BS	G	●			24 B4
4674 Sixes River	Edson Creek	BS	E	●		●	25 B5
4677 Sixes River	Mid-drift	BS	G	●			25 B5
4680 Sixes River	Sixes River Store	BS	G			●	25 B5
4683 Skipanon River	Warrenton Marina	BT	C	●	●	●	70 C2
4686 Smith Reservoir	Smith Reservoir	T	G	●		●	49 B8
4689 Smith River	Bolon Island	BDMST	C	●		●	32 C4
4692 Smith River	Lower Drift Take-out	BDST	P	●			40 B2
4695 Smith River	Noel Ranch Boat Launch	BDST	C	●			40 B1
4698 Smith River	Riverside	BDST	C	●		●	40 B1
4701 Snake River	Adrian Ramp	W	G	●			79 B8
4704 Snake River	Dug Bar	STW	C	●		●	88 A2
4707 Snake River	Hells Canyon Cr Rec Site	S	C	●		●	88 C2
4710 Snake River	Nyssa Ramp	W	C	●		●	79 A8
4713 Snake River	Oasis	W	E	●			83 C8
4716 Snake River	Ontario Ramp	W	A	●		●	88 D4
4719 Snake River	Pittsburgh Landing	ABSTW	C	●		●	88 B3
4728 Snake River	Tunnel Ramp	S	C	●		●	88 D1
4737 South Santiam River	Gills Landing	BST	C	●			54 D1
4740 South Santiam River	Santiam Marine Park	TW	A	●		●	48 A3
4743 South Santiam River	Waterloo Park	BST	C	●		●	48 A2
4746 South Santiam River	Wiley Creek Park	BST	C	●		●	48 A3
4749 South Twin Lake	South Twin Boating	T	C	●		●	44 C2
4752 South Umpqua River	Canyonville Park	SW	C	●		●	26 A6
4755 South Umpqua River	Fairgrounds	BSW	C	●		●	35 C6
4758 South Umpqua River	Happy Valley	BSW	C	●			35 C5
4761 South Umpqua River	Three C Rock	BST	E	●		●	28 A1
4764 South Umpqua River	Weigle Landing	BSW	E	●			35 D5
4767 South Yamhill River	Kiwanis Marine Park	BST	C	●		●	59 C7
4770 Sparks Lake	Sparks Lake	T	C	●		●	50 D3
4773 Spaulding Reservoir	Spaulding Res Access	T	E	●			73 D7
4776 Sturgeon Lake	Sturgeon Lake	W	A	●			66 C2
4779 Summit Lake	Summit Lake Campgd	T	E	●		●	37 A7
4782 Sunset Lake	Sunset Lake Park	TW	G	●			70 D2
4785 Suttle Lake	Blue Bay Campground	T	C	●		●	50 A3
4788 Suttle Lake	Link Creek Campgd	T	C	●		●	50 A2
4791 Suttle Lake	South Shore Campgd	T	C	●		●	50 A3
4794 Suttle Lake	Water Ski Area	T	C	●		●	50 A2
4797 Sutton Lake	Sutton Launch	BTW	A	●		●	32 D2
4800 Swan Island Lagoon	Swan Island Boat Ramp	ABSW	A	●		●	66 D3
4803 Taft Miller Reservoir	Taft Miller Access	W	E	●			73 B7
4806 Tahkenitch Lake	Tahkenitch Landing	BTW	A	●		●	32 B4
4809 Tahkenitch Lake	Tahkenitch Ramp	BTW	G	●		●	32 B4
4812 Tenmile Creek	Lakeside #1	BS	A				32 D3
4815 Tenmile Creek	Lakeside #2	BDSTW	A				32 D3
4818 Tenmile Creek	Spinreel	BDSTW	P	●		●	32 D3
4821 Tenmile Lake	La Playa Marina	BDTW	O	●	●	●	32 D3
4824 Tenmile Lake	North Lake Resort	BDTW	C	●	●	●	32 D3
4827 Tenmile Lake	Tenmile Lake Park	BDTW	C	●	●	●	33 D3
4830 Thief Valley Reservoir	Thief Valley	TW	C	●		●	87 D5
4833 Thompson Reservoir	East Bay Campground	T	C	●		●	31 A8
4836 Thompson Reservoir	Thompson Res Campgd	T	C	●		●	31 A8
4839 Three Creek Lake	Three Cr L Campgd	T	E	●			50 D3
4842 Tillamook Bay	Garibaldi Marina	BCMS	A	●			64 D1
4845 Tillamook Bay	Memaloose Point	BCMS	C	●	●	●	58 A1
4848 Tillamook Bay	Port of Bay City	BCMS	C	●	●	●	64 D1
4851 Tillamook River	Big Barn Marina	BST	G	●	●	●	58 A2
4854 Tillamook River	Burton Frasier Ramp	BST	C	●		●	58 A2
4857 Timothy Lake	Gone Creek Campgd	T	E	●		●	62 D2
4860 Timothy Lake	Hood View Campgd	T	E	●		●	62 D2
4863 Timothy Lake	Oak Fork Camp	T	C	●		●	62 D2
4866 Timothy Lake	Pine Point Ramp	T	C	●		●	62 D2
4869 Toketee Reservoir	Toketee Lake	T	G	●		●	37 B5
4872 Town Lake	Town Lake	TW	G	●			58 C1
4875 Trail Bridge Reservoir	Trail Bridge	T	G	●		●	49 B8
4878 Trask River	Carnahan Park	BST	C	●		●	58 A2
4881 Trask River	Cedar Creek Ramp	BST	G	●			58 A3
4884 Trask River	Lorens Drift	BST	G	●			58 A3
4887 Trask River	Lower Peninsula	BST	G				58 A3
4890 Trask River	Lower Trask	BST	C	●			58 A2
4893 Trask River	Stone Camp	BST	P				58 A3
4896 Trask River	Upper Peninsula	BST	G				58 A3
4899 Triangle Lake	Triangle Lake	TW	C	●			46 C4
4902 Trillium Lake	Trillium Lake Camp	T	E	●		●	62 B3
4905 Tualatin River	Cook Park	BSTW	C	●		●	60 A2
4908 Tualatin River	Tualatin City Park	BSTW	C	●		●	60 A2
4911 Umatilla River	Nugent Park	SW	A	●		●	85 A7
4920 Umpqua River	Cleveland Rapids	BSW	C	●		●	35 B5
4923 Umpqua River	Gardiner	ABDMS	A	●			32 C4
4926 Umpqua River	James Wood	BSTW	C	●		●	34 A4
4927 Umpqua River	Osprey Ramp	BSTW	C	●		●	34 A4
4929 Umpqua River	Rainbow Plaza	BDMST	C	●		●	32 C2
4932 Umpqua River	River Forks Park	BSW	C	●		●	35 B5
4933 Umpqua River	Salmon Harbor—E	ABCDM	C	●	●	●	32 C3
4934 Umpqua River	Salmon Harbor—W	ABCDM	C	●	●	●	32 C3
4935 Umpqua River	Sawyers Rapids	BSW	C	●		●	40 C3
4938 Umpqua River	Scott Creek	BSW	C	●		●	40 C3
4941 Umpqua River	Scottsburg Park	ABDSW	A	●		●	40 C2
4942 Umpqua River	Templin Beach	BSTW	C	●		●	35 C6
4944 Umpqua River	Umpqua Landing	BSW	C	●		●	35 B5
4947 Umpqua River	Umpqua State Scenic Cor	ABDSW	A	●		●	40 C1
4953 Umpqua River	Yellow Creek	BSW	C	●		●	35 A5
4956 Unity Reservoir	Unity Lake State Rec Site	TW	A	●		●	82 B4
4959 Upper Klamath Lake	Eagle Ridge	T	C	●		●	22 A1
4962 Upper Klamath Lake	Hagelstein Park	T	C	●		●	22 A2
4965 Upper Klamath Lake	Harrimans Lodge	T	C	●	●	●	21 A8
4968 Upper Klamath Lake	Howard Bay	T	C	●		●	22 B1
4971 Upper Klamath Lake	Klamath Yacht Club	T	A	●			22 C2
4974 Upper Klamath Lake	Moore Park Marina #1	T	C	●		●	22 C2
4977 Upper Klamath Lake	Moore Park Marina #2	T	C	●		●	22 C2
4980 Upper Klamath Lake	Odessa Campground	TW	E	●			21 A8
4983 Upper Klamath Lake	Pelican Marina	T	A	●		●	22 C2
4986 Upper Klamath Lake	Rocky Point Landing	T	A	●		●	21 A8
4989 Upper Klamath Lake	Rocky Point Resort	T	C				21 A8
4995 Waldo Lake	Islet	T	A	●		●	43 B8
4998 Waldo Lake	North Waldo	T	A	●		●	43 B8
5001 Waldo Lake	Shadow Bay	T	C	●		●	43 C8
5004 Wallowa Lake	North Wallowa Lake	T	C	●		●	87 C8
5007 Wallowa Lake	Wallowa Lake SRA	T	A	●		●	87 C8
5010 Walton Lake	Walton Lake	T	G	●		●	80 C3
5013 Warm Springs Res	Warm Springs Landing	TW	C	●		●	78 B4
5019 Wickiup Reservoir	Gull Point Campground	T	C	●		●	44 C2
5022 Wickiup Reservoir	North Davis Creek	T	E			●	44 C2
5025 Wickiup Reservoir	North Wickiup Boating	T	C	●		●	44 C2
5028 Wickiup Reservoir	Reservoir Campground	T	C	●		●	44 C2
5031 Wickiup Reservoir	Sheeps Bridge	T	G	●		●	44 C2
5034 Wickiup Reservoir	West South Twin	T	E			●	44 C2
5035 Wickiup Reservoir	Wickiup Butte	T	A	●		●	44 C3
5036 Willamette R, Mid Fk	Clearwater Landing	BST	A	●		●	48 D1
5037 Willamette R, Mid Fk	Jasper Bridge	BST	G	●			42 A1
5038 Willamette R, Mid Fk	Pengra Access	BST	C	●		●	42 A2
5040 Willamette River	Baker Park	BST	E	●		●	47 D8
5043 Willamette River	Bernert Landing	ABSW	C	●		●	60 B3
5049 Willamette River	Boones Ferry Landing	BSW	C	●		●	60 B2
5052 Willamette River	Bowman Park	BSW	C	●		●	53 C8
5055 Willamette River	Browns Landing	BST	P	●			47 C7
5058 Willamette River	Bryant Park	BST	A	●		●	53 C8
5061 Willamette River	Buena Vista County Park	BSW	C	●		●	53 B7
5064 Willamette River	Cathedral Park	ABSW	C	●		●	66 D2
5067 Willamette River	Cedar Oak	ABSW	C	●		●	60 A3
5070 Willamette River	Christensens Landing	BSW	C	●		●	47 C7
5072 Willamette River	Clackamette Park	ABSW	C	●		●	60 B4
5076 Willamette River	Corvallis Ramp	BSTW	A	●			53 D6
5079 Willamette River	Harrisburg	BSW	O	●		●	47 B7
5082 Willamette River	Hebb Park	ABSW	C	●		●	60 B3
5085 Willamette River	Hileman Landing	BST	G				47 C7
5088 Willamette River	Hyak Park	BSW	C	●		●	53 C7
5091 Willamette River	Island Park	BST	C	●		●	47 D8
5097 Willamette River	Jefferson Street	ABSW	C	●		●	60 A3
5100 Willamette River	Marshall Island Access	BSW	C	●		●	47 C7
5103 Willamette River	McCartney Park	BSTW	C	●		●	47 B7
5106 Willamette River	Meldrum Bar Park	ABSW	C	●		●	60 B4
5109 Willamette River	Molalla River State Park	BSTW	C				60 B3
5112 Willamette River	Oak Grove Boat Ramp	ABSW	C	●		●	60 A3
5118 Willamette River	Peoria Park	BSTW	C	●		●	47 A7
5121 Willamette River	Riverview Park	BSW	C	●		●	53 B7
5124 Willamette River	Rogers Landing	BSW	C	●		●	60 B1
5127 Willamette River	San Salvador	BSW	C	●		●	59 C8
5130 Willamette River	Sportcraft Landing	ABSW	C	●		●	60 B4
5131 Willamette River	Takena Landing	BST	C	●		●	53 C8
5133 Willamette River	Wallace Marine Park	BSW	C	●		●	53 A8
5136 Willamette River	Wallace Marine	BSE	C	●		●	53 A8
5139 Willamette River	Western Oregon Marine	BSW	A			●	60 B2
5142 Willamette River	Wheatland Ferry	BSW	C	●			59 D8
5145 Willamette River	Whitely Landing	BST	A	●			47 D8
5148 Willamette River	Willamette Mission SP	BSW	C	●		●	59 D8
5151 Willamette River	Willamette Park	BSTW	C	●		●	53 D6
5154 Willamette River	Willamette Park	ABSW	C	●	●	●	60 B2
5157 Willamette River	Willamette Park	ABSW	C	●	●	●	60 A3
5160 Williamson River	Chiloquin Access	T	E	●		●	30 D1
5163 Williamson River	Waterwheel Park	T	E	●	●	●	30 D1
5166 Willow Creek Res	Willow Creek Lake	TW	C	●		●	85 C6
5169 Willow Lake	Willow Lake	TW	C	●		●	21 A5
5172 Willow Valley Res	Willow Valley Access	TW	G	●			23 D8
5175 Wilson River	Herd Hole	BST	P				58 A3
5178 Wilson River	Mills Bridge	BST	G	●		●	58 A3
5181 Wilson River	Siskeyville	BST	P	●			58 A3
5184 Wilson River	Sollie Smith	BST	C	●		●	58 A2
5187 Woahink Lake	East Woahink Lake	T	C	●		●	32 A4
5190 Woahink Lake	West Woahink Lake	T	A	●		●	32 A4
5193 Wolf Creek Reservoir	Wolf Creek	T	C	●		●	86 D4
5196 Yachats River	Yachats Landing	BST	C	●			32 B2
5199 Yamhill River	Dayton Boat Ramp	BST	C	●			59 C8
5202 Yaquina Bay	Idaho Point Marina	BCM	C	●	●	●	32 D1
5205 Yaquina Bay	Newport Marina	BCM	A	●	●	●	32 C1
5208 Yaquina Bay	River Bend Moorage	BCM	H	●	●	●	32 D1
5211 Yaquina Bay	Sawyers Moorage	BCM	H	●	●	●	32 D1
5214 Yaquina Bay	South Beach Marina	BCM	C	●	●	●	32 D1
5217 Yaquina River	Cannon Park	BST	C	●		●	52 D1
5220 Yaquina River	Elk City Dock and Ramp	BST	A	●		●	52 D2
5223 Yaquina River	Toledo Boat Launch	BST	C	●		●	52 D1
5226 Yellow Jacket Res	Yellow Jacket Landing	T	G	●		●	77 A7
5229 Youngs Bay	Tide Point Ramp	BT	A	●	●	●	70 C3
5235 Youngs Bay	Yacht Club	BT	C	●		●	70 C3

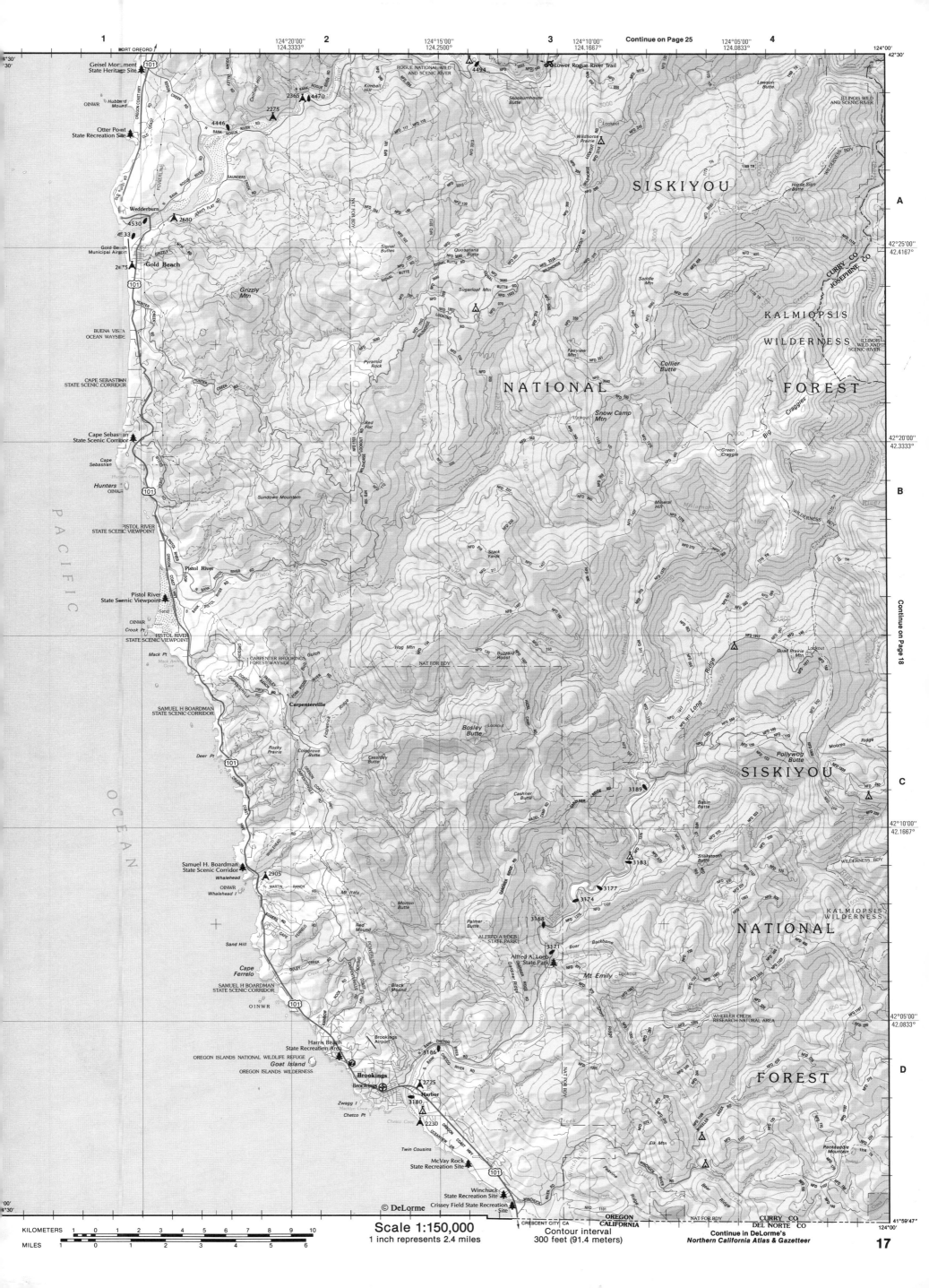

PACIFIC

OCEAN

SISKIYOU

NATIONAL

FOREST

KALMIOPSIS
WILDERNESS

KALMIOPSIS
WILDERNESS

SISKIYOU

NATIONAL

FOREST

Gold Beach

Pistol River

Carpenterville

Brookings
Harbor

Continue on Page 18

© DeLorme

Scale 1:150,000
1 inch represents 2.4 miles

Contour interval
300 feet (91.4 meters)

KILOMETERS
MILES

OREGON
CALIFORNIA

CURRY CO
DEL NORTE CO

Continue in DeLorme's
Northern California Atlas & Gazetteer

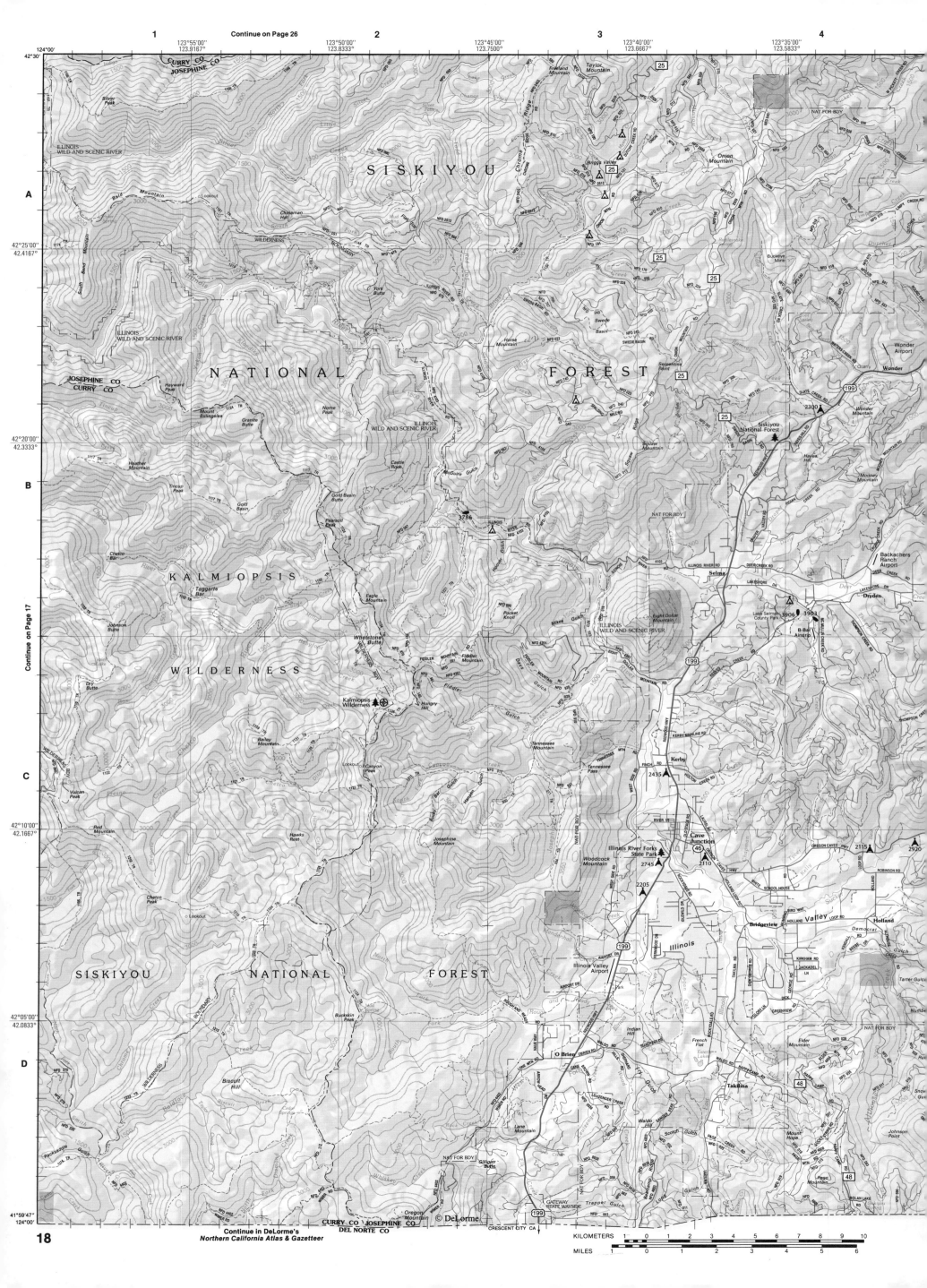

Continue on Page 17

Continue in DeLorme's
Northern California Atlas & Gazetteer

Continue on Page 27

Continue on Page 20

Continue in DeLorme's
Northern California Atlas & Gazetteer

Scale 1:150,000
1 inch represents 2.4 miles

Contour interval
300 feet (91.4 meters)

© DeLorme

19

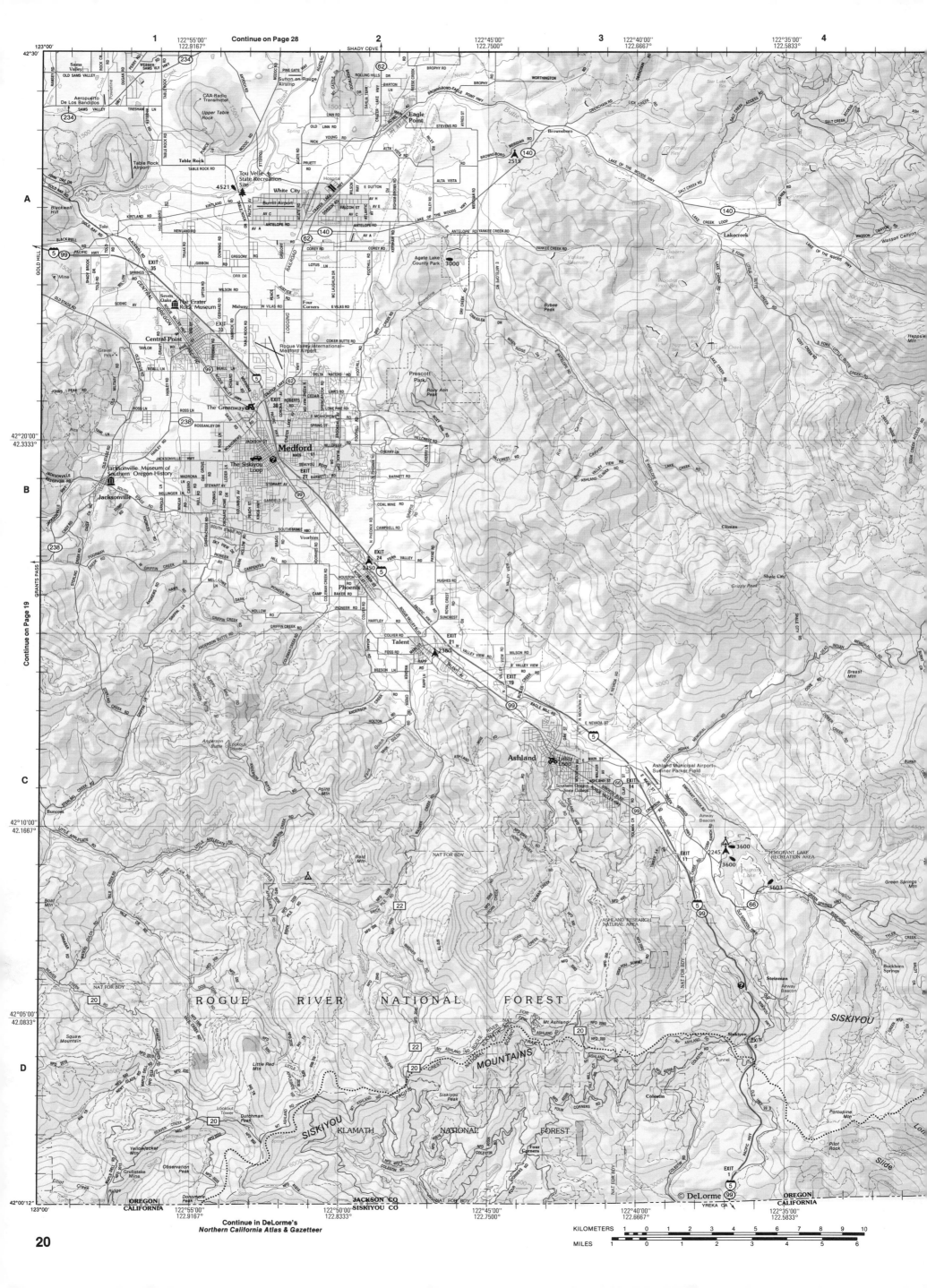

Continue on Page 19

Continue in DeLorme's
Northern California Atlas & Gazetteer

ROGUE RIVER NATIONAL FOREST

SISKIYOU   KLAMATH   NATIONAL   FOREST

MOUNTAINS

SISKIYOU

Medford

Central Point

Jacksonville

Phoenix

Talent

Ashland

Eagle Point

Brownsboro

White City

Lakecreek

KILOMETERS

MILES

© DeLorme

OREGON
CALIFORNIA

Continue on Page 29

Continue on Page 22

ROGUE

RIVER

NATIONAL

FOREST

WINEMA

NATIONAL

FOREST

Mt. McLoughlin
ELEV 9495 ft
2894 m

Brown Mountain Lava Field

Brown Mtn

Mountain Lakes Wilderness

MOUNTAIN LAKES WILDERNESS

Mount Hartman

Upper Klamath Lake
ELEV 4140 ft
1262 m

UPPER KLAMATH

NATIONAL

WILDLIFE REFUGE

Upper Klamath National Wildlife Refuge

MOUNTAINS

Keene

Creek Ridge

Pine Ridge

Continue in DeLorme's
Northern California Atlas & Gazetteer

OREGON
CALIFORNIA

KLAMATH CO
SISKIYOU CO

JACKSON CO
KLAMATH CO

SISKIYOU CO
JACKSON CO

© DeLorme

Scale 1:150,000
1 inch represents 2.4 miles

Contour interval
300 feet (91.4 meters)

Continue on Page 21

Continue in DeLorme's
Northern California Atlas & Gazetteer

KILOMETERS
MILES

© DeLorme

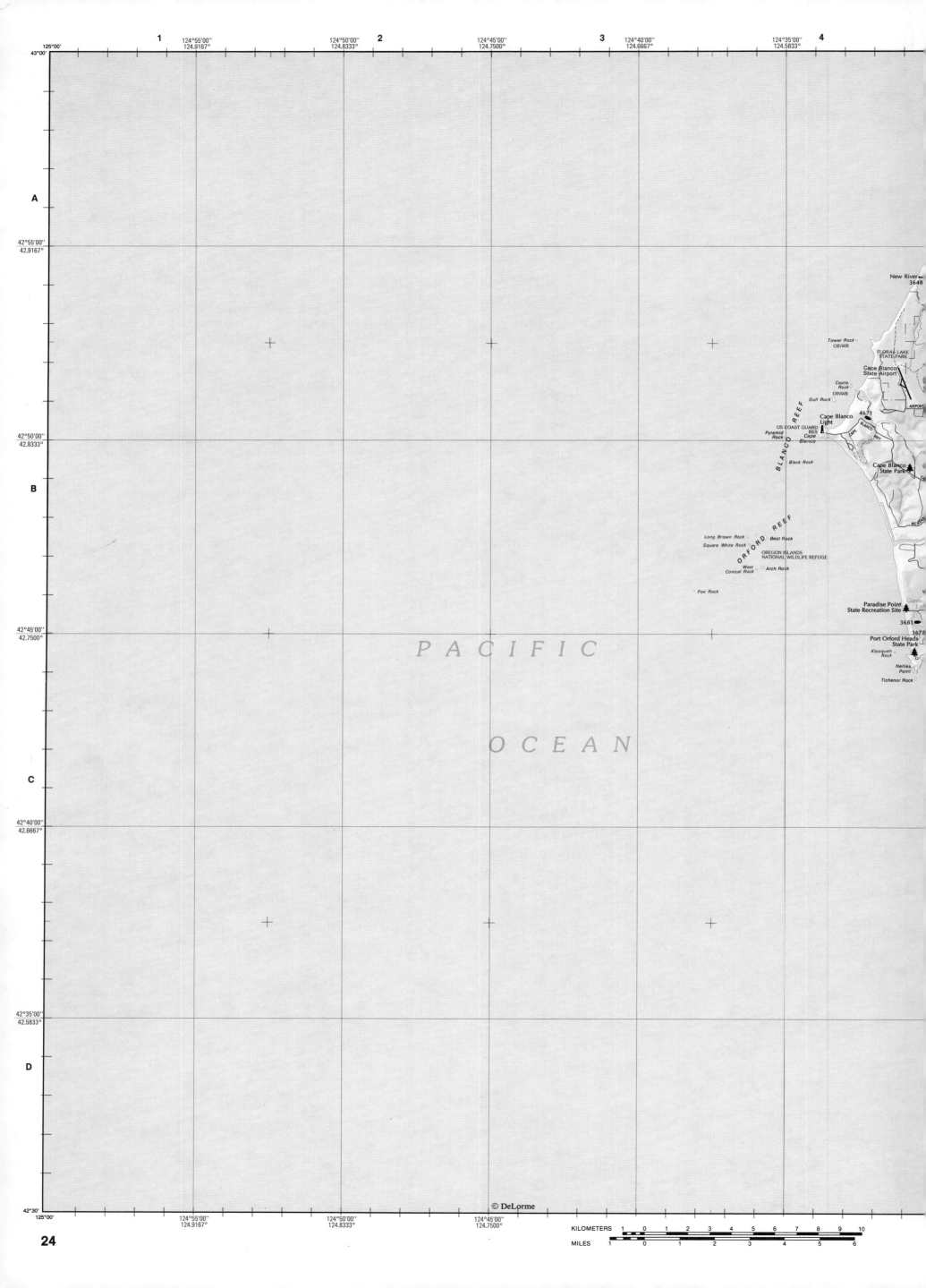

125°00'
124°55'00'' 124.9167°
124°50'00'' 124.8333°
124°45'00'' 124.7500°
124°40'00'' 124.6667°
124°35'00'' 124.5833°

43°00'

A

42°55'00'' 42.9167°

New River 3648

Tower Rock OINWR

FLORAS LAKE STATE PARK

Cape Blanco State Airport

Castle Rock OINWR

Gull Rock

AIRPORT

Cape Blanco Light 4671

US COAST GUARD RES

Pyramid Rock

Cape Blanco

42°50'00'' 42.8333°

BLANCO REEF

Black Rock

B

Cape Blanco State Park

ORFORD REEF

Long Brown Rock   Best Rock

Square White Rock

OREGON ISLANDS NATIONAL WILDLIFE REFUGE

West Conical Rock   Arch Rock

Fox Rock

Garris

Paradise Point State Recreation Site 3681

3678

42°45'00'' 42.7500°

PACIFIC

Port Orford Heads State Park

Klooqueh Rock

Nellies Point

Tichenor Rock

OCEAN

C

42°40'00'' 42.6667°

42°35'00'' 42.5833°

D

42°30'

125°00'
124°55'00'' 124.9167°
124°50'00'' 124.8333°
124°45'00'' 124.7500°

© DeLorme

KILOMETERS   1   0   1   2   3   4   5   6   7   8   9   10

MILES   1   0   1   2   3   4   5   6

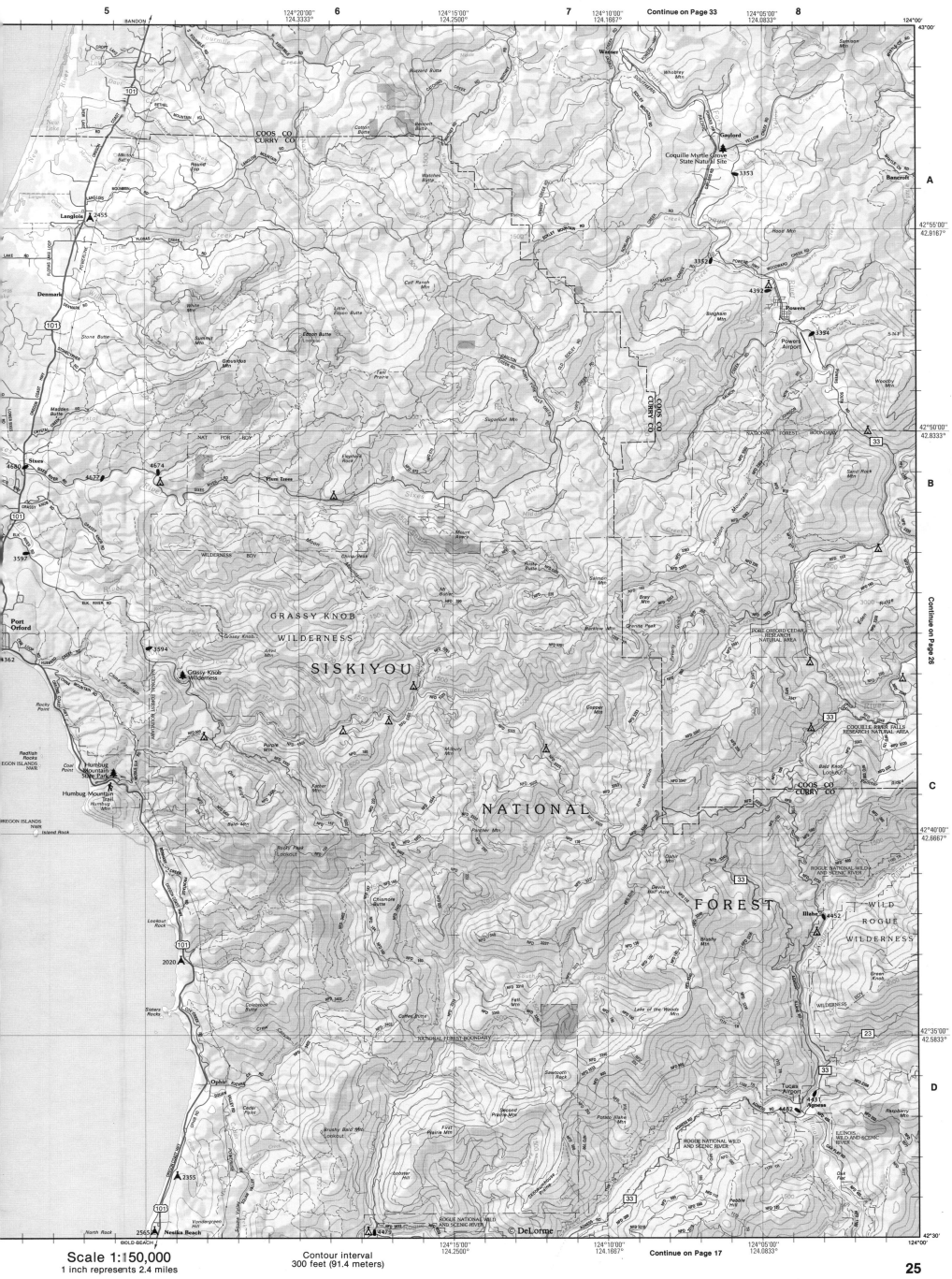

124°20'00''
124.3333°

124°15'00''
124.2500°

124°10'00''
124.1667°

124°05'00''
124.0833°

124°00'

43°00'

BANDON

Coal Knob

New Lake

101

BETHEL

MOUNTAIN RD

Round Top

COOS CO
CURRY CO

Buzzard Butte

Cotton Butte

Benett Butte

Watches Butte

Watner

Whobrey Mtn

Samson Mtn

Gaylord

Coquille Myrtle Grove
State Natural Site

3353

Bancroft

A

Langlois
2455

Denmark

101

White Mtn

Summit Mtn

Gabouslous Mtn

Calf Ranch Mtn

Little Edson Butte

Edson Butte Lookout

Tent Prairie

Carlton

Hood Mtn

42°55'00''
42.9167°

3352

4392

Bingham Mtn

Powers

Powers Airport

3354

Woodby Mtn

S N F

Madden Butte

Stone Butte

Sixes
4680

4677

4674

NAT FOR BDY

Plum Trees

Sugarloaf Mtn

42°50'00''
42.8333°

33

NATIONAL FOREST BOUNDARY

Elephant Rock

Sixes

Sand Rock Mtn

B

3597

Port Orford

4362

WILDERNESS BDY

GRASSY KNOB

China Peak

Mt Butler

NFD 590

Moon

Mount Avery

Rusty Butte

Salmon Mtn

Bray Mtn

Granite Peak

Barklow Mtn

PORT ORFORD CEDAR
RESEARCH NATURAL AREA

Eden Ridge

3594

WILDERNESS

Grassy Knob
Wilderness

Anvil Mtn

SISKIYOU

Copper Mtn

Coquille River Falls
Research Natural Area

33

C

Redfish Rocks
OREGON ISLANDS NWR

Coal Point

Humbug Mountain State Park

Humbug Mountain Trail

Humbug Mtn

Bald Mtn

Milbury Mtn

Father Mtn

NATIONAL

Bald Knob Lookout

COOS CO
CURRY CO

Island Rock
OREGON ISLANDS NWR

Rocky Point

Rocky Peak Lookout

Panther Mtn

Ophir Mtn

42°40'00''
42.6667°

ROGUE NATIONAL WILD
AND SCENIC RIVER

33

Lookout Rock

2020

101

Chismore Butte

FOREST

Devils Half Acre

Illahe
4452

WILD

ROGUE

WILDERNESS

Green Knob

Sisters Rocks

Colebrook Butte

Brushy Mtn

Lake of the Woods Mtn

WILDERNESS

23

2355

Ophir

Cedar Point

Fall Mtn

Coffee Butte

NATIONAL FOREST BOUNDARY

Sawtooth Rock

Tucas Airport

42°35'00''
42.5833°

33

D

Brushy Bald Mtn Lookout

First Prairie Mtn

Second Prairie Mtn

Potato Illahe Mtn

Agness

4931

4482

ROGUE NATIONAL
WILD AND SCENIC RIVER

ILLINOIS
WILD AND SCENIC
RIVER

Raspberry Mtn

Lobster Hill

Oak Flat

Pebble Hill

2565

North Rock

Nesika Beach

GOLD BEACH

101

4479

ROGUE NATIONAL WILD
AND SCENIC RIVER

© DeLorme

33

42°30'

124°15'00''
124.2500°

124°10'00''
124.1667°

124°05'00''
124.0833°

Continue on Page 17

124°00'

Scale 1:150,000
1 inch represents 2.4 miles

Contour interval
300 feet (91.4 meters)

25

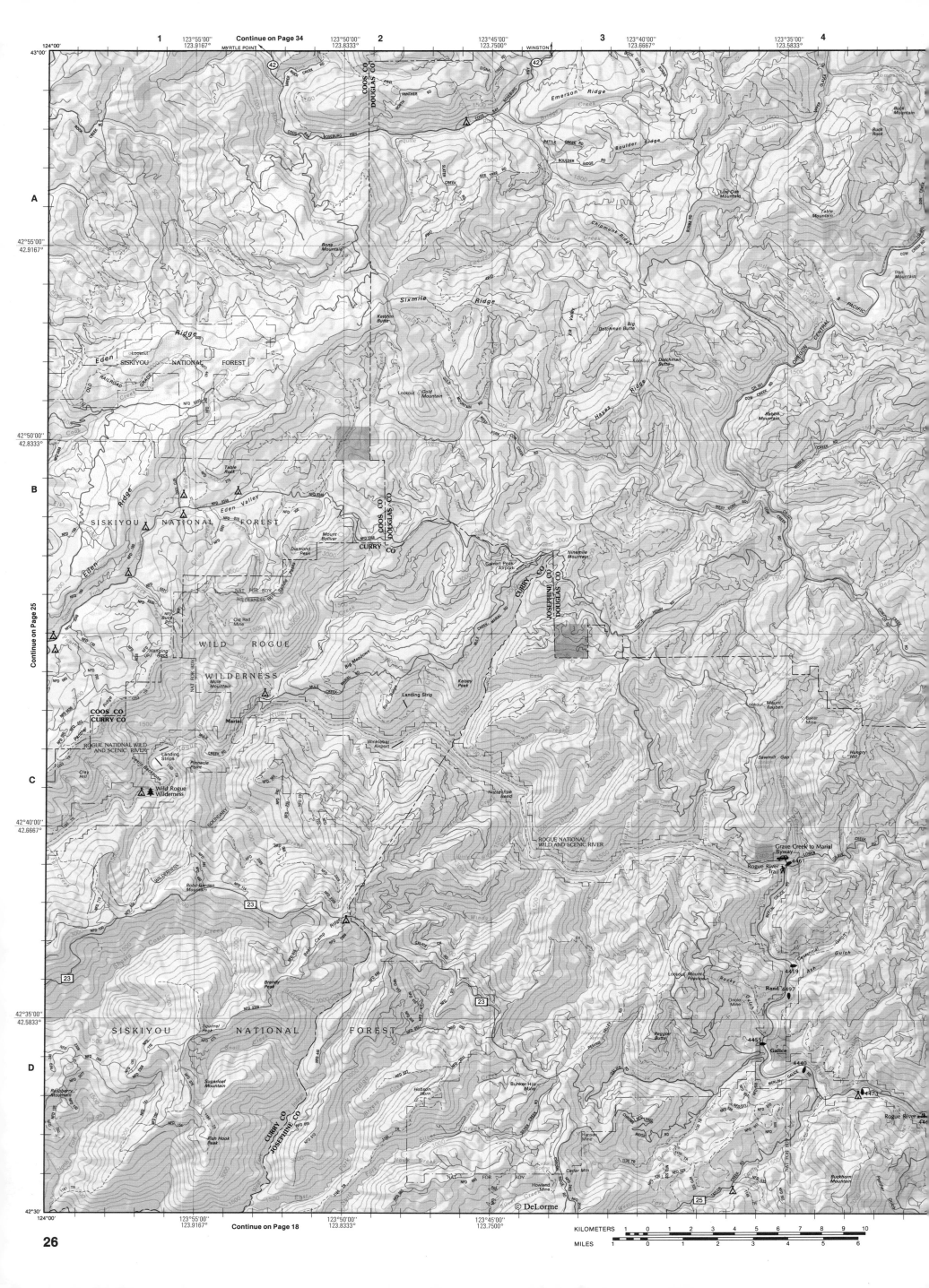

© DeLorme

KILOMETERS
MILES

Continue on Page 28

Continue on Page 19

Scale 1:150,000
1 inch represents 2.4 miles

Contour interval
300 feet (91.4 meters)

© DeLorme

43°00'

ROGUE UMPQUA DIVIDE WILDERNESS

A

42°55'00"
42.9167°

U M P Q U A   N A T I O N A L

DOUGLAS CO
JACKSON CO

F O R E S T

R O G U E   R I V E R

42°50'00"
42.8333°

B

Continue on Page 27

DOUGLAS CO
JACKSON CO

C

42°40'00"
42.6667°

ROGUE RIVER NAT FOR

Joseph H Stewart State Recreation Area

42°35'00"
42.5833°

D

42°30'
123°00'

© DeLorme

KILOMETERS   1   0   1   2   3   4   5   6   7   8   9   10

MILES   1   0   1   2   3   4   5   6

122°45'00"
122.7500°

Continue on Page 30

Scale 1:150,000
1 inch represents 2.4 miles

Contour interval
300 feet (91.4 meters)

© DeLorme

Continue on Page 38

DIAMOND LAKE JUNCTION

121°55'00"
121.9167°

121°45'00"
121.7500°

121°40'00"
121.6667°

121°35'00"
121.5833°

122°00'

43°00'

Beer Butte

Scout Hill

Lookout Butte

CRATER LAKE NATIONAL PARK

Pothole Butte

Dry Butte

WINEMA

NATIONAL

FOREST

Sand Ridge

ANTELOPE DESERT

Baundacy Butte

SUN PASS STATE FOREST

Jackson F. Kimball State Recreation Site

Sun Pass State Forest

Fort Klamath

Fort Klamath Jct

Sugar Hill

Agency Hill

Klamath Agency

Collier Memorial State Park
Logging Museum and Pioneer Village

Pine Ridge

Chiloquin State Airport

Chiloquin

Winema National Forest

Cave Mountain

Brasmill

THE DALLES-CALIFORNIA HWY

PACIFIC

Lena

Chinchalo

Fuego

Kirk

Calimus

Soloman Flat

Soloman Butte

Applegate Butte

Little Applegate Butte

KLAMATH MARSH

NATIONAL

WILDLIFE

REFUGE

Klamath Marsh National Wildlife Refuge

NAT FOR BDY

Rocky Point

Bloddy Point

WINEMA

Wildhorse Ridge

NATIONAL

FOREST

Haystack

WINEMA

NATIONAL

Crawford Butte

Lookout Butte

Calimus Butte

Lone Pine

42°55'00"
42.9167°

42°50'00"
42.8333°

42°40'00"
42.6667°

42°35'00"
42.5833°

A

B

C

D

Continue on Page 29

CRATER LAKE NATIONAL PARK

Agency Lake
ELEV 4139 ft
1262 m

UPPER KLAMATH NAT WILDLIFE REF

3009

3006

3003

5163

2900

2890

3160 Gaging Station

© DeLorme

122°00'
42°30'

121°55'00"
121.9167°

KLAMATH FALLS

Continue on Page 22

121°50'00"
121.8333°

121°45'00"
121.7500°

KILOMETERS 1 0 1 2 3 4 5 6 7 8 9 10

MILES 1 0 1 2 3 4 5 6

Continue on Page 39

Continue on Page 72

Continue on Page 23

Scale 1 150,000
1 inch represents 2.4 miles

Contour interval
300 feet (91.4 meters)

© DeLorme

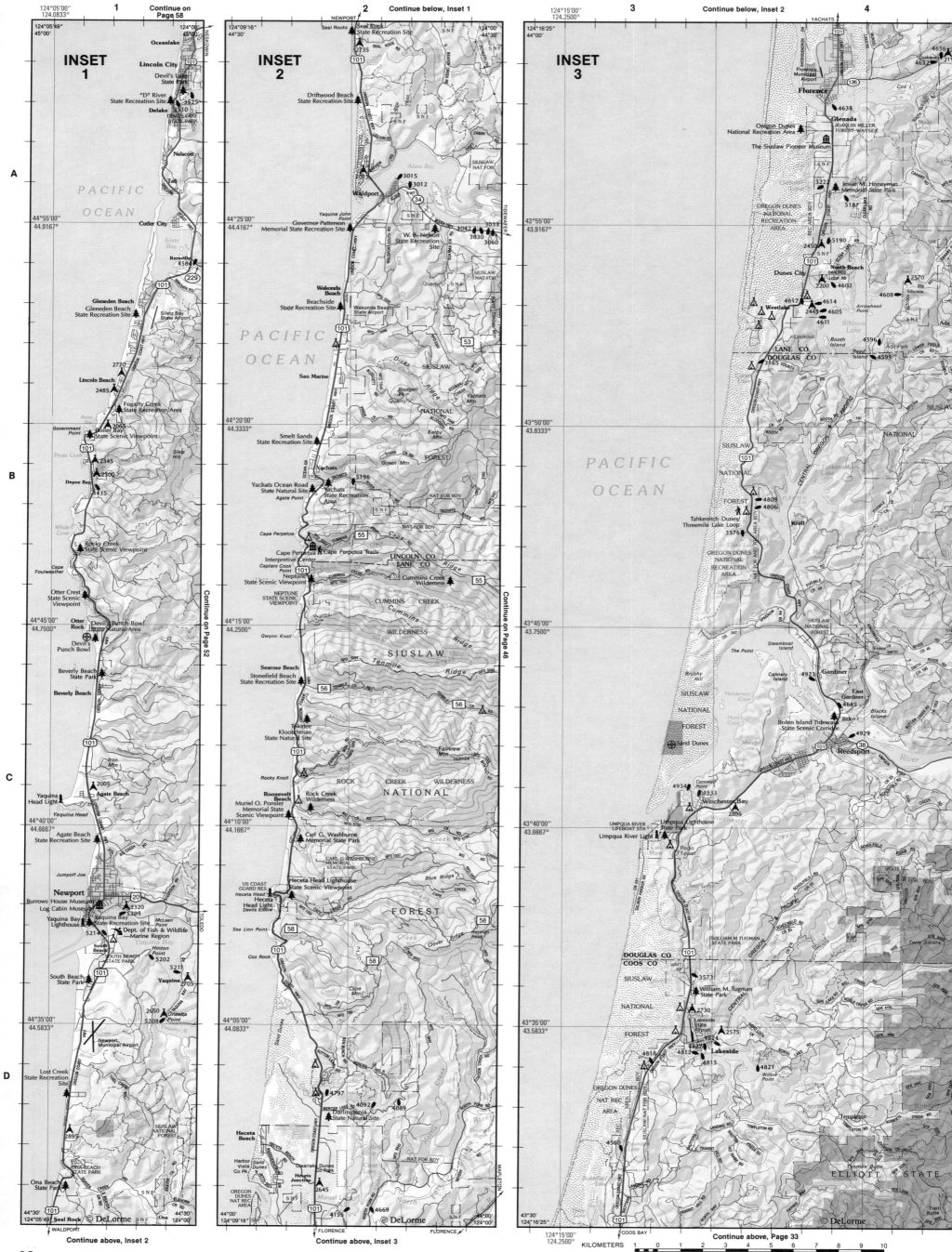

INSET 1

PACIFIC OCEAN

Oceanlake
Lincoln City
Devil's Lake State Park
"D" River State Recreation Site
Delake
Nelscott
Taft
Cutler City
Kernville
Gleneden Beach
Gleneden Beach State Recreation Site
Siletz Bay State Airport
Lincoln Beach
Fogarty Creek State Recreation Area
Boiler Bay State Scenic Viewpoint
Government Point
Depoe Bay
Rocky Creek State Scenic Viewpoint
Cape Foulweather
Otter Crest State Scenic Viewpoint
Otter Rock
Devil's Punch Bowl State Natural Area
Devil's Punch Bowl
Beverly Beach State Park
Beverly Beach
Yaquina Head Light
Agate Beach
Yaquina Head
Agate Beach State Recreation Area
Jumpoff Joe
Newport
Burrows House Museum
Log Cabin Museum
Yaquina Bay Lighthouse
Yaquina Bay State Recreation Site
Dept. of Fish & Wildlife Marine Region
South Beach
SOUTH BEACH STATE PARK
South Beach State Park
Yaquina
McLean Point
Hinton Point
Onsatta Point
Newport Municipal Airport
SIUSLAW NATIONAL FOREST
Lost Creek State Recreation Site
Ona Beach State Park
ONA BEACH STATE PARK
Seal Rock
WALDPORT
Ona

Continue on Page 58
Continue on Page 52
Continue on Page 46
Continue above, Inset 2

INSET 2

NEWPORT
Seal Rock State Recreation Site
Seal Rocks
Driftwood Beach State Recreation Site
SNF
Alsea Bay
SIUSLAW NAT FOR
Waldport
Yaquina John Point
Governor Patterson Memorial State Recreation Site
W. B. Nelson State Recreation Site
Wakonda Beach
Beachside State Recreation Site
Wakonda Beach State Airport
San Marine
PACIFIC OCEAN
Dicks Ridge
SIUSLAW
Blodgett Quarry
Yachats Mtn
NATIONAL
Smelt Sands State Recreation Site
Yachats
Yachats Ocean Road State Natural Site
Agate Point
Yachats State Recreation Area
Cape Perpetua
Green Mtn
NAT FOR BDY
FOREST
Cape Perpetua Trails
Cape Perpetua Interpretive Center
Captain Cook Point
Neptune State Scenic Viewpoint
NEPTUNE STATE SCENIC VIEWPOINT
LINCOLN CO
LANE CO
Cummins Creek Wilderness
CUMMINS CREEK WILDERNESS
Cummins Ridge
SIUSLAW
Searose Beach
Stonefield Beach State Recreation Site
Tenmile Ridge
Gwynn Knoll
Tokatee Klootchman State Natural Site
Rocky Knoll
ROCK CREEK WILDERNESS
Fairview Mtn
Roosevelt Beach
Muriel O. Ponsler Memorial State Scenic Viewpoint
Rock Creek Wilderness
NATIONAL
Carl G. Washburne Memorial State Park
CARL G WASHBURNE MEMORIAL STATE PARK
Blue Ridge
Heceta Head Lighthouse State Scenic Viewpoint
Heceta Head
Heceta Head Light
Devils Elbow
US COAST GUARD RES
Sea Lion Point
Cox Rock
Cape Mtn
FOREST
Clover Ridge
Herman Peak
Silver Dunes
Darlingtonia State Natural Site
Heceta Beach
Harbor Vista Co Pk
Sand Dunes Co Park
Clearlake
Heceta Junction
OREGON DUNES NAT REC AREA
SNF
Munsel Lake
FLORENCE

Continue below, Inset 1
Continue above, Inset 3
Continue below, Inset 2

INSET 3

YACHATS
Florence Municipal Airport
Florence
Glenada
JOAQUIN MILLER FOREST WAYSIDE
Oregon Dunes National Recreation Area
The Siuslaw Pioneer Museum
Jessie M. Honeyman Memorial State Park
OREGON DUNES NATIONAL RECREATION AREA
SNF
Dunes City
North Beach
Siltcoos
Westlake
Arrowhead Point
Booth Island
Ada Park
Reed Island
LANE CO
DOUGLAS CO
Lookout
SIUSLAW NATIONAL FOREST
Kroll
Tahkenitch Dunes Threemile Lake Loop
OREGON DUNES NATIONAL RECREATION AREA
PACIFIC OCEAN
Steamboat Island
Brushy Hill
The Point
SIUSLAW NATIONAL FOREST
Cannery Island
Gardiner
East Gardiner
Blacks Island
Bolon Island Tideways State Scenic Corridor
Henderson Cove
Sand Dunes
Reedsport
Winchester Bay
Cornwall
UMPQUA RIVER LIFEBOAT STA
Umpqua Lighthouse State Park
Umpqua River Light
Radio Tower
WILLIAM M TUGMAN STATE PARK
DOUGLAS CO
COOS CO
SIUSLAW NATIONAL FOREST
William M. Tugman State Park
Lakeside State Airport
Lakeside
Willow Point
OREGON DUNES NAT REC AREA
ELLIOTT STATE
Tenmile Butte
COOS BAY
FLORENCE

Continue below, Inset 2
Continue above, Page 33

KILOMETERS 1 0 1 2 3 4 5 6 7 8 9 10
MILES 1 0 1 2 3 4 5 6

32

DeLorme

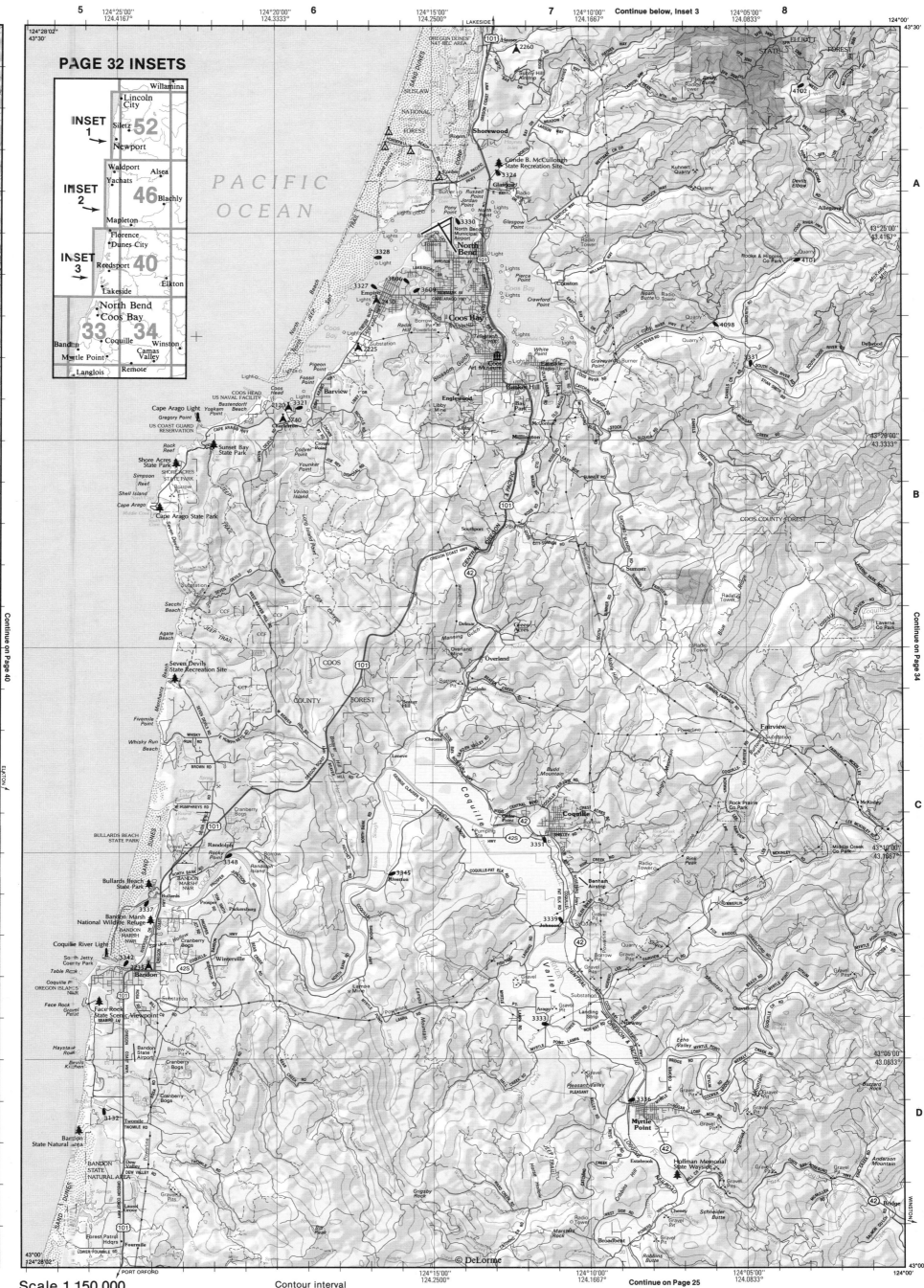

PAGE 32 INSETS

INSET 1
Willamina
Lincoln City
Siletz **52**
Newport

INSET 2
Waldport   Alsea
Yachats
46 Blachly
Mapleton

INSET 3
Florence
Dunes City
Reedsport **40**
Lakeside   Elkton

North Bend
Coos Bay
33 Coquille **34** Winston
Bandon   Camas Valley
Myrtle Point   Remote
Langlois

PACIFIC OCEAN

North Bend

Coos Bay

Charleston

Barview

Coquille

Bandon

Myrtle Point

Continue on Page 40
Continue on Page 34

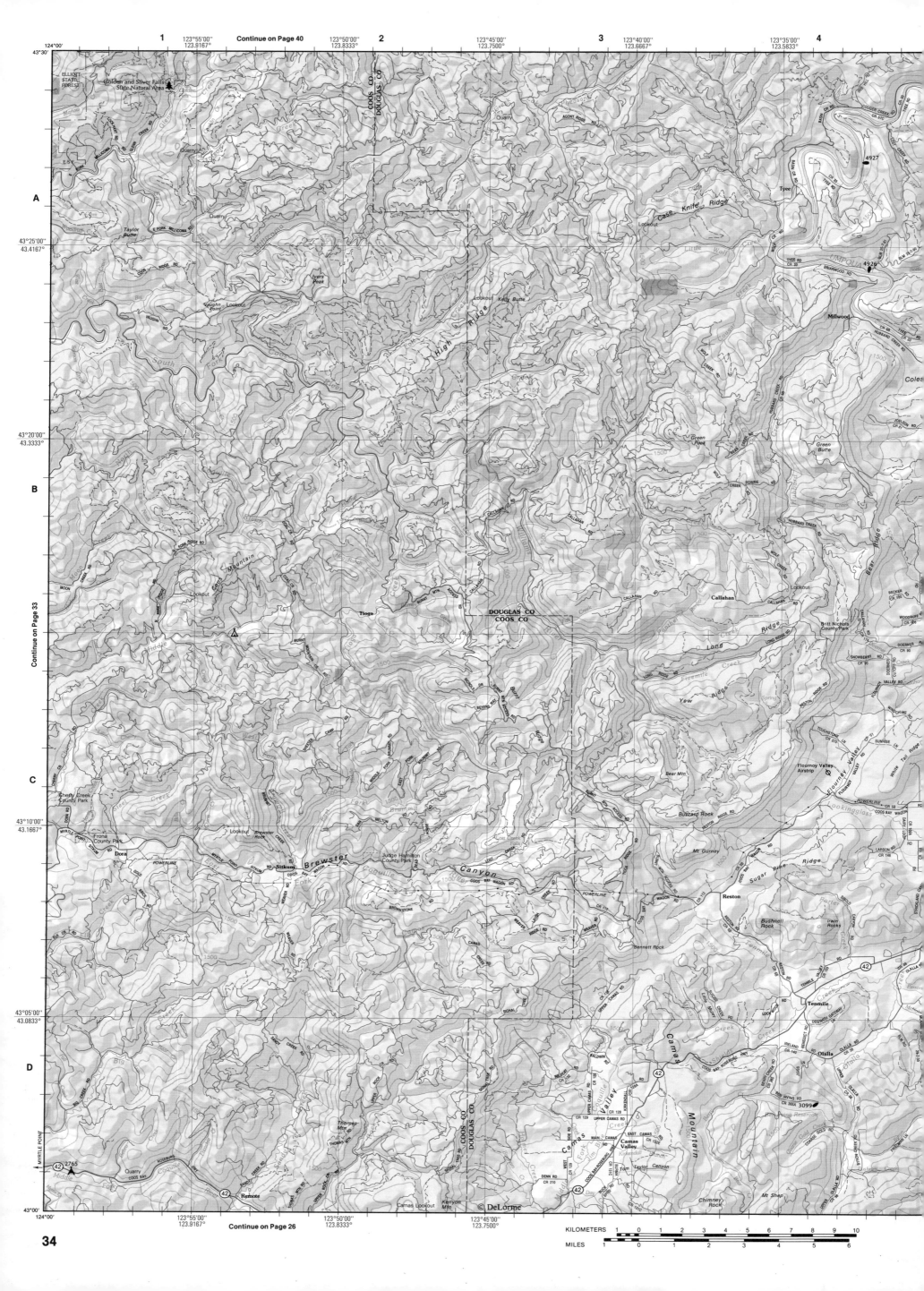

Continue on Page 40

123°55'00''
123.9167°

123°50'00''
123.8333°

123°45'00''
123.7500°

123°40'00''
123.6667°

123°35'00''
123.5833°

124°00'

43°30'

A

43°25'00''
43.4167°

B

43°20'00''
43.3333°

Continue on Page 33

C

43°10'00''
43.1667°

D

43°05'00''
43.0833°

43°00'

124°00'

123°55'00''
123.9167°

Continue on Page 26

123°50'00''
123.8333°

123°45'00''
123.7500°

© DeLorme

ELLIOTT STATE FOREST

Golden and Silver Falls State Natural Area

Taylor Butte

Ivers Peak

Vaughn Point Lookout

Kelly Butte Lookout

High Ridge

Green Peak

Green Butte

Coles

DOUGLAS CO / COOS CO

Tioga

Callahan

Long Ridge

Yew Ridge

Sugar Pine Ridge

Bear Mtn

Buzzard Rock

Mt Gurney

Reston

Bushnell Rock

Irwin Rocks

Bennett Rock

Brewster

Sitkum

Dora

Frona County Park

Cherry Creek County Park

Judge Hamilton County Park

Camas Canyon

Remote

Camas Valley

Thomas Mtn

Camas Lookout

Kenyon Mtn

Chimney Rock

Mt Shep

Tenmile

Otalla

Tyee

Millwood

Case Knife Ridge

UMPQUA

Britt Nichols County Park

Flournoy Valley Airstrip

4927

4926

3099

2765

KILOMETERS   1   0   1   2   3   4   5   6   7   8   9   10

MILES   1   0   1   2   3   4   5   6

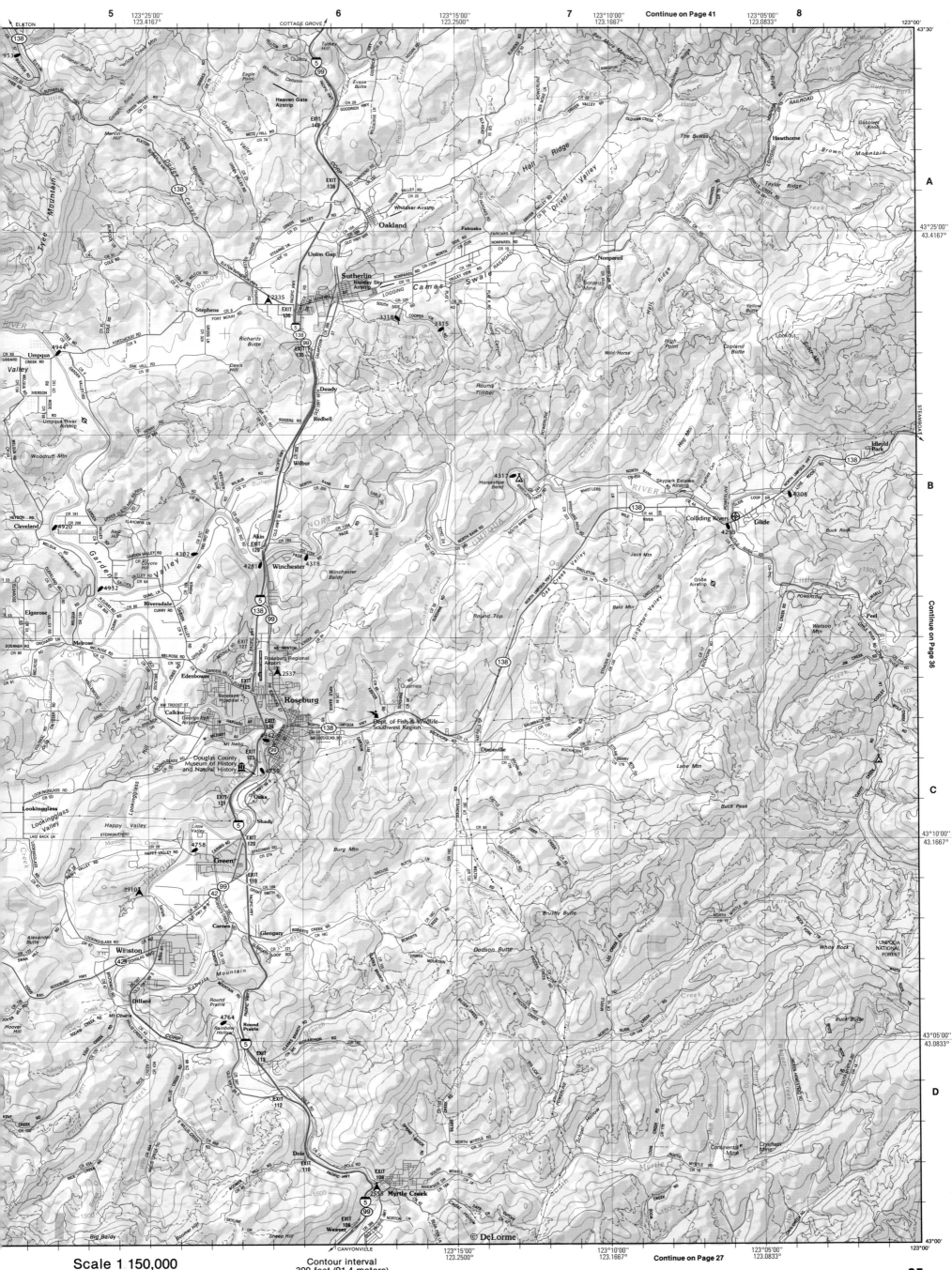

Continue on Page 41

Continue on Page 36

Continue on Page 27

Scale 1 150,000
1 inch represents 2.4 miles

Contour interval
300 feet (91.4 meters)

© DeLorme

35

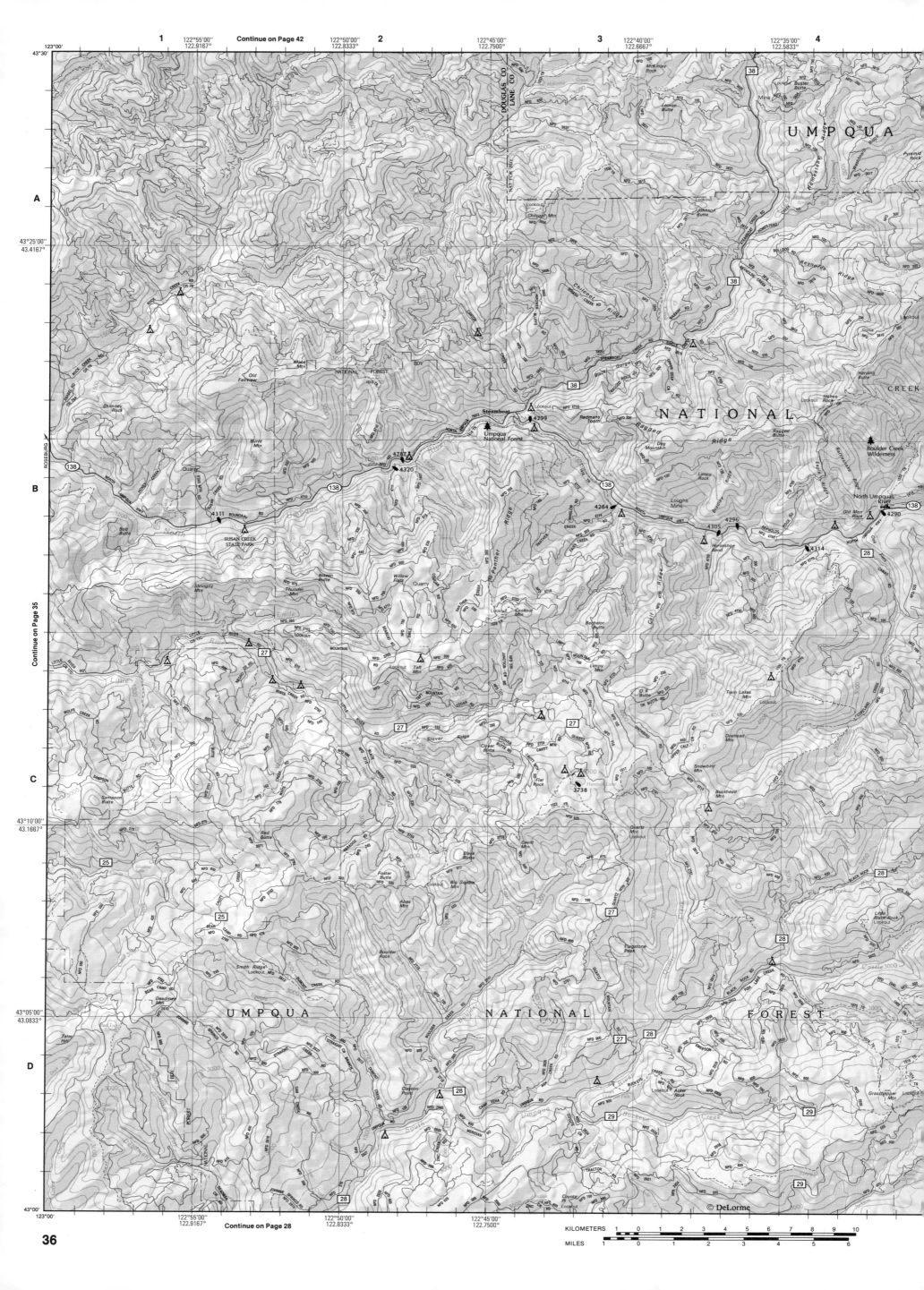

Continue on Page 42

Continue on Page 35

Continue on Page 28

KILOMETERS   1   0   1   2   3   4   5   6   7   8   9   10

MILES   1   0   1   2   3   4   5   6

© DeLorme

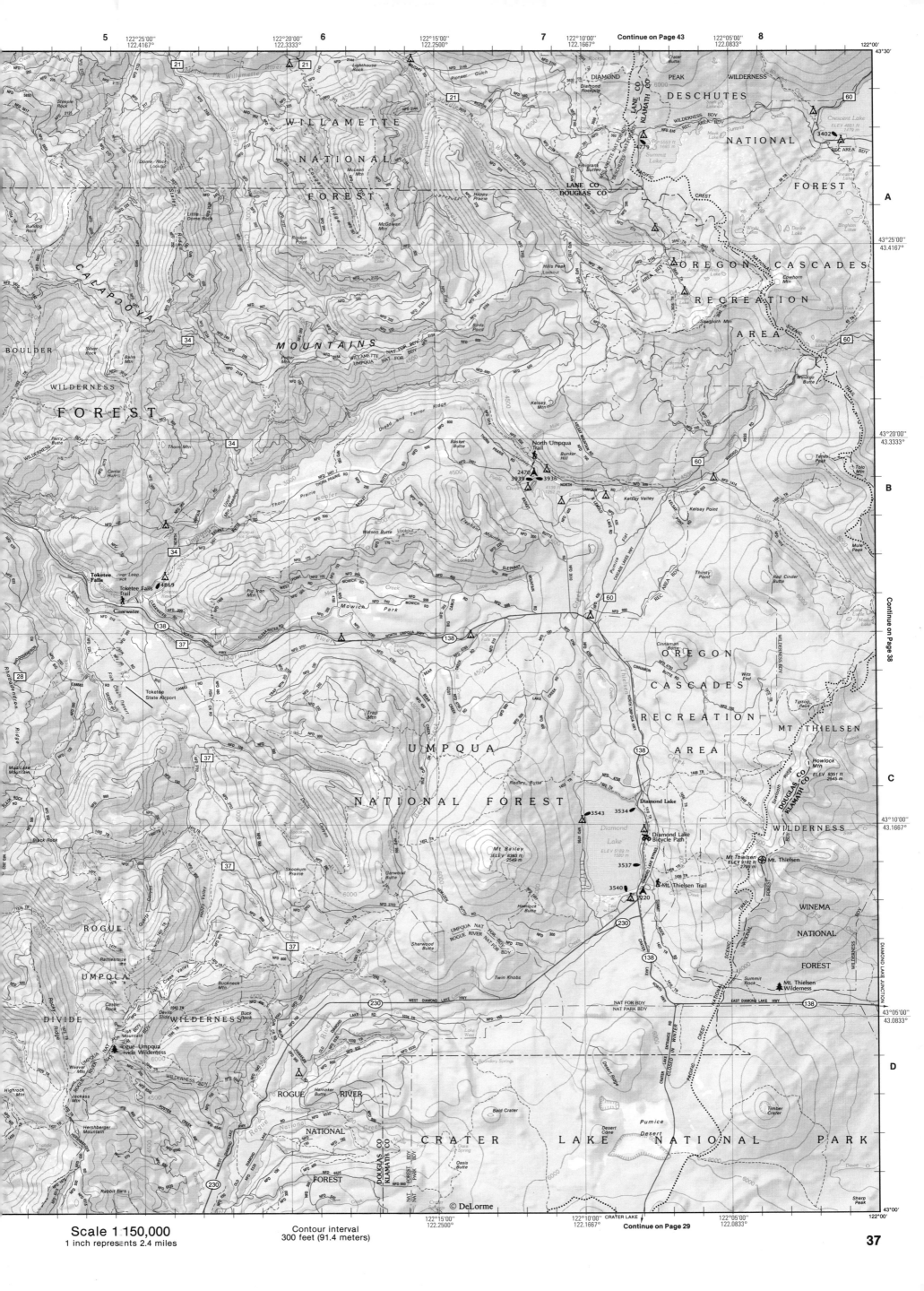

Continue on Page 43

Continue on Page 38

Continue on Page 29

Scale 1:150,000
1 inch represents 2.4 miles

Contour interval
300 feet (91.4 meters)

© DeLorme

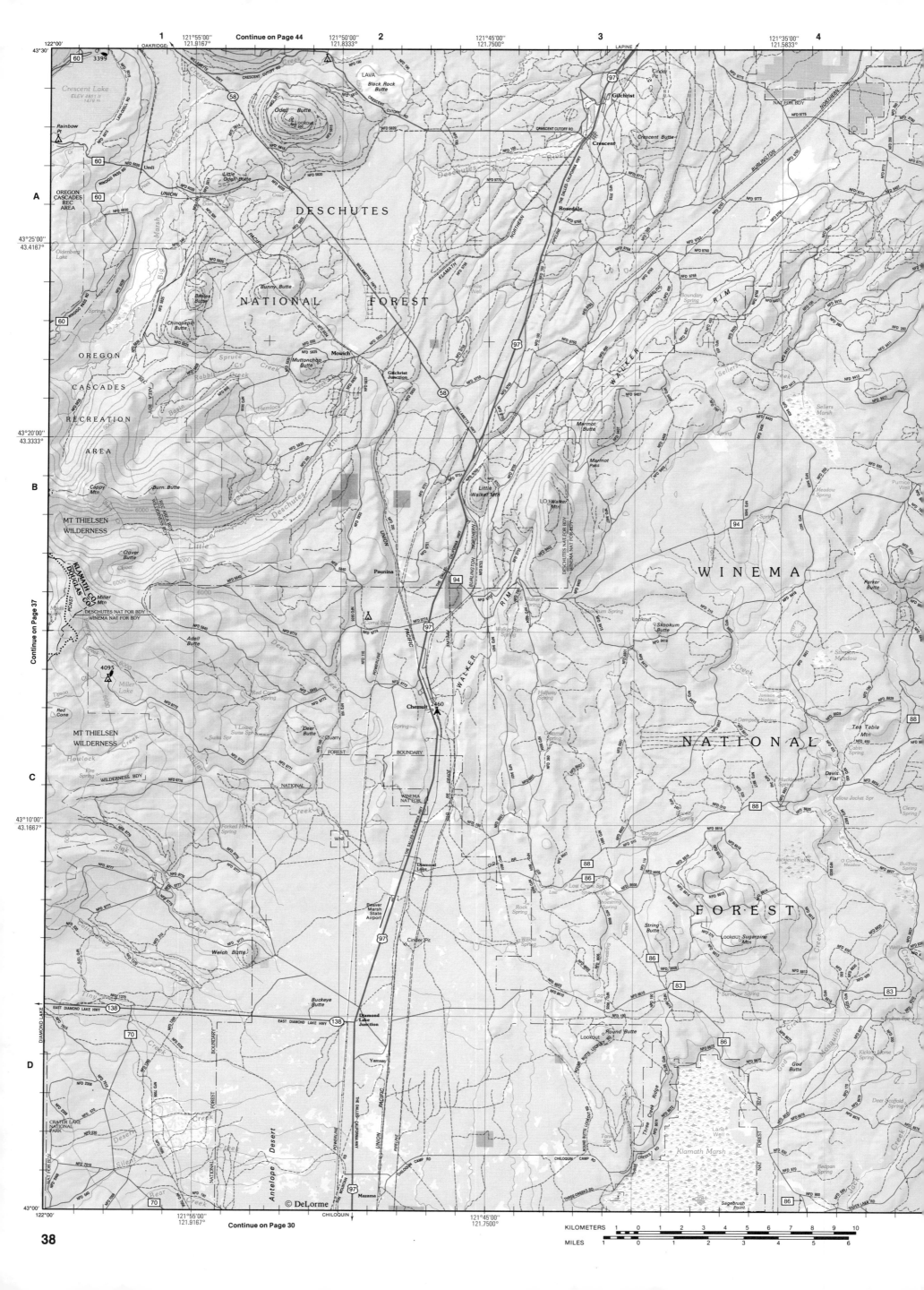

Continue on Page 37

© DeLorme

121°25'00''
121.4167°

121°20'00''
121.3333°

121°15'00''
121.2500°

121°10'00''
121.1667°

121°05'00''
121.0833°

121°00'

43°30'

LAPINE

DESCHUTES NATIONAL FOREST

A

43°25'00''
43.4167°

Big Hole Butte Lookout

Hole-in-the-Ground

Fort Rock State Monument

Fort Rock State Natural Area

FORT ROCK VALLEY

Christmas Valley Byway

43°20'00''
43.3333°

B

FREMONT NATIONAL

Conley Hills

Continue on Page 76

FOREST

C

43°10'00''
43.1667°

Paulina Marsh

43°05'00''
43.0833°

Silver Lake Landing Field

D

FREMONT NATIONAL FOREST

© DeLorme

Continue on Page 31

121°15'00''
121.2500°

121°10'00''
121.1667°

121°05'00''
121.0833°

121°00'
43°00'

Scale 1:150,000
1 inch represents 2.4 miles

Contour interval
300 feet (91.4 meters)

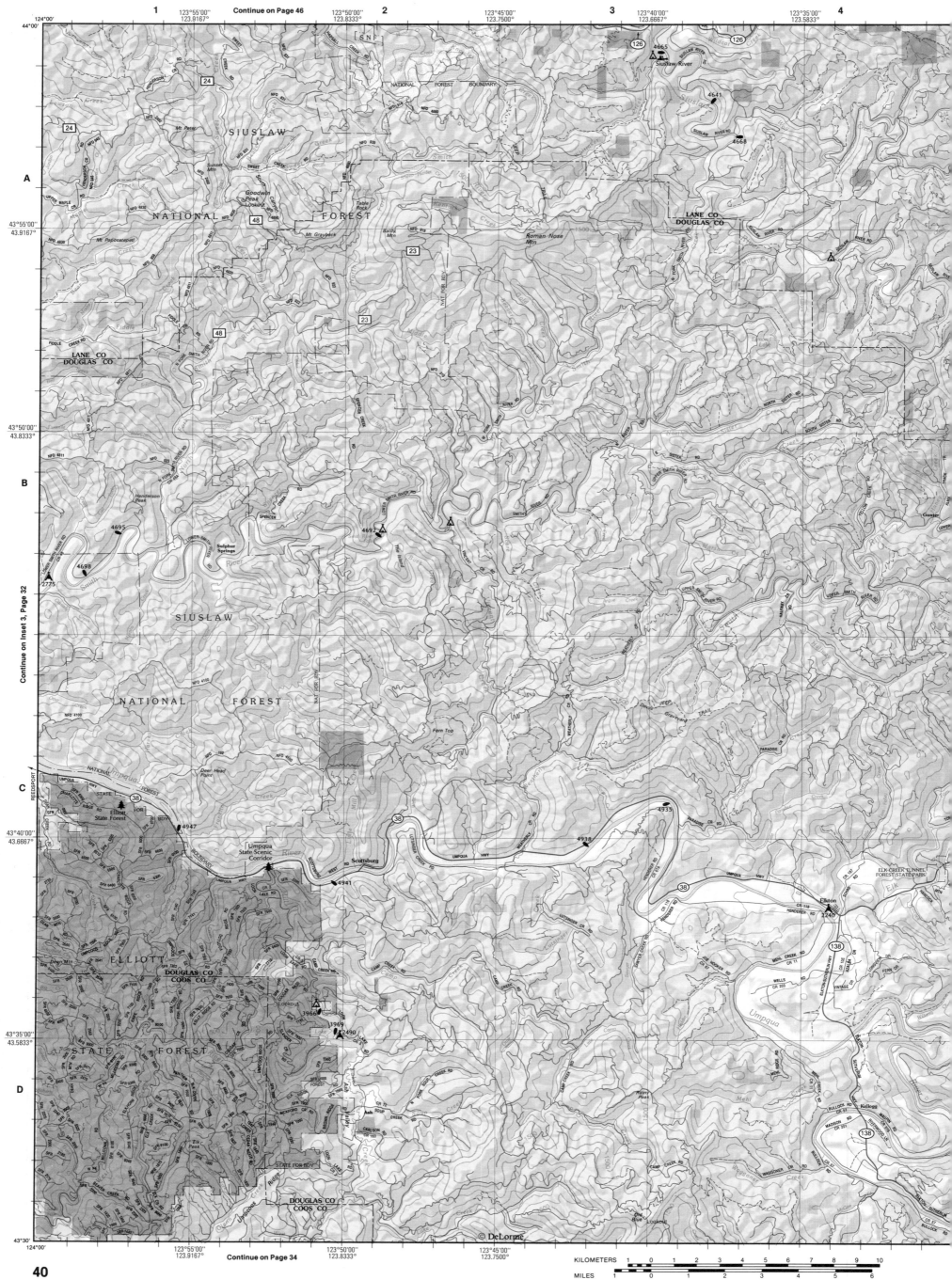

Continue on Inset 3, Page 32

© DeLorme

KILOMETERS 1 0 1 2 3 4 5 6 7 8 9 10
MILES 1 0 1 2 3 4 5 6

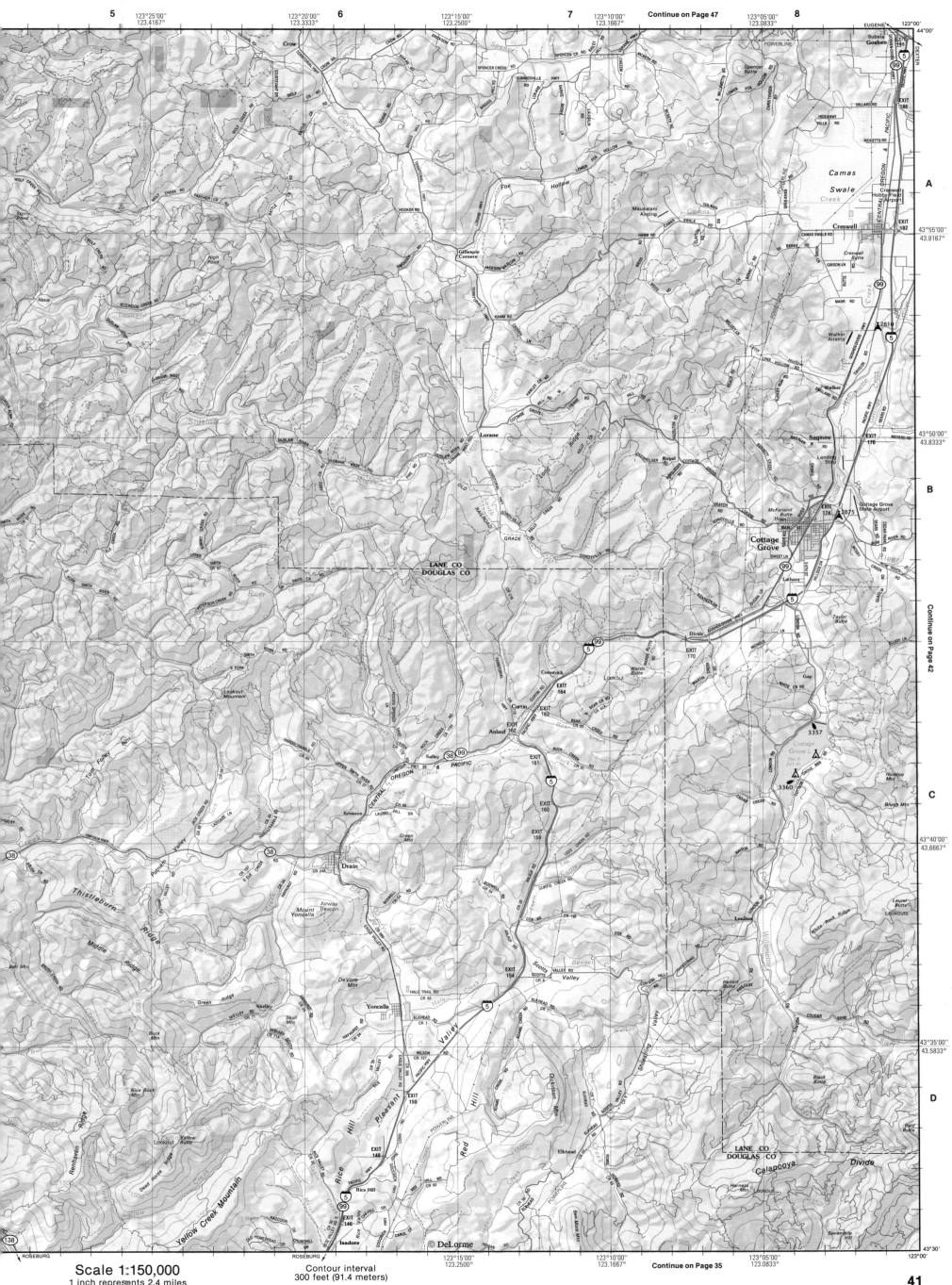

Continue on Page 42

Continue on Page 35

Scale 1:150,000
1 inch represents 2.4 miles

Contour interval
300 feet (91.4 meters)

© DeLorme

Continue on Page 48

Continue on Page 41

Continue on Page 36

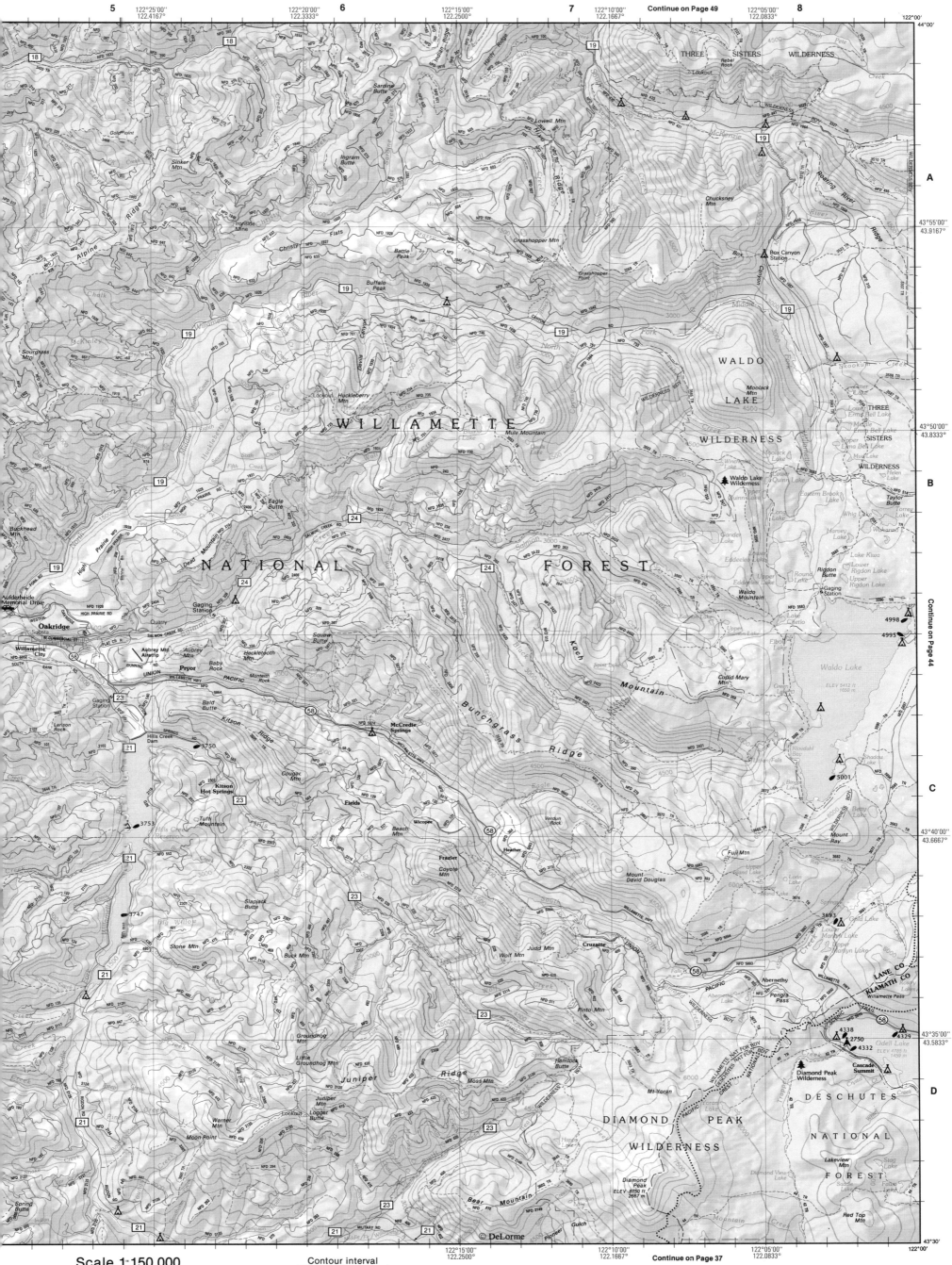

Continue on Page 44

Scale 1:150,000
1 inch represents 2.4 miles

Contour interval
300 feet (91.4 meters)

© DeLorme

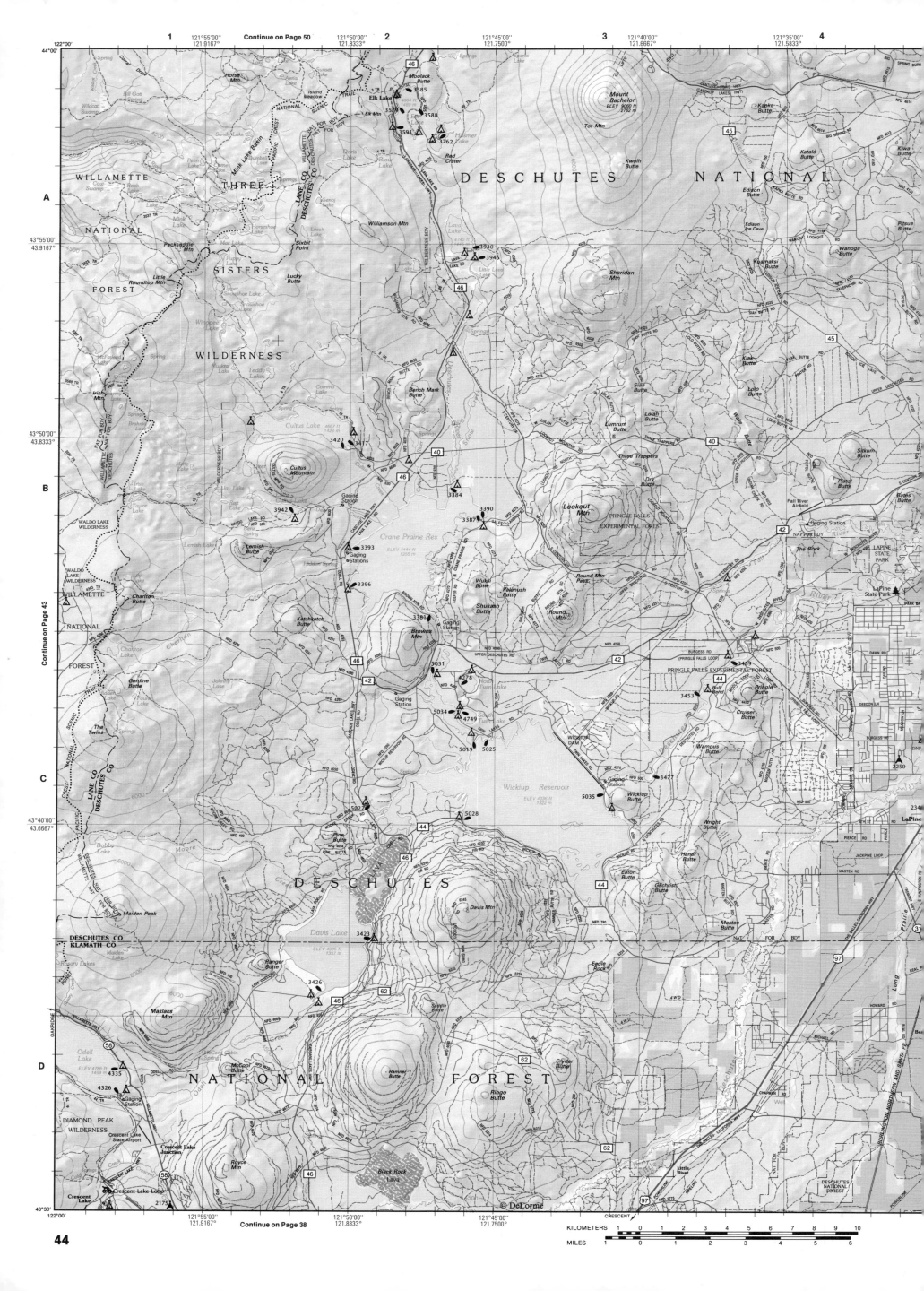

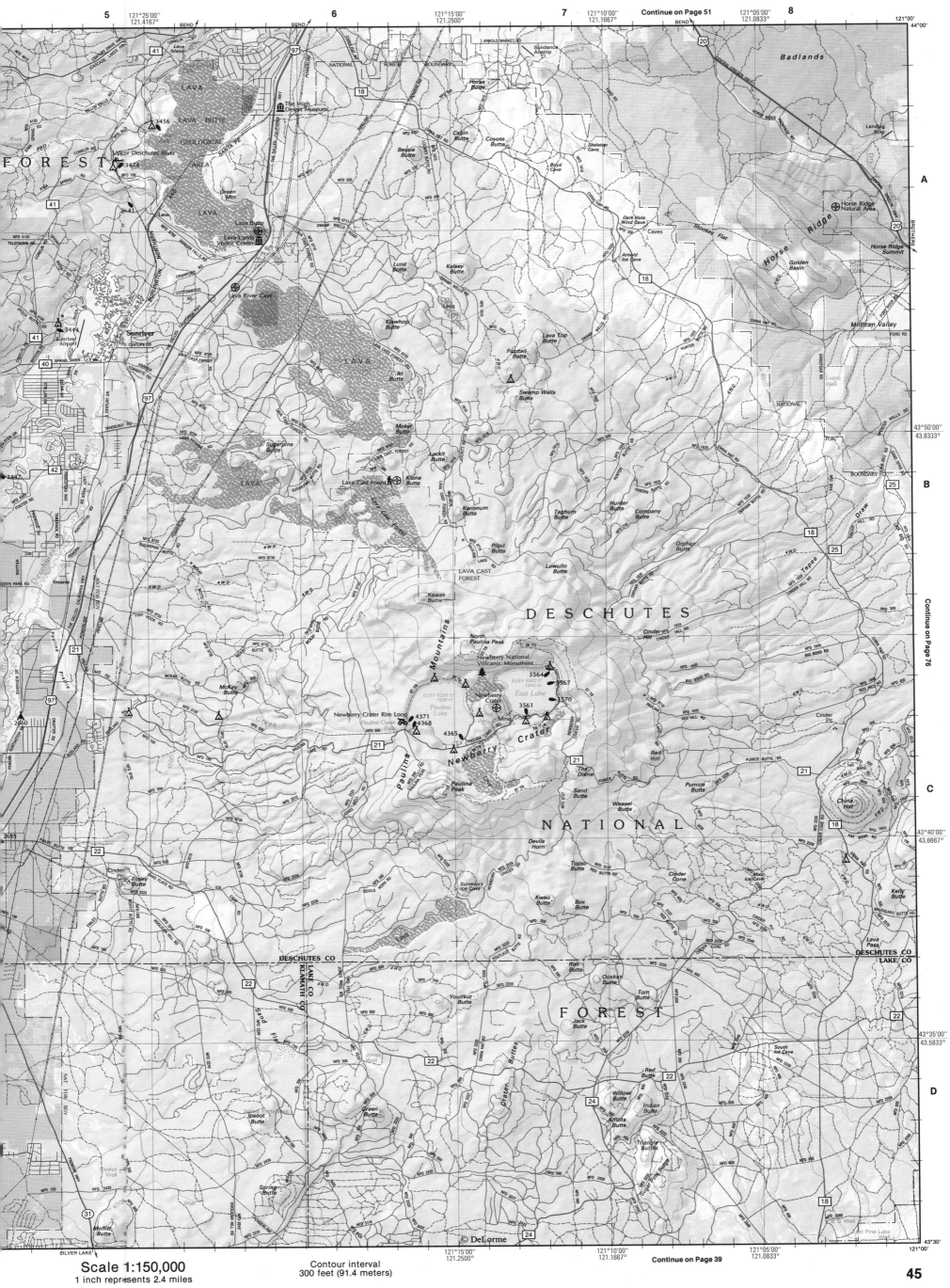

Continue on Page 51

Continue on Page 76

Continue on Page 39

Scale 1:150,000
1 inch represents 2.4 miles

Contour interval
300 feet (91.4 meters)

© DeLorme

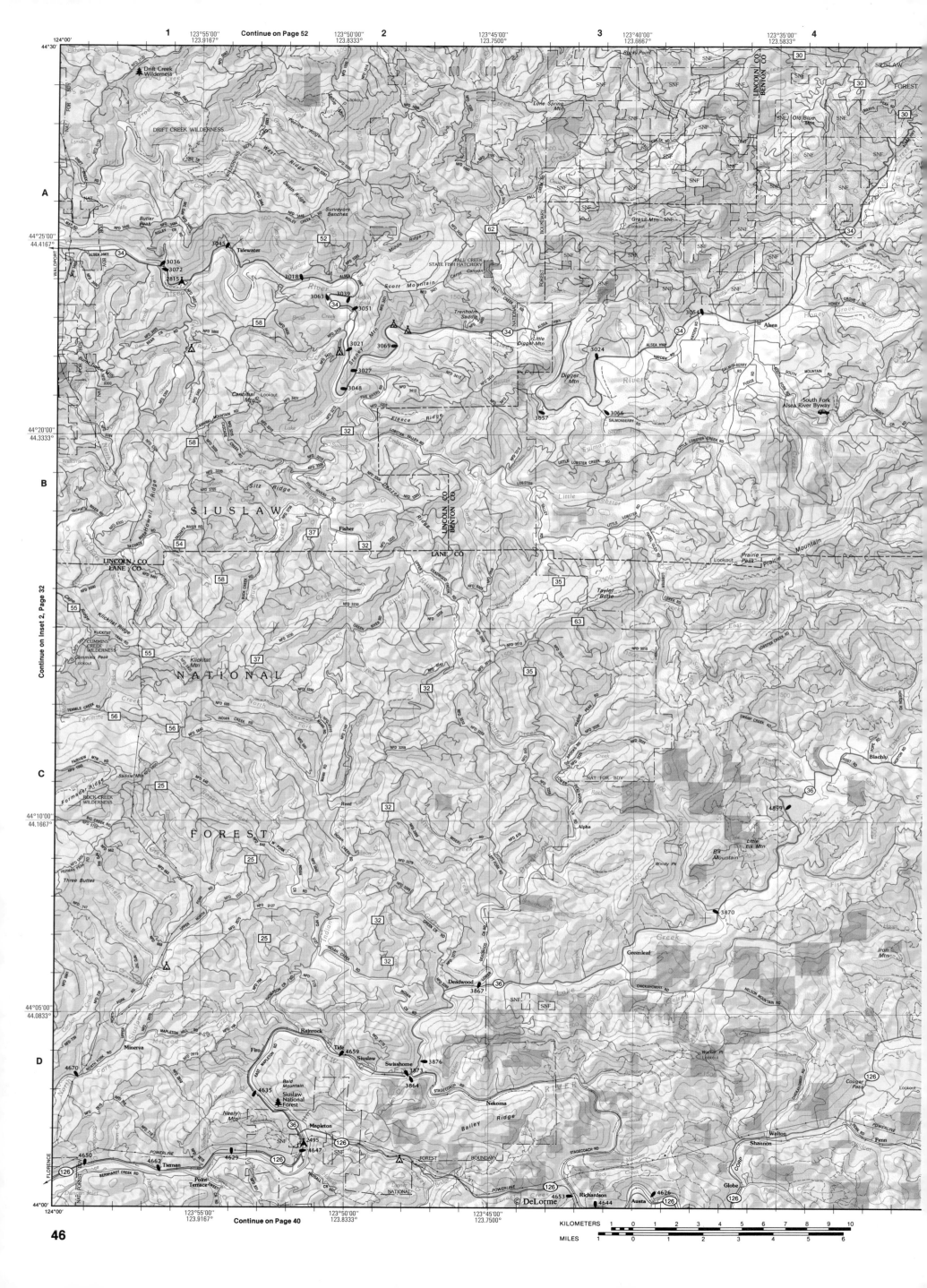

Continue on Inset 2, Page 32

© DeLorme

KILOMETERS

MILES

Continue on Page 53

Continue on Page 48

Continue on Page 41

Scale 1:150,000
1 inch represents 2.4 miles

Contour interval
300 feet (91.4 meters)

© DeLorme

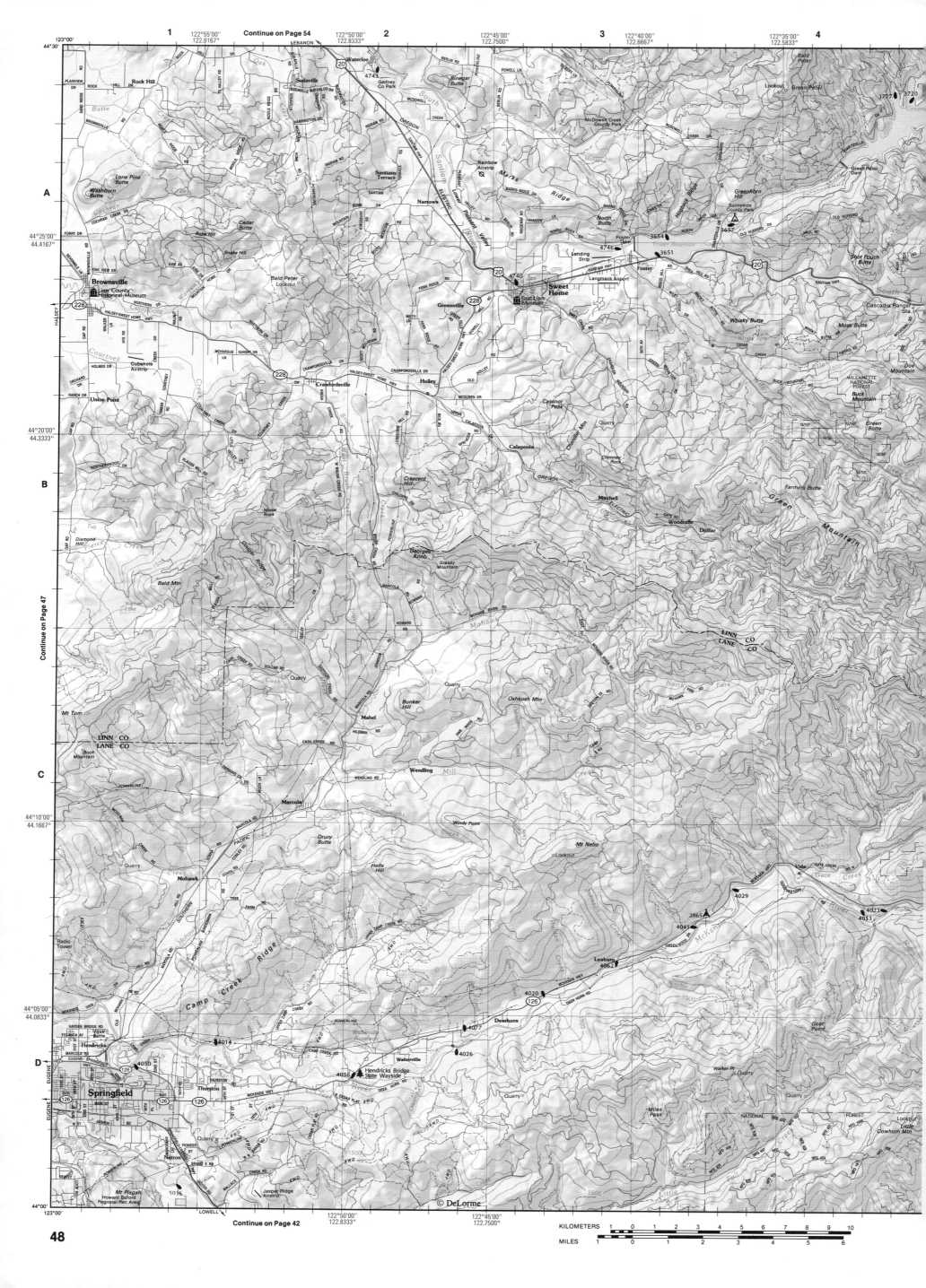

Continue on Page 54

122.9167°   122.8333°   122.7500°   122.6667°   122.5833°

123°00'
44°30'

A

44°25'00"
44.4167°

B

Continue on Page 47

44°20'00"
44.3333°

C

44°10'00"
44.1667°

D

44°05'00"
44.0833°

44°00'
123°00'

© DeLorme

Continue on Page 42

122°50'00"
122.8333°

122°45'00"
122.7500°

KILOMETERS 1 0 1 2 3 4 5 6 7 8 9 10
MILES 1 0 1 2 3 4 5 6

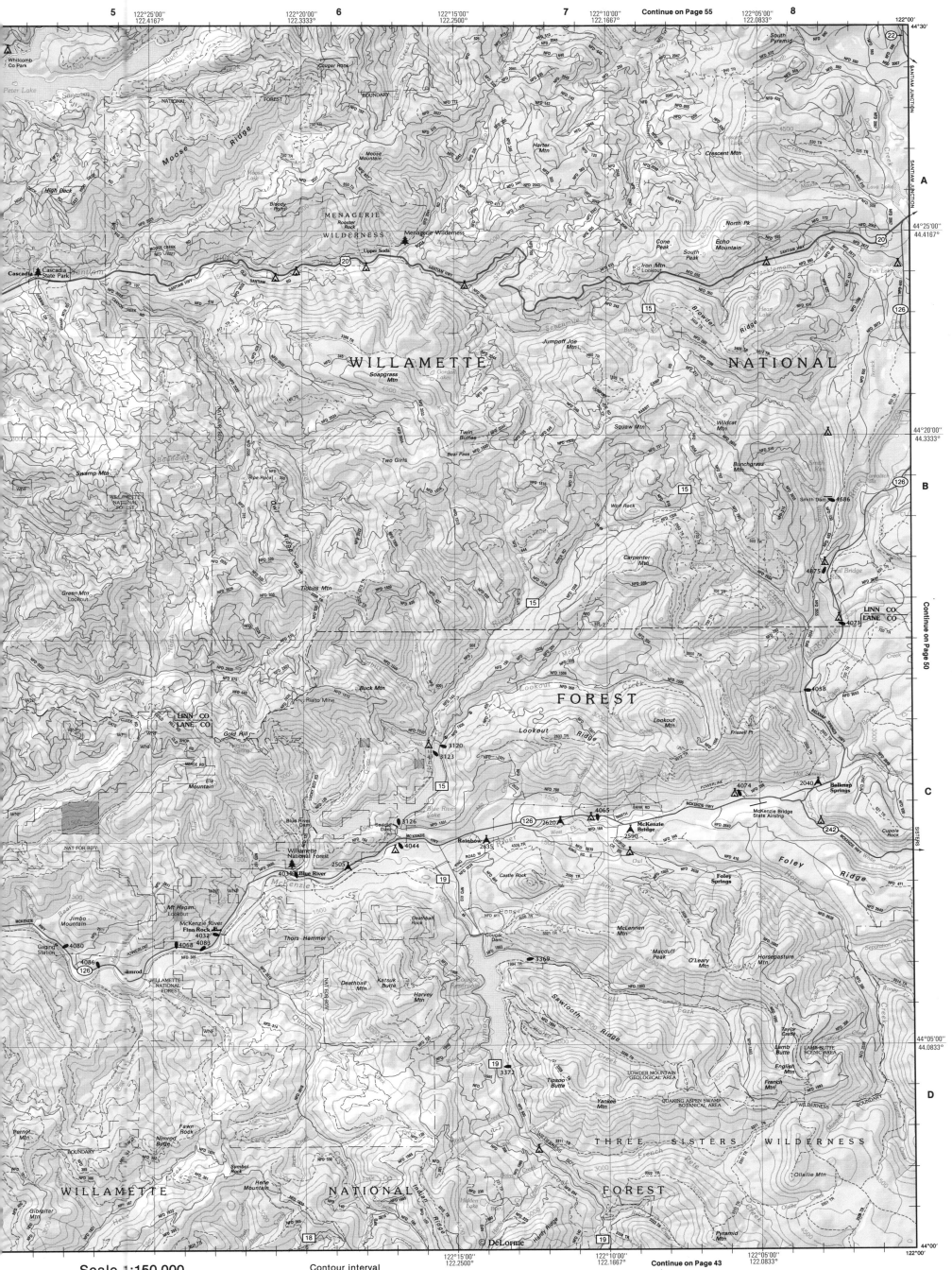

Continue on Page 50

Scale 1:150,000
1 inch represents 2.4 miles

Contour interval
300 feet (91.4 meters)

© DeLorme

49

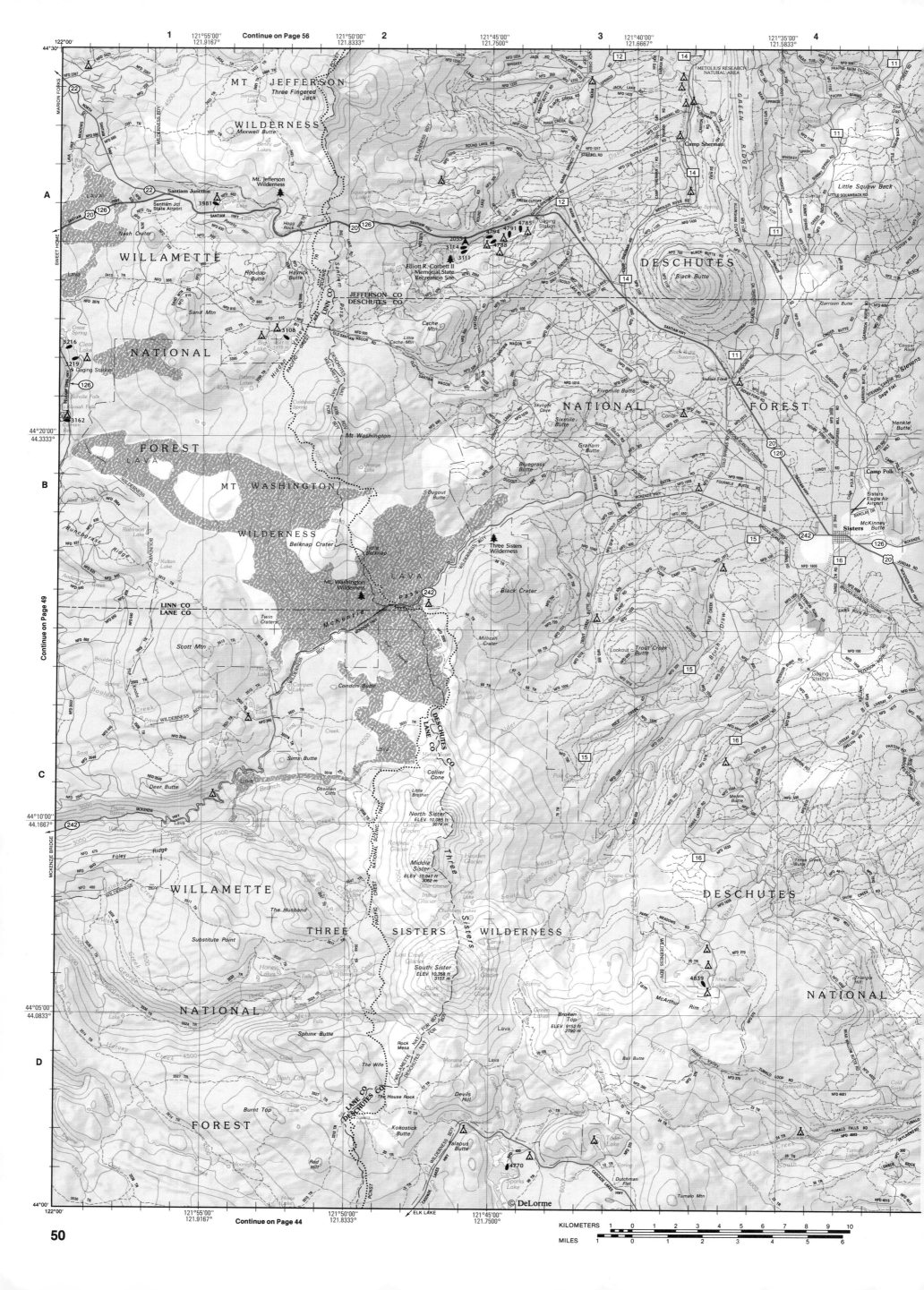

Continue on Page 49
Continue on Page 44

DeLorme

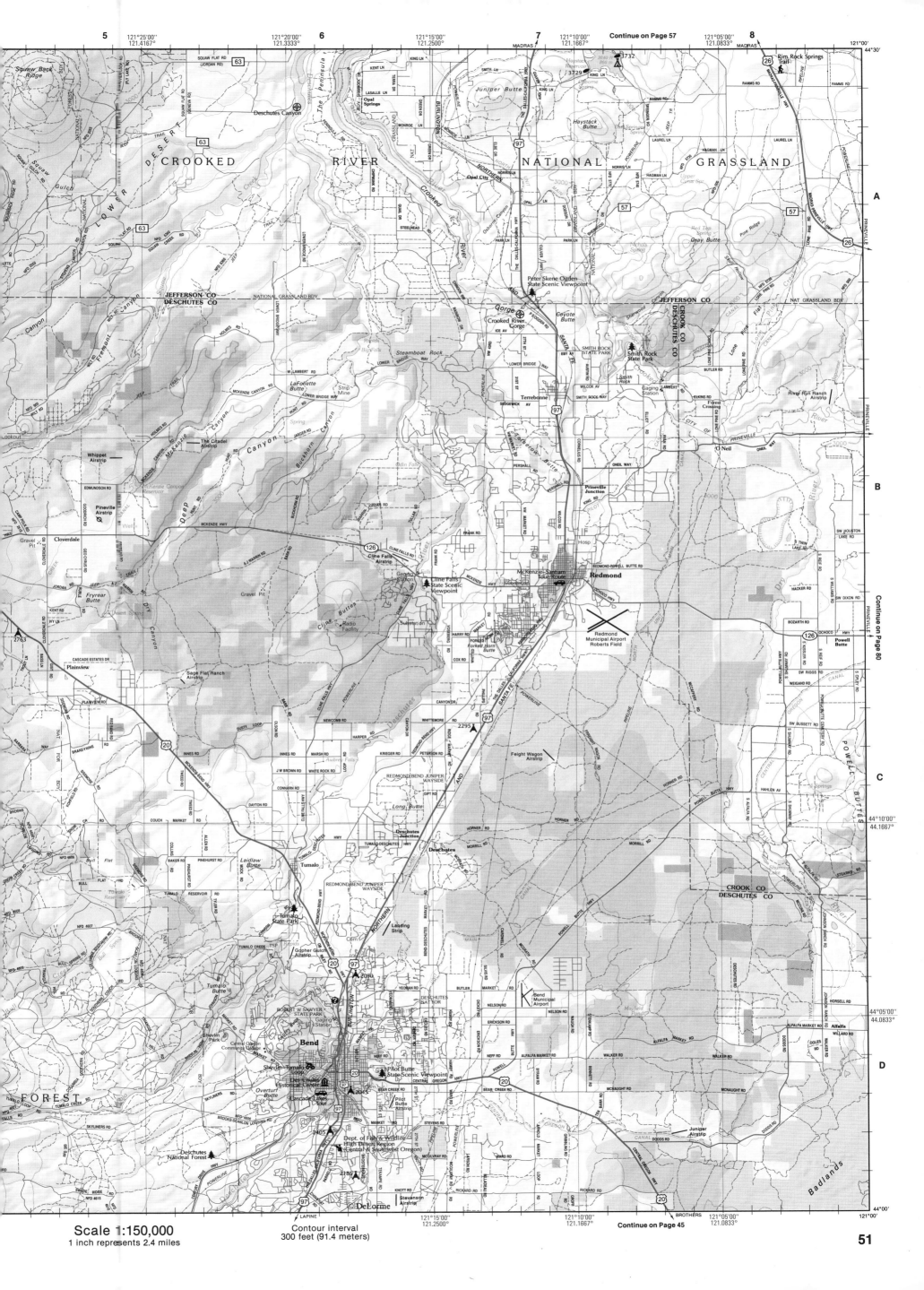

Scale 1:150,000
1 inch represents 2.4 miles

Contour interval
300 feet (91.4 meters)

Continue on Page 57
Continue on Page 80
Continue on Page 45

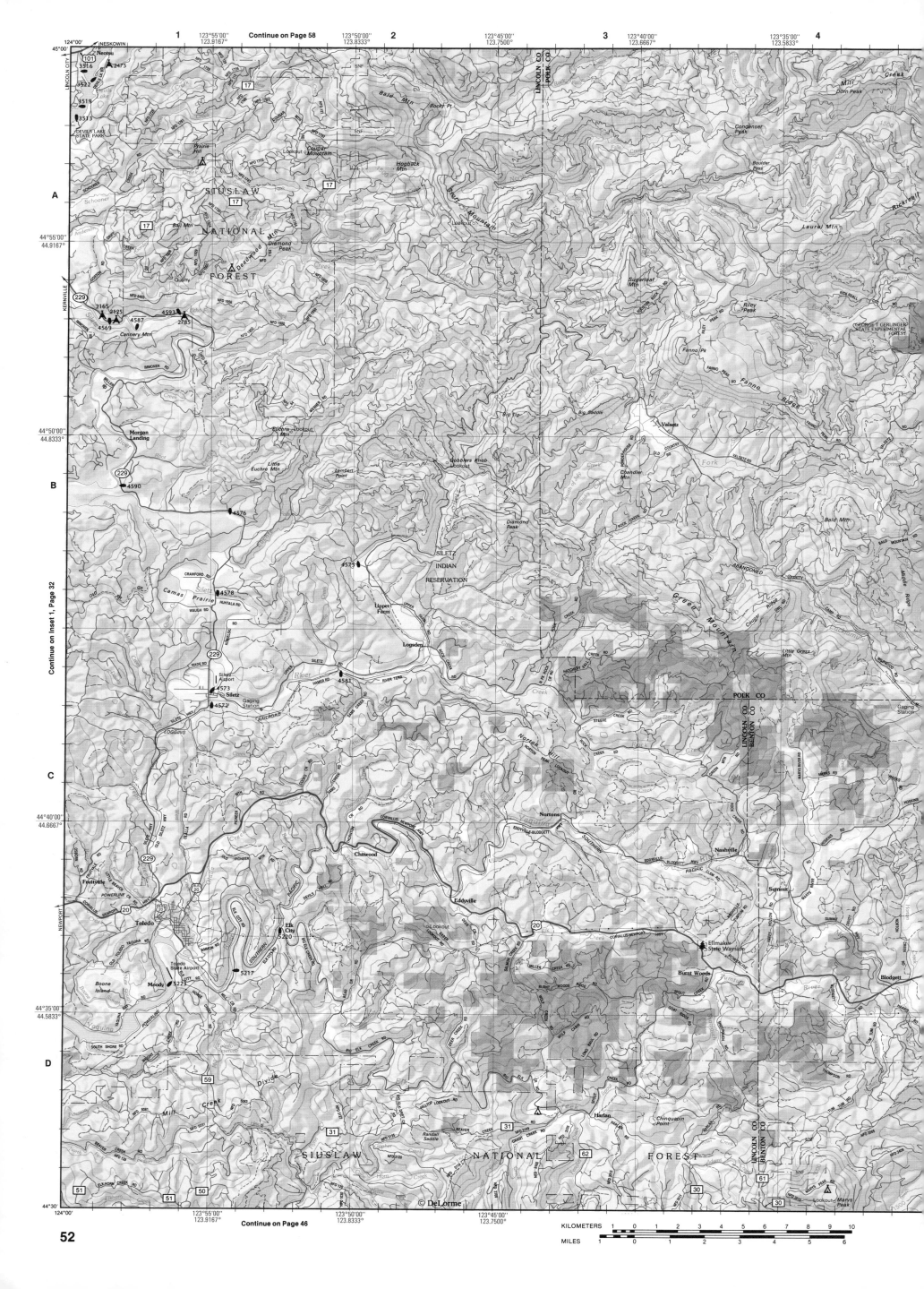

123°55'00''
123.9167°

123°50'00''
123.8333°

123°45'00''
123.7500°

123°40'00''
123.6667°

123°35'00''
123.5833°

124°00'

45°00'

A

44°55'00''
44.9167°

B

44°50'00''
44.8333°

C

44°40'00''
44.6667°

44°35'00''
44.5833°

D

44°30'
124°00'

SIUSLAW NATIONAL FOREST

SILETZ INDIAN RESERVATION

LINCOLN CO / POLK CO

GEORGE T. GERLINGER STATE EXPERIMENTAL FOREST

Continue on Inset 1, Page 32

Neotsu

Lincoln City

Kernville

Devils Lake State Park

Siletz

Siletz Airport

Toledo

Elk City

Moody

Fruitvale

Chitwood

Eddyville

Nortons

Nashville

Summit

Burnt Woods

Blodgett

Valsetz

Harlan

© DeLorme

123°55'00''
123.9167°

123°50'00''
123.8333°

123°45'00''
123.7500°

KILOMETERS   1   0   1   2   3   4   5   6   7   8   9   10

MILES   1   0   1   2   3   4   5   6

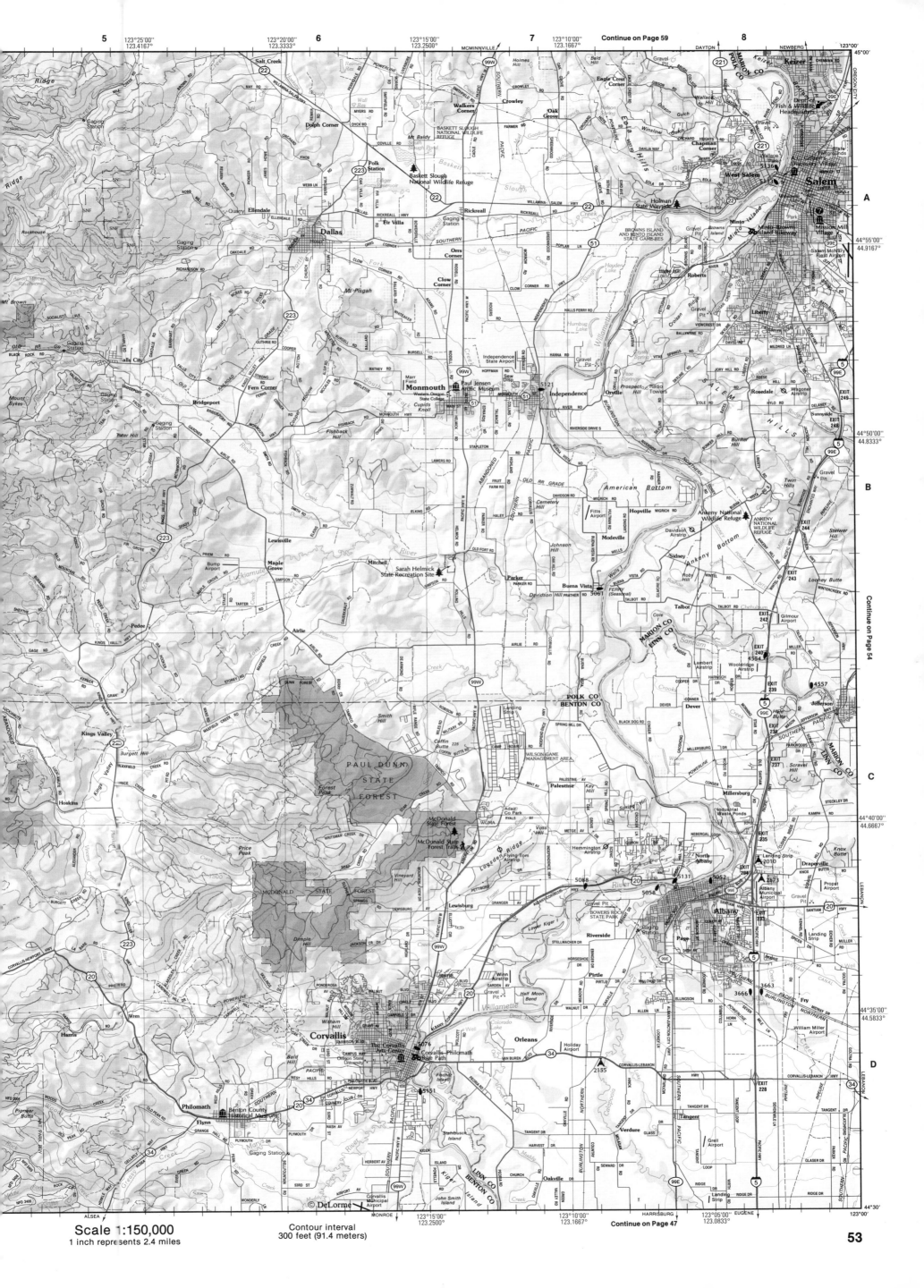

Continue on Page 54

Continue on Page 47

Scale 1:150,000
1 inch represents 2.4 miles

Contour interval
300 feet (91.4 meters)

© DeLorme

53

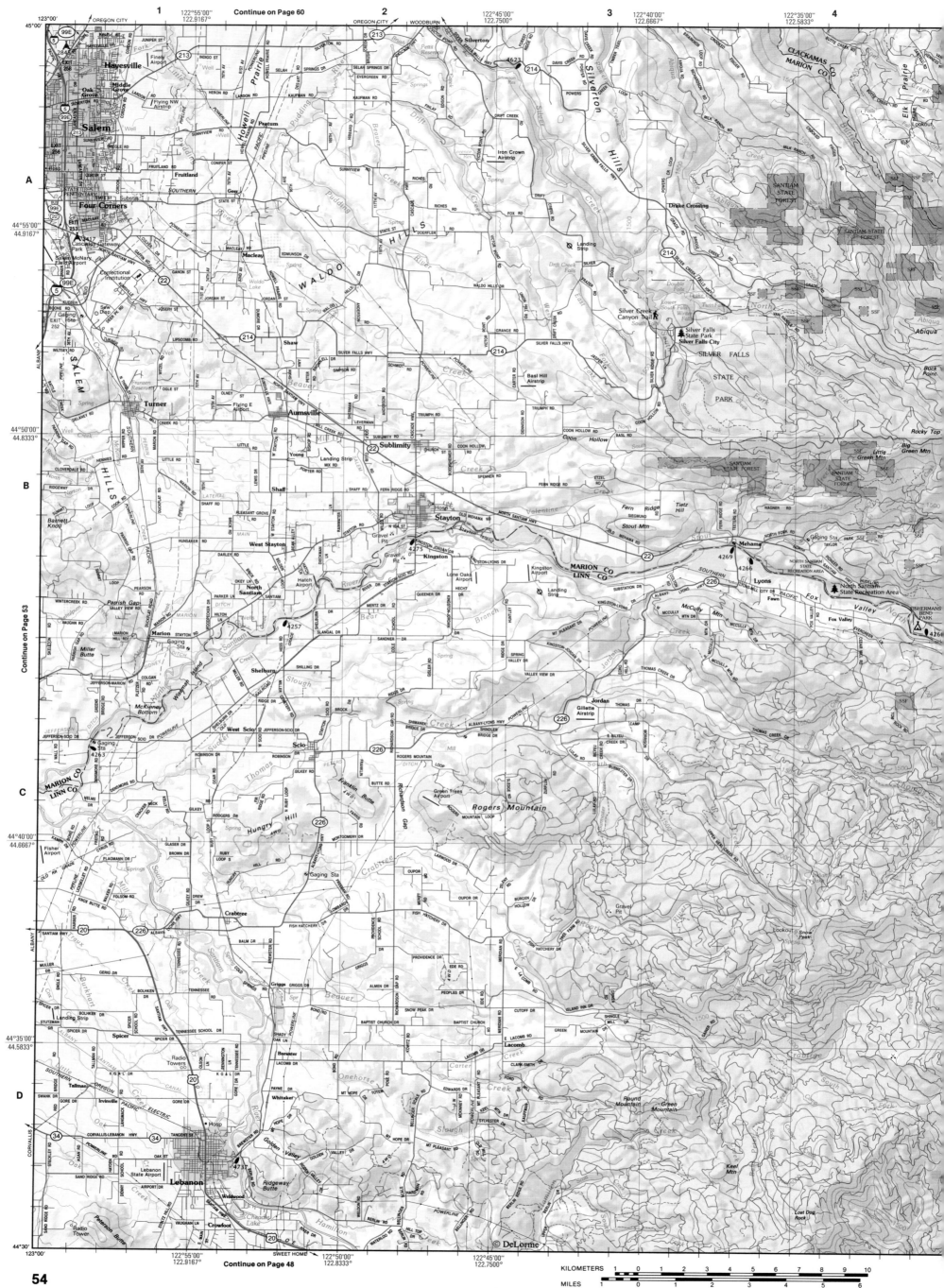

Continue on Page 53
Continue on Page 48

KILOMETERS

MILES

© DeLorme

Scale 1:150,000
1 inch represents 2.4 miles

Contour interval
300 feet (91.4 meters)

Continue on Page 49

© DeLorme

MT HOOD

NATIONAL   FOREST

WARM

WILLAMETTE

NATIONAL

FOREST

MT   JEFFERSON

WILDERNESS

DESCHUTES

NATIONAL   FOREST

GREEN RIDGE

© DeLorme

KILOMETERS   1 0 1 2 3 4 5 6 7 8 9 10

MILES   1 0 1 2 3 4 5 6

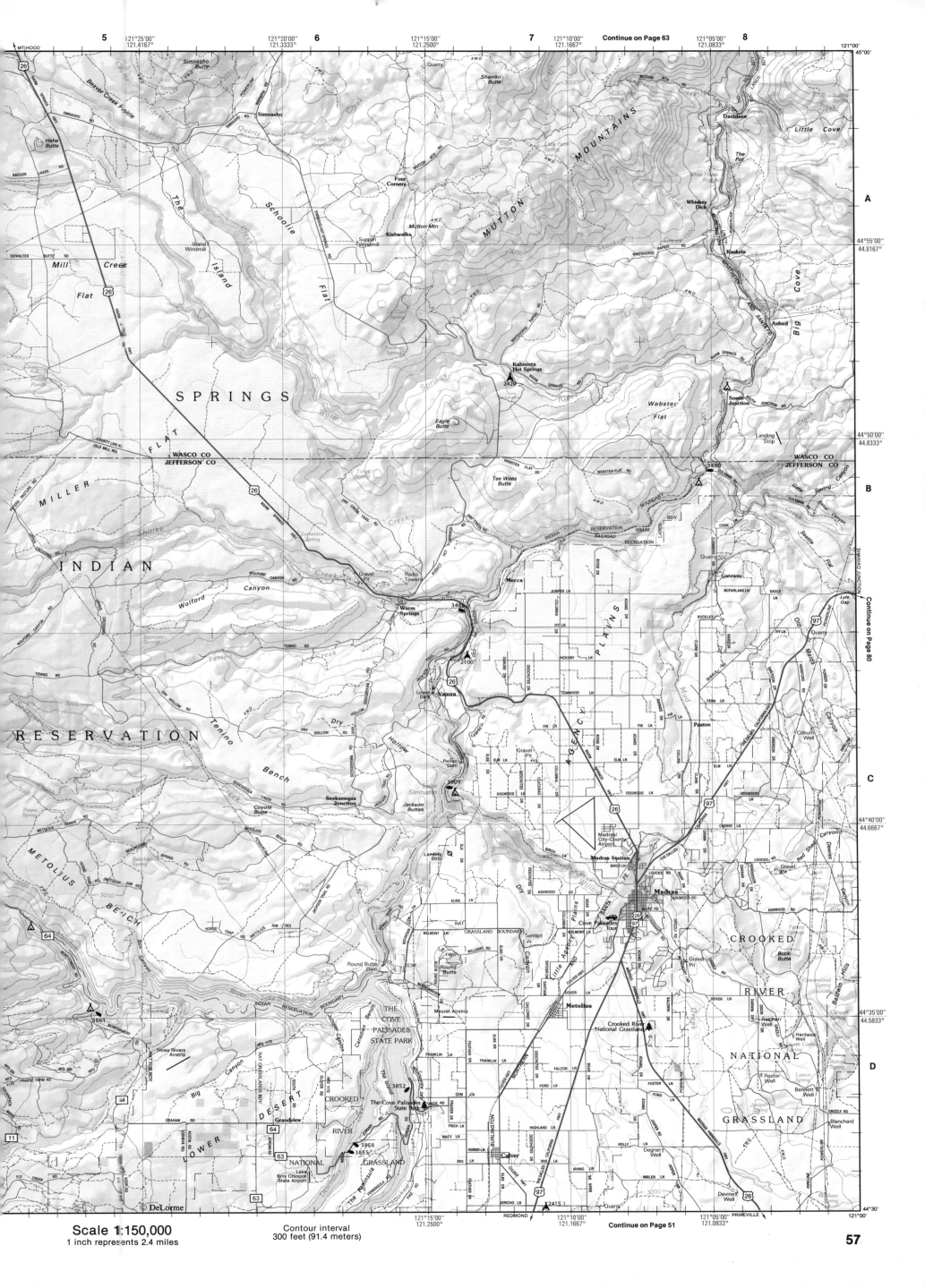

121°25'00" 121°20'00" 121°15'00" 121°10'00" 121°05'00"
121.4167° 121.3333° 121.2500° 121.1667° 121.0833°

Continue on Page 63

121°00'

45°00'

MT HOOD

A

44°55'00"
44.9167°

Continue on Page 80

44°50'00"
44.8333°

B

WASCO CO
JEFFERSON CO

C

44°40'00"
44.6667°

44°35'00"
44.5833°

D

44°30'

121°15'00" 121°10'00" 121°05'00" PRINEVILLE 121°00'
121.2500° 121.1667° 121.0833°

Continue on Page 51

Scale 1:150,000
1 inch represents 2.4 miles

Contour interval
300 feet (91.4 meters)

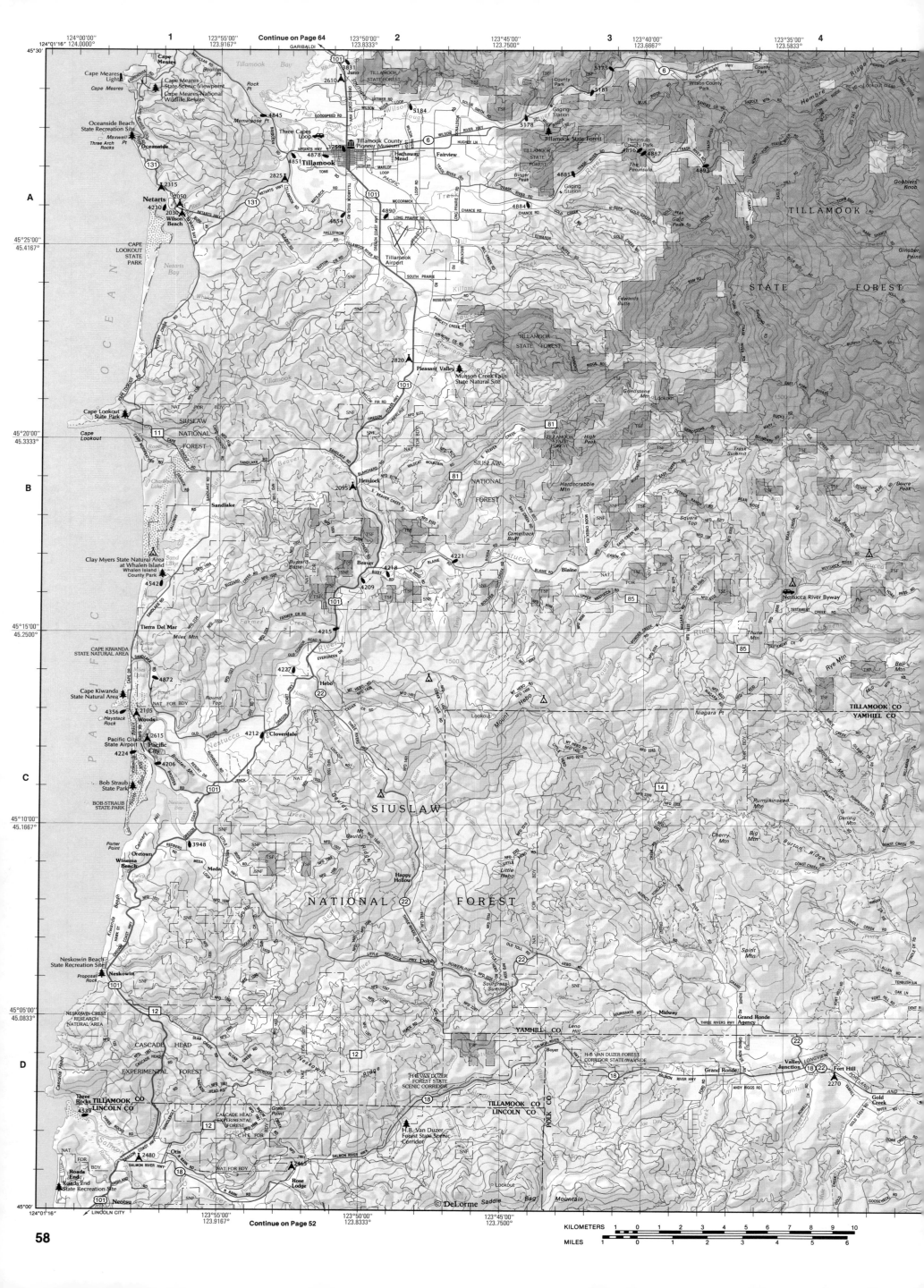

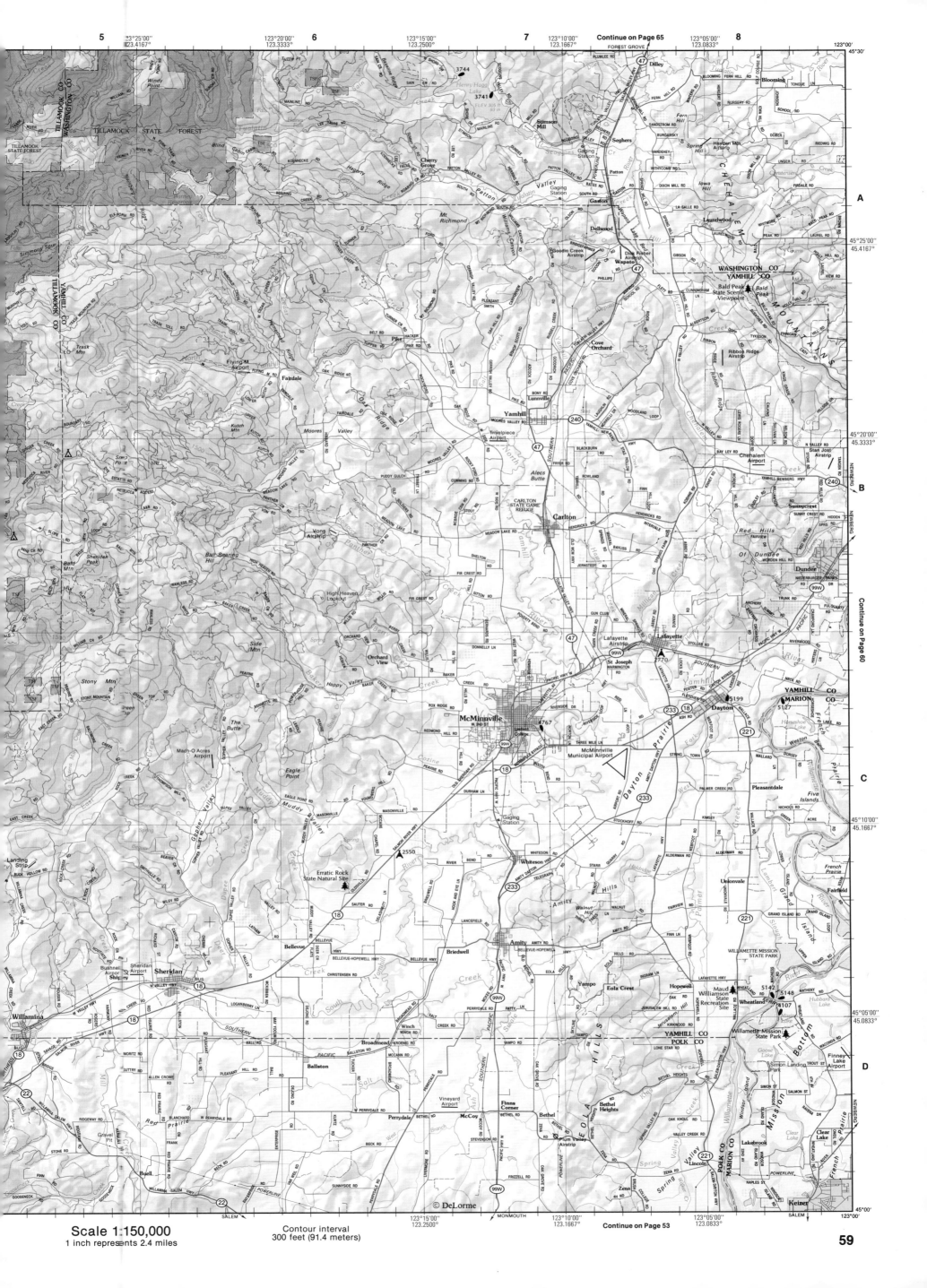

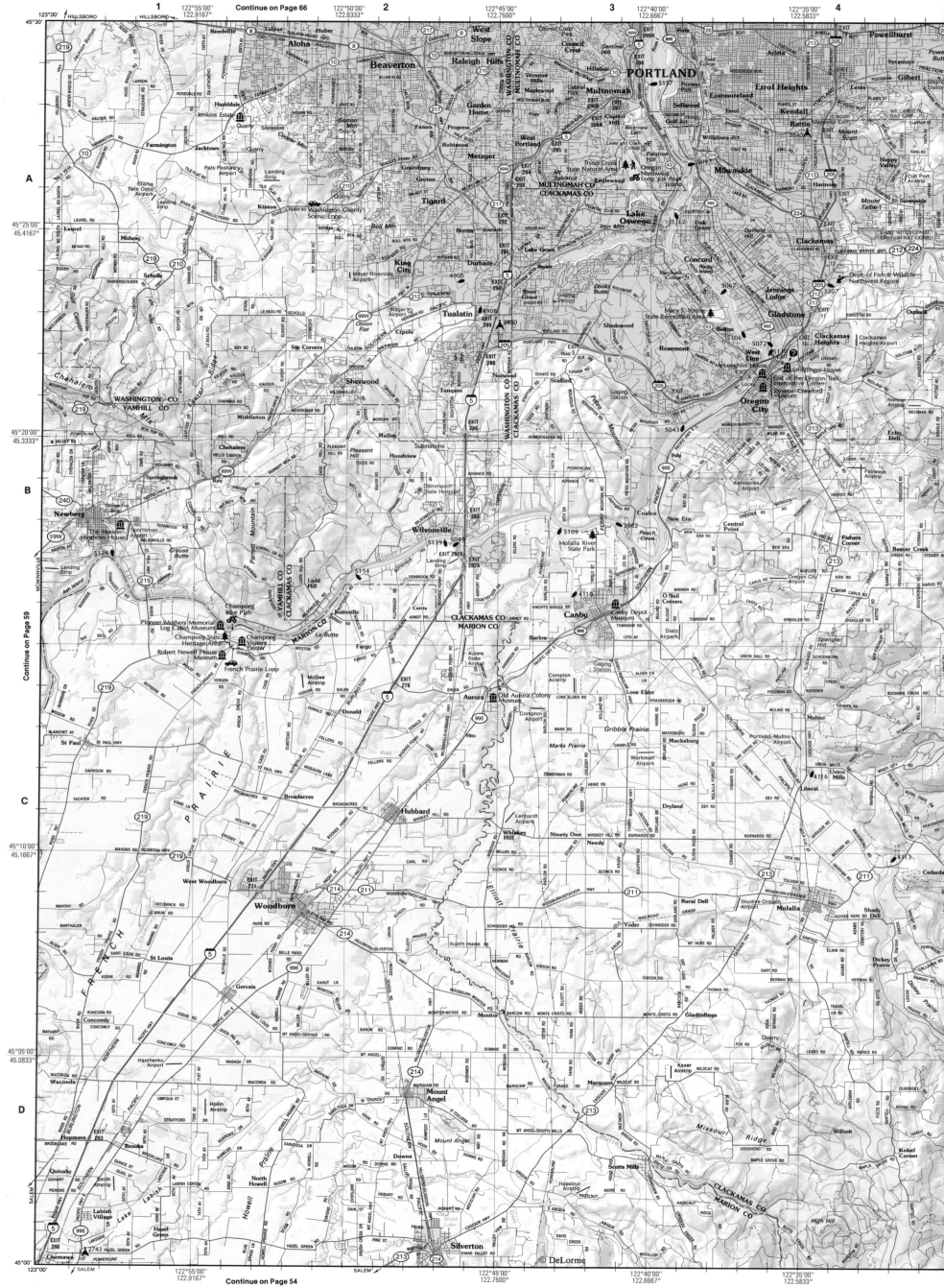

Continue on Page 59

5   6   7   Continue on Page 67   8

122°25'00"
122.4167°

122°20'00"
122.3333°

122°15'00"
122.2500°

122°10'00"
122.1667°

122°05'00"
122.0833°

122°00'

45°30'

Gresham

MULTNOMAH CO
CLACKAMAS CO

MT HOOD

MULTNOMAH CO
CLACKAMAS CO

NATIONAL   FOREST

A

45°25'00"
45.4167°

Sandy

SALMON-HUCKLEBERRY

WILDERNESS

B

45°20'00"
45.3333°

Estacada

Continue on Page 62

C

45°10'00"
45.1167°

MT HOOD

NATIONAL   FOREST

D

45°05'00"
45.0833°

Ripplebrook

45°00'

122°15'00"
122.2500°

122°10'00"
122.1667°

Continue on Page 55

122°05'00"
122.0833°

122°00'

Scale 1:150,000
1 inch represents 2.4 miles

Contour interval
300 feet (91.4 meters)

© DeLorme

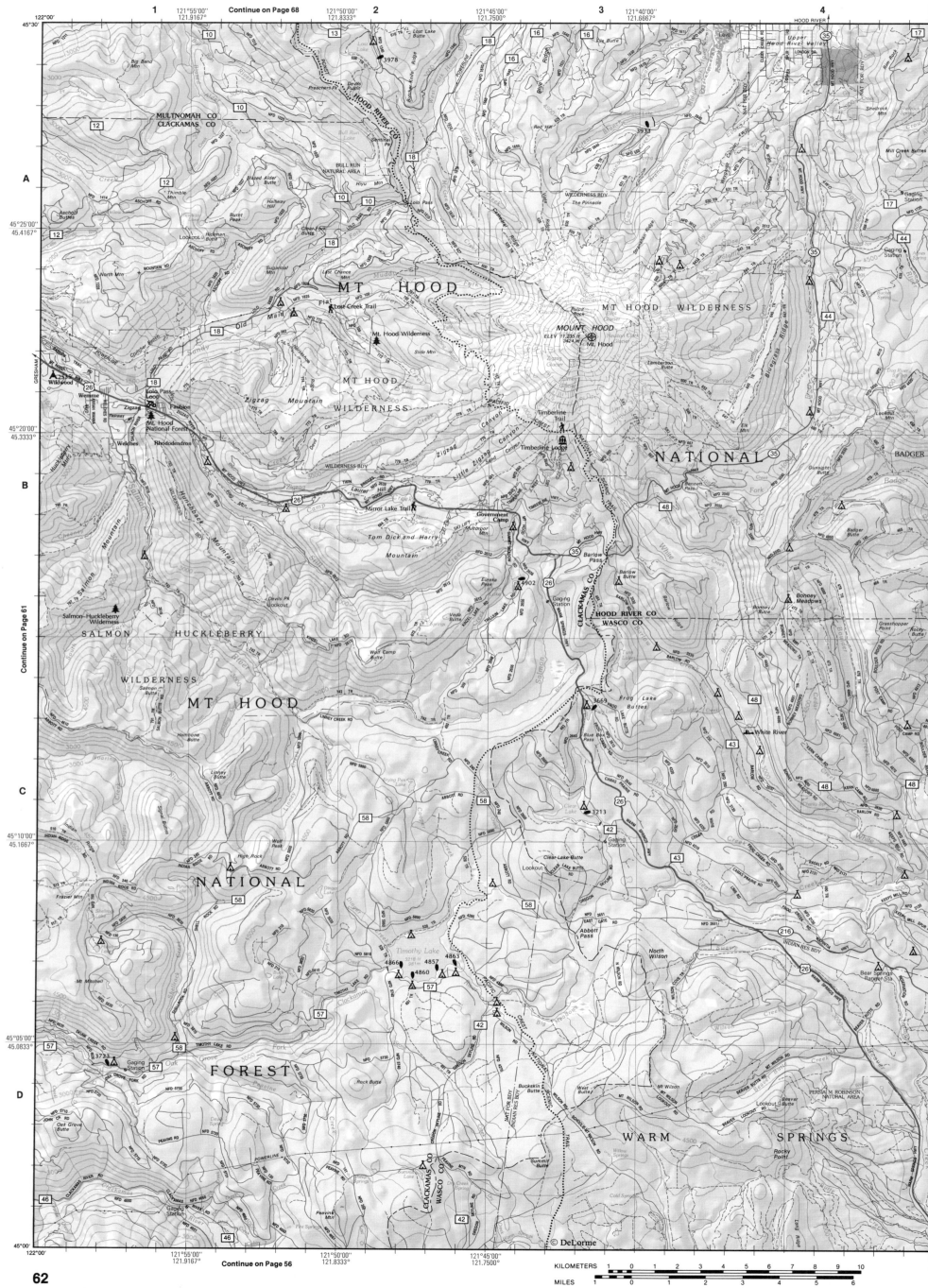

Continue on Page 61

KILOMETERS

MILES

© DeLorme

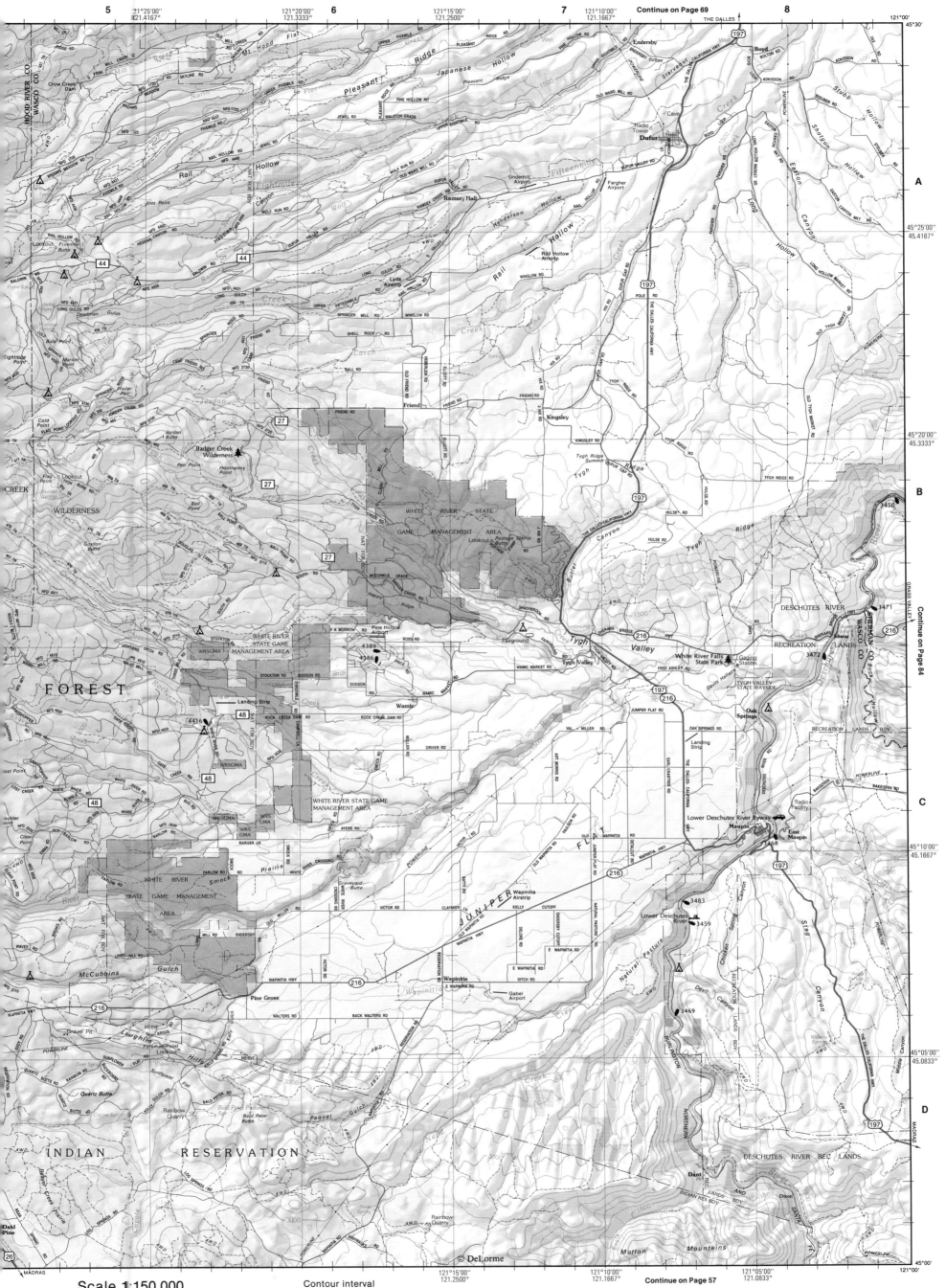

Continue on Page 69

Continue on Page 84

Scale 1:150,000
1 inch represents 2.4 miles

Contour interval
300 feet (91.4 meters)

121°15'00"   121°10'00"   121°05'00"   121°00'
121.2500°   121.1667°   121.0833°   45°00'

Continue on Page 57

63

© DeLorme

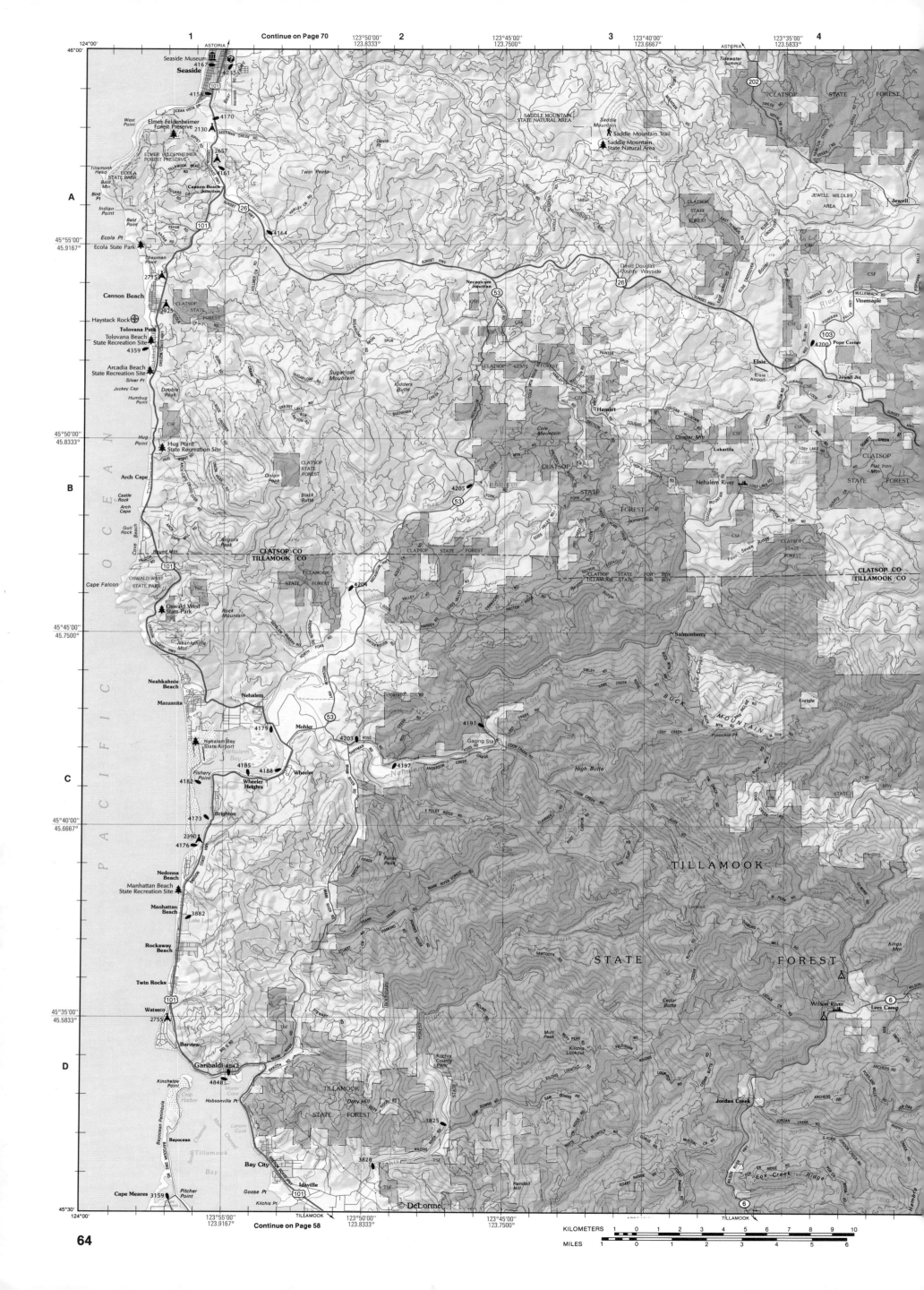

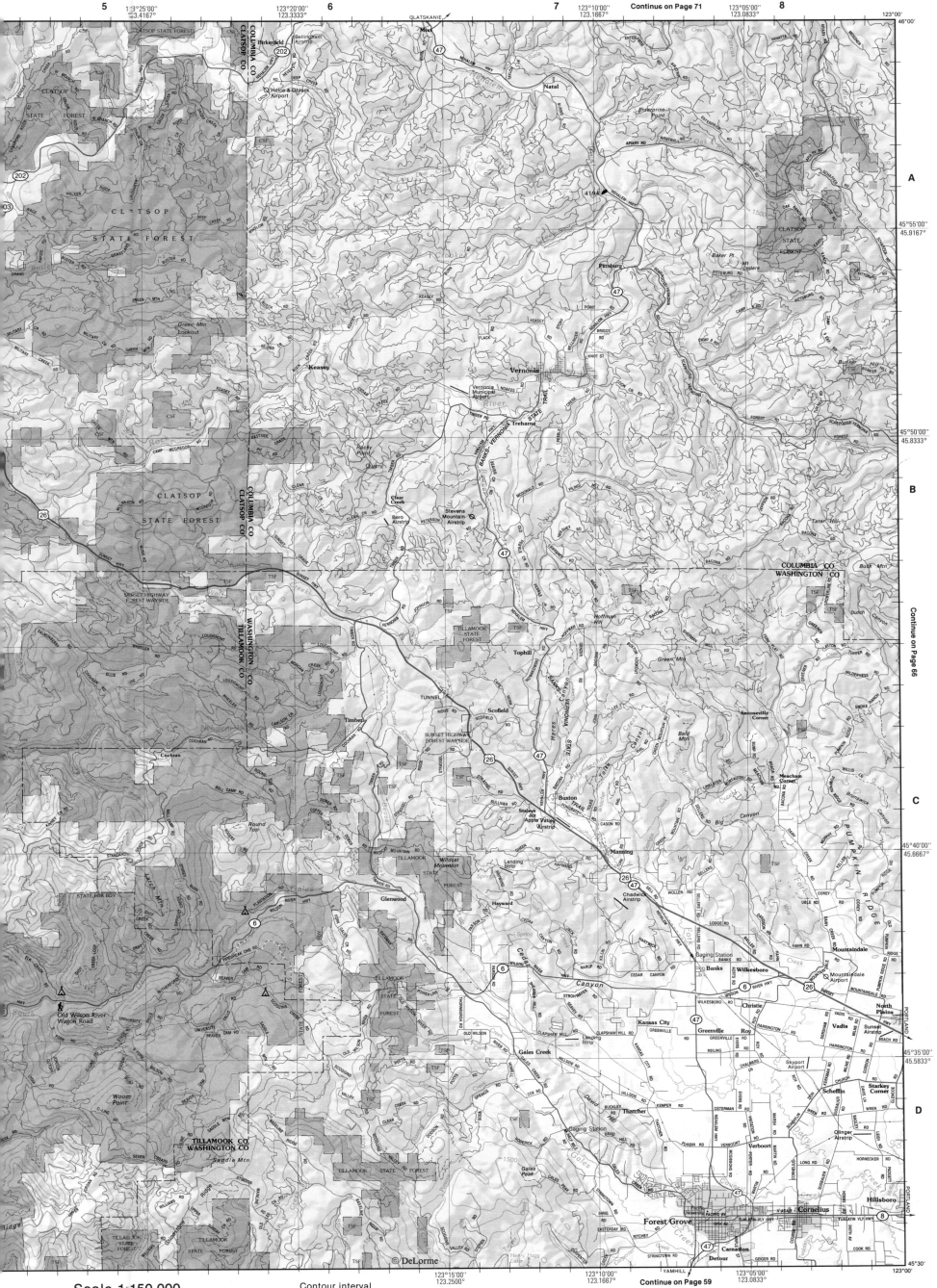

Continue on Page 66

Continue on Page 59

Scale 1:150,000
1 inch represents 2.4 miles

Contour interval
300 feet (91.4 meters)

© DeLorme

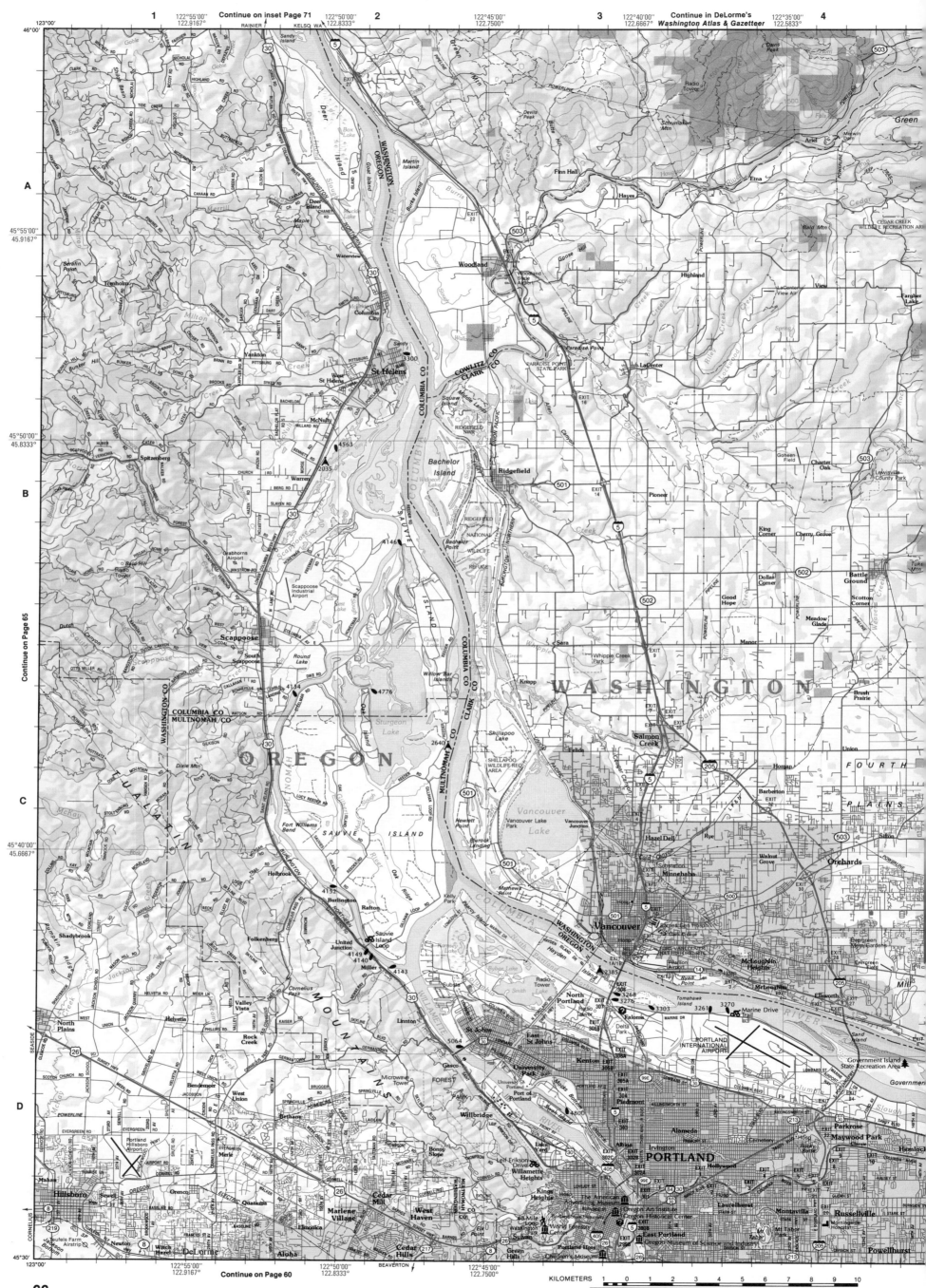

Continue on Page 65

Continue on Page 60

KILOMETERS 1 0 1 2 3 4 5 6 7 8 9 10

MILES 1 0 1 2 3 4 5 6

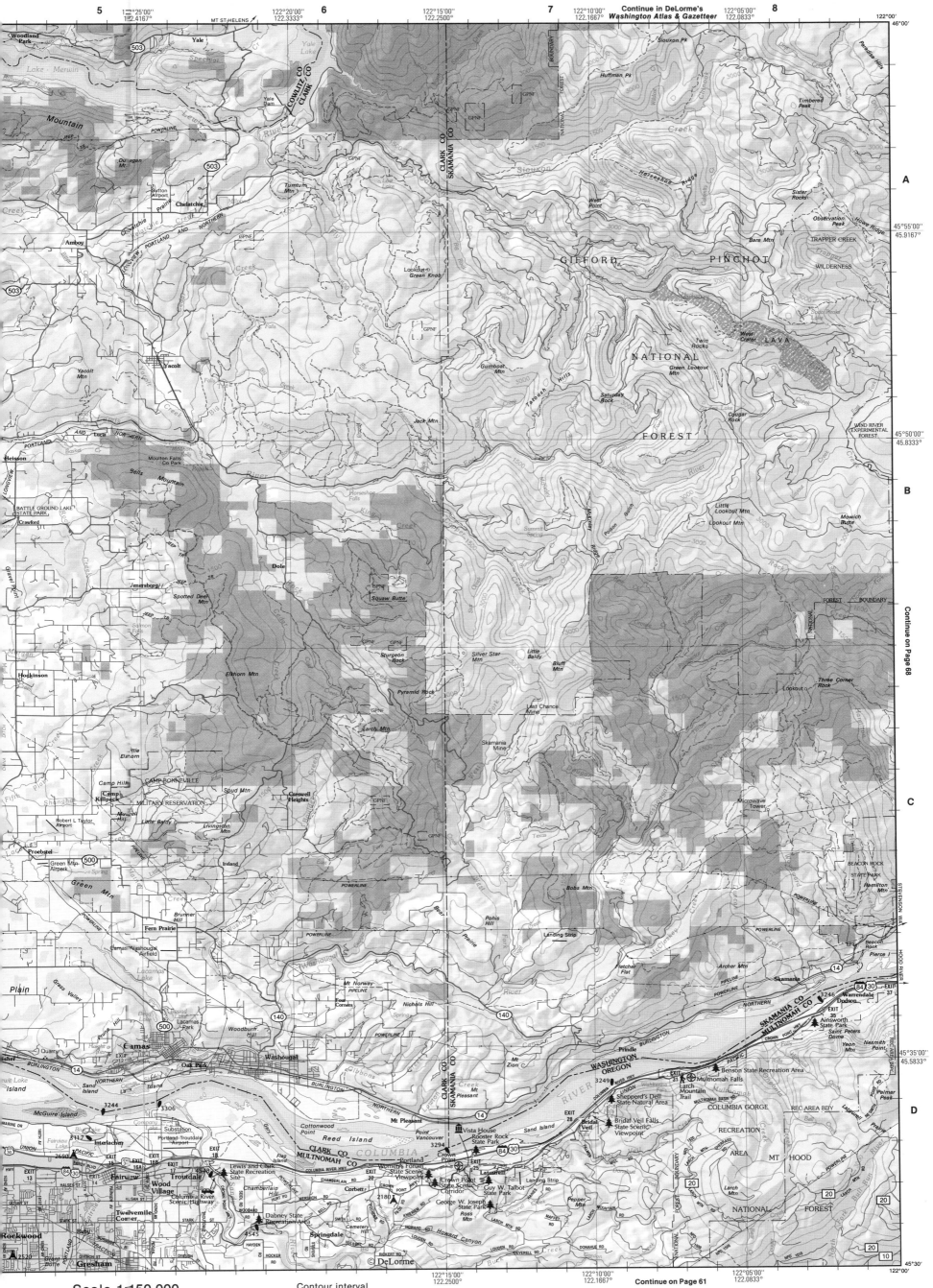

MT ST HELENS

GIFFORD PINCHOT

NATIONAL

FOREST

WIND RIVER EXPERIMENTAL FOREST

TRAPPER CREEK WILDERNESS

Continue on Page 68

COLUMBIA RIVER

WASHINGTON
OREGON

COLUMBIA GORGE
RECREATION AREA

MT HOOD
NATIONAL FOREST

Continue on Page 61

Scale 1:150,000
1 inch represents 2.4 miles

Contour interval
300 feet (91.4 meters)

©DeLorme

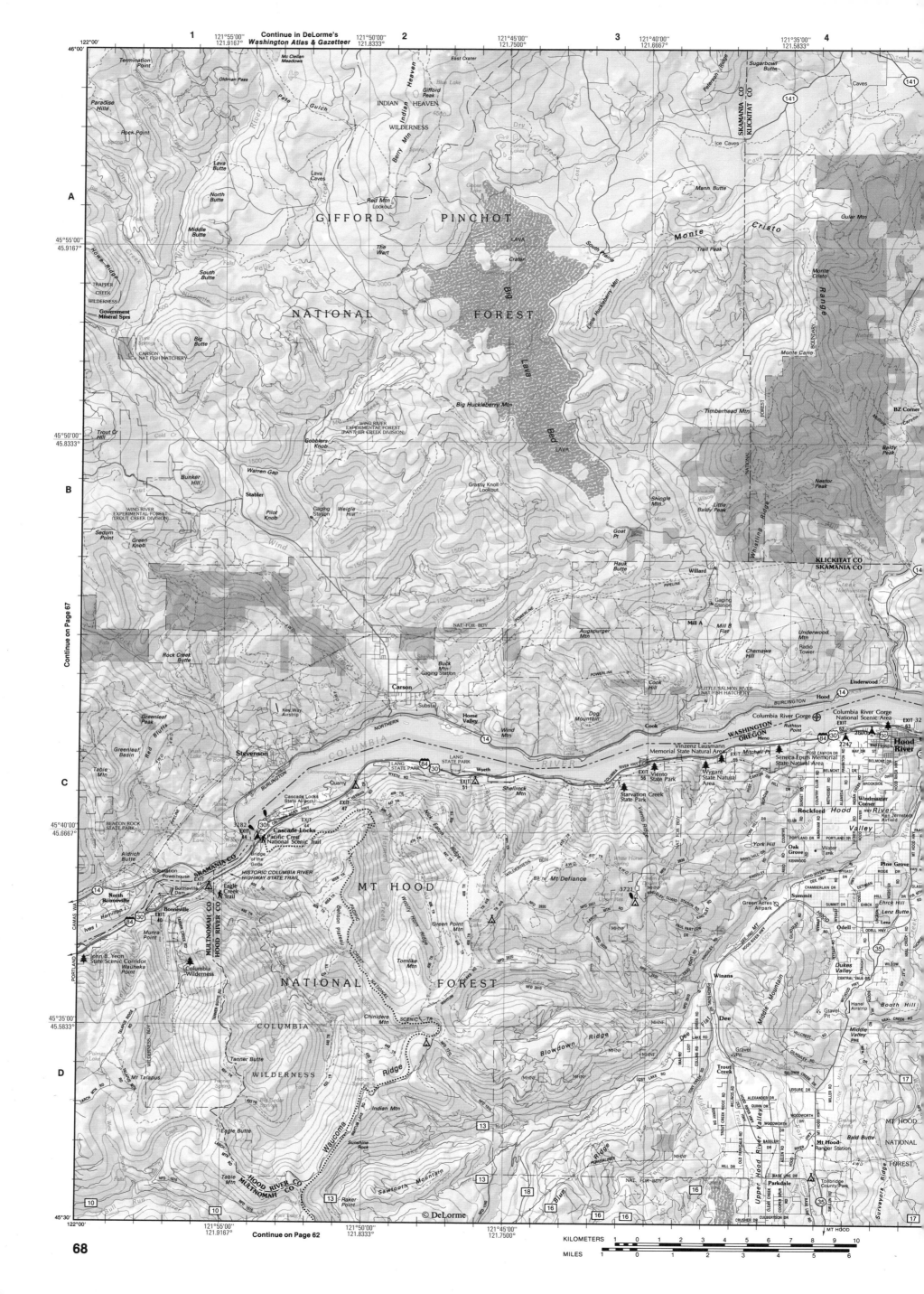

KILOMETERS   1   0   1   2   3   4   5   6   7   8   9   10

MILES   1   0   1   2   3   4   5   6

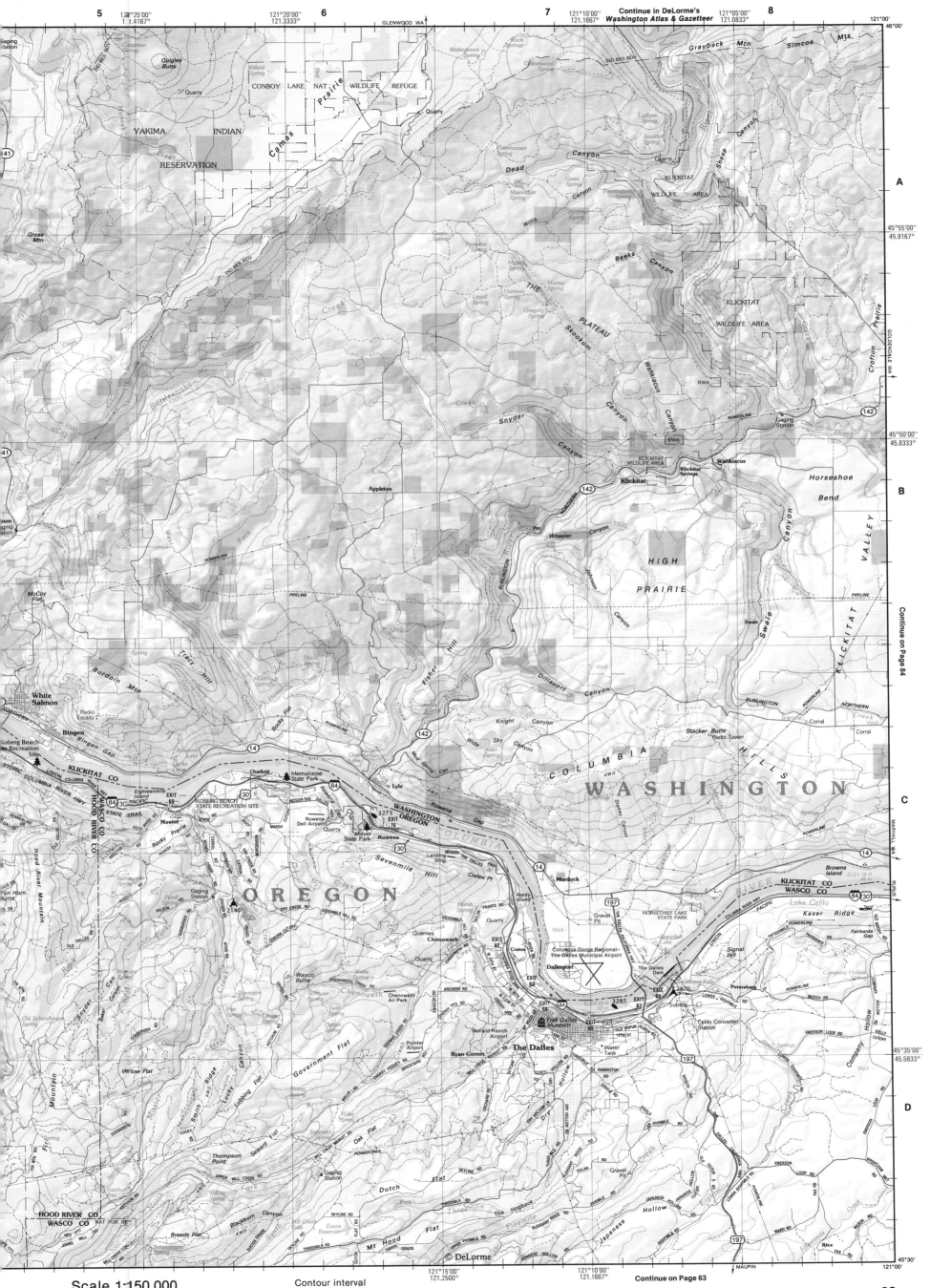

123°25'00'' 121°20'00'' 121°15'00'' 121°10'00'' 121°05'00'' 121°00'

GLENWOOD WA

46°00'

YAKIMA INDIAN RESERVATION

CONBOY LAKE NAT'L WILDLIFE REFUGE

Camas Prairie

Quigley Butte

Grayback Mtn   Simcoe Mts

Quarry

THE PLATEAU

KLICKITAT WILDLIFE AREA

Dead Canyon

Gross Mtn

A

45°55'00''
45.9167°

Beeks Canyon

KLICKITAT WILDLIFE AREA

Appleton

KWA

Klickitat   Wahkiacus
Klickitat Springs

142

45°50'00''
45.8333°

B

Gaging Station

142

HIGH PRAIRIE

HORSESHOE BEND

KLICKITAT VALLEY

McCoy Flat

Burdoin Mtn

Dillacort Canyon

Stacker Butte Radio Tower

Knight Canyon

BURLINGTON

NORTHERN

Corral

White Salmon

Bingen

KLICKITAT CO
HOOD RIVER CO

Charfield
Memaloose State Park

Lyle

14

Rowena

84

**WASHINGTON
OREGON**

COLUMBIA HILLS

WASHINGTON

4WD

C

45°45'00''

Koberg Beach State Recreation Site

Mosier

30

Rowena Dell Airport
Mayer State Park
Rowena

EXIT 76

Sevenmile Hill

Murdock

14

197

HORSETHIEF LAKE STATE PARK

KLICKITAT CO
WASCO CO

Lake Celilo

Kaser Ridge

Fairbanks Gap

30 84

OREGON

2140

Chenoweth

Chenoweth Air Park

Crates Pt

Rocky Island

Columbia Gorge Regional–
The Dalles Municipal Airport

Dallesport

The Dalles Dam

Signal Hill

Petersburg

Celilo Converter Station

Wasco Butte

Chenoweth

EXIT 82

EXIT 83

2870

EXIT 88

MCCOY RD

D

Government Flat

Fort Dalles Museum

The Dalles

Ryan Corner

Water Tank

197

45°35'00''
45.5833°

Thompson Point

Dutch Flat

Threemile Flat

Japanese Hollow

Maupin

197

© DeLorme

121°15'00''
121.2500°

121°10'00''
121.1667°

Continue on Page 63

121°00'
45°30'

Continue on Page 84

Scale 1:150,000
1 inch represents 2.4 miles

Contour interval
300 feet (91.4 meters)

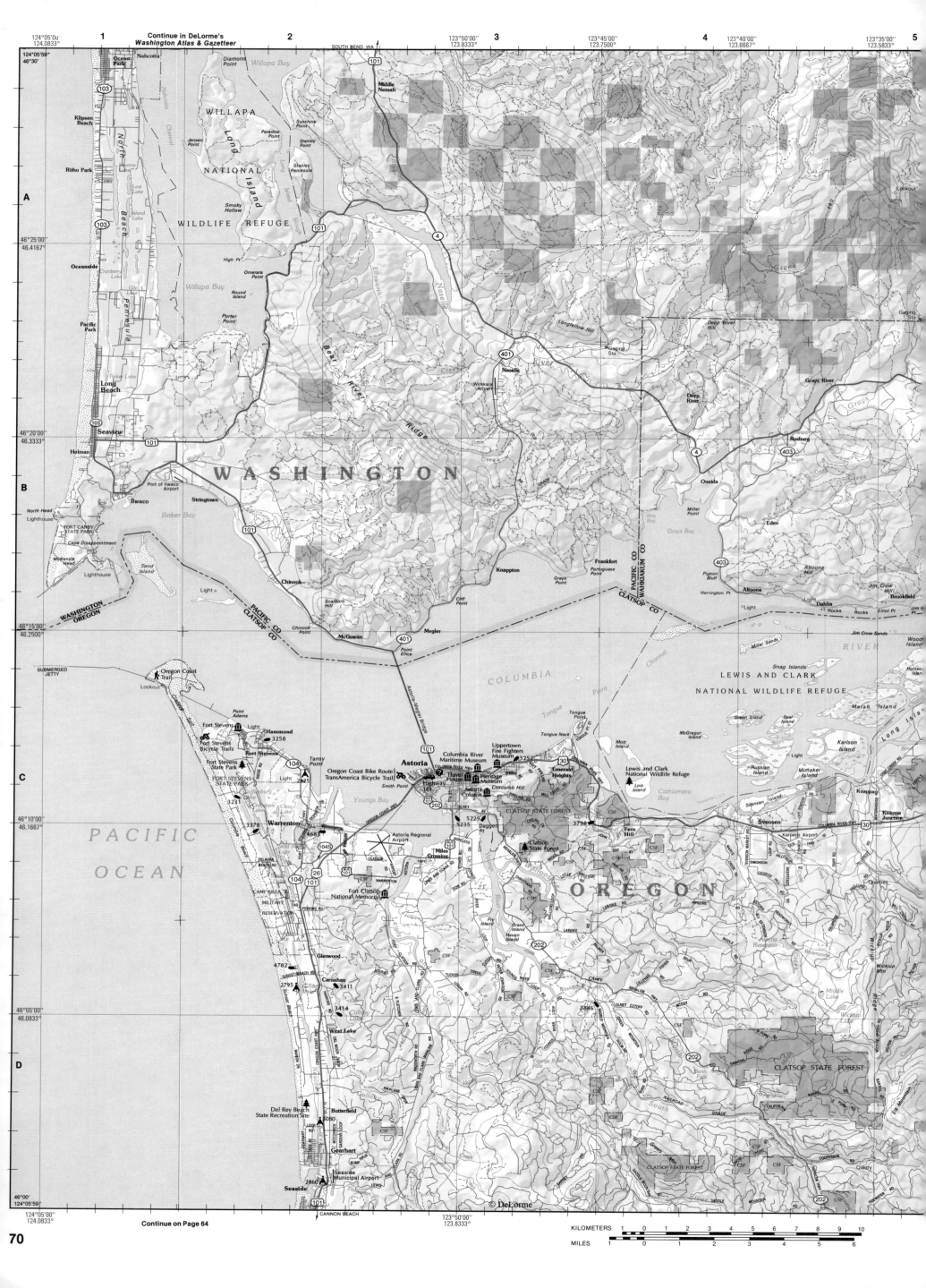

124°05'0u
124.0833°

46°30'

46°25'00"
46.4167°

A

46°20'00"
46.3333°

B

46°15'00"
46.2500°

46°10'00"
46.1667°

C

46°05'00"
46.0833°

D

46°00'
124°05'59"

SOUTH BEND WA

WILLAPA

NATIONAL

WILDLIFE REFUGE

WASHINGTON

WASHINGTON
OREGON

PACIFIC CO
CLATSOP CO

PACIFIC
OCEAN

COLUMBIA

RIVER

LEWIS AND CLARK
NATIONAL WILDLIFE REFUGE

Lewis and Clark
National Wildlife Refuge

CLATSOP STATE FOREST

OREGON

CLATSOP STATE FOREST

CLATSOP STATE FOREST

Long Beach

Seaview

Holman

Ilwaco

Chinook

McGowan

Megler

Astoria

Warrenton

Hammond

Seaside

Gearhart

Naselle

Rosburg

Oneida

Svensen

© DeLorme

123°50'00"
123.8333°

123°45'00"
123.7500°

123°40'00"
123.6667°

123°35'00"
123.5833°

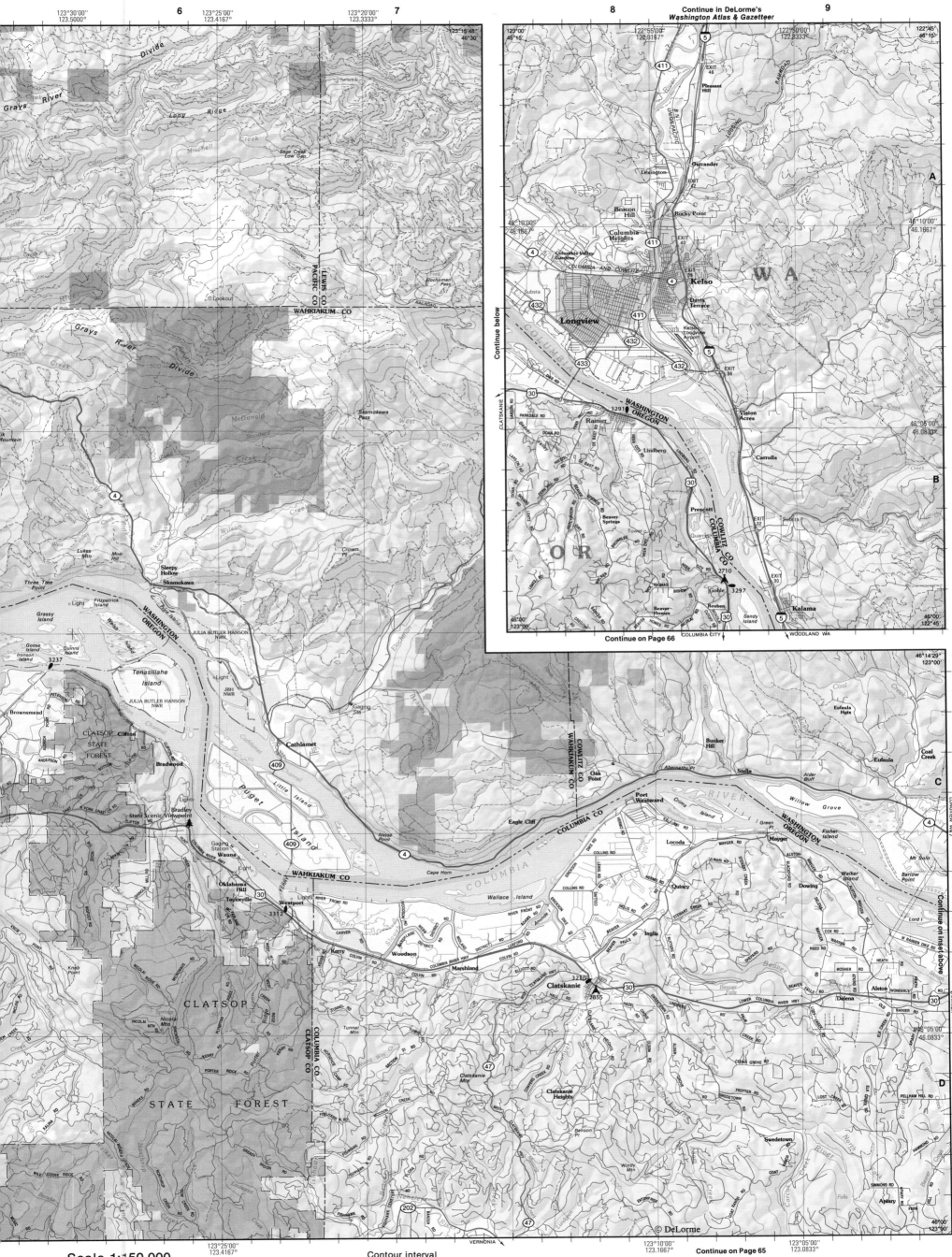

Continue in DeLorme's
Washington Atlas & Gazetteer

Scale 1:150,000
1 inch represents 2.4 miles

Contour interval
300 feet (91.4 meters)

Continue on Page 66
Continue on Page 65
Continue below
Continue on Inset above

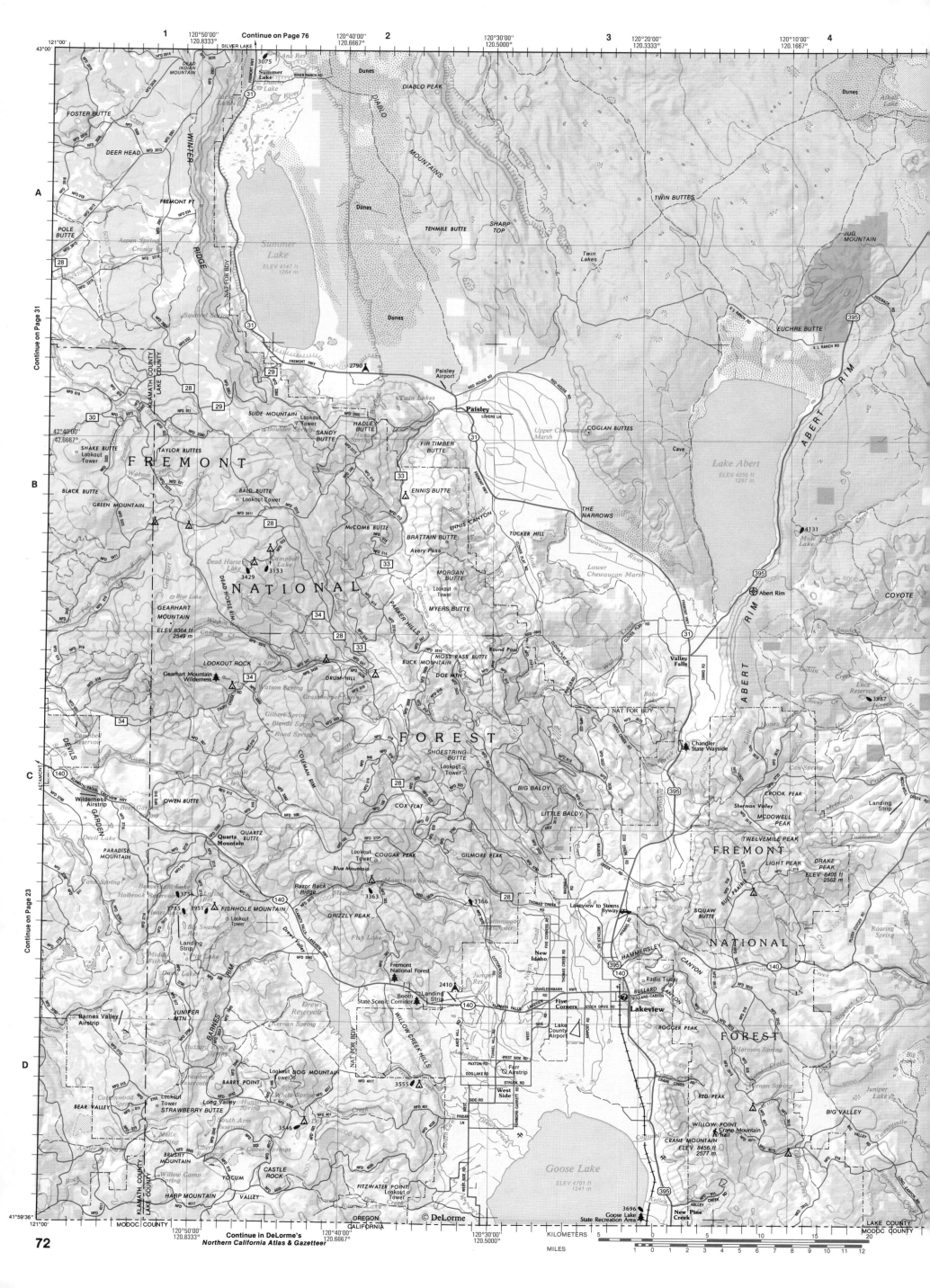

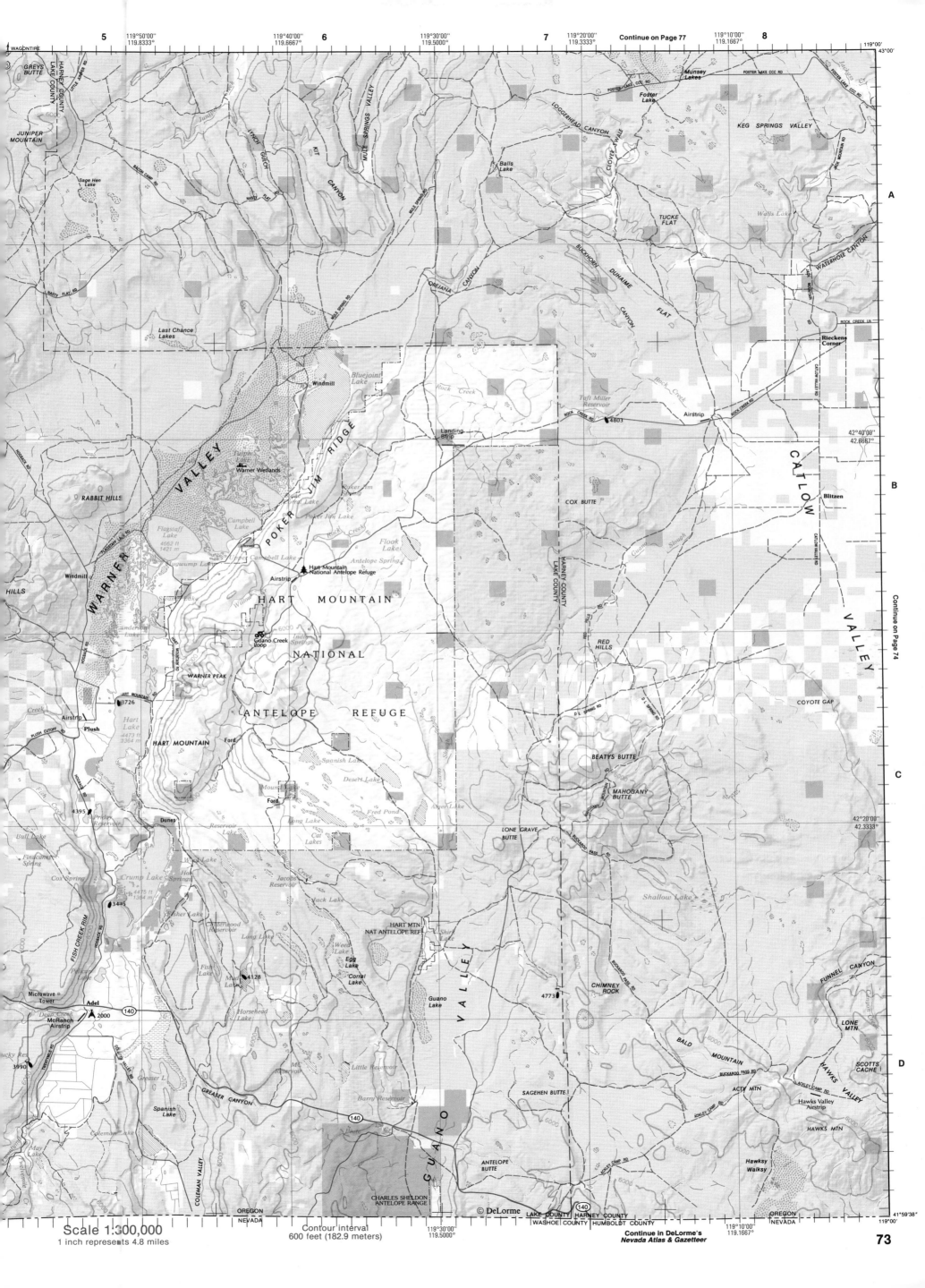

43°00'

GREYS
BUTTE

HARNEY
LAKE COUNTY

JUNIPER
MOUNTAIN

WAGONTIRE

Munsey
Lakes

FOSTER LAKE CCC RD

Foster
Lake

FOSTER LAKE CCC RD

KEG SPRINGS VALLEY

LOGGERHEAD CANYON

Sage Hen
Lake

Last Chance
Lakes

LYNCH GULCH

KIT CANYON

MULE SPRINGS VALLEY

Balls
Lake

TUCKE
FLAT

Walls Lake

A

Windmill

Bluejoint
Lake

OREJANA CANYON

CLOVER SWALE

Rock Creek

Taft Miller
Reservoir

BUCKHORN

DUHAIME
FLAT

WATERHOLE CANYON

Rieckens
Corner

ROCK CREEK LN

42°40'00"
42.6667°

Warner Wetlands

POKER JIM RIDGE

Poker Jim
Lake

Landing
Strip

Rock Creek

Airstrip
4803

ROCK CREEK RD

CATLOW

B

RABBIT HILLS

WARNER

VALLEY

Flagstaff
Lake
4662 ft
1421 m

Campbell
Lake

Flook
Lake

Hart Mountain
National Antelope Refuge

Antelope Spring

Airstrip

COX BUTTE

HARNEY COUNTY
LAKE COUNTY

Guano Slough

Blitzen

CATLOW VALLEY RD

VALLEY

Continue on Page 74

HILLS

Windmill

HART   MOUNTAIN

Guano Creek
Loop

Indian
Springs

RED
HILLS

COYOTE GAP

WARNER PEAK

NATIONAL

C

Airstrip
Plush

3726

Hart Mountain
4473 ft
1364 m

ANTELOPE   REFUGE

Spanish Lake

Desert Lake

Fred Pond

Mount Lyle

Ford

BEATYS BUTTE

MAHOGANY
BUTTE

42°20'00"
42.3333°

4395

Dunes

Reservoir
Lake

Long Lake

Cat Lakes

 Augen Lake

LONE GRAVE
BUTTE

Bull Lake

Finnicum
Spring

Cox Spring

Crump Lake
4473 ft
1364 m

Hot
Springs

Jacobs
Reservoir

Jack Lake

SHALLOW Lake

FUNNEL CANYON

3425

Fisher Lake

Cottonwood
Reservoir

Long Lake

HART MTN
NAT ANTELOPE REF

Shirk

GUANO

CHIMNEY
ROCK

4773

BUCKAROO PASS RD

LONE
MTN

Microwave
Tower

Fish
Lake

4128

Weed
Lake

Egg
Lake

Corral
Lake

VALLEY

SCOTTS
CACHE

D

3990

Adel

2000

McRanch
Airstrip

140

Horsehead
Lake

Mud
Reservoir

Guano
Lake

Little Reservoir

SAGEHEN BUTTE

BALD
MOUNTAIN

ACTY MTN

ACKLEY CAMP RD

Hawks Valley
Airstrip

HAWKS VALLEY

HAWKS MTN

Spanish
Lake

GREASER CANYON

Barry Reservoir

140

ANTELOPE
BUTTE

Hawksy
Walksy

May
Lake

COLEMAN VALLEY

Coleman Lake

CHARLES SHELDON
ANTELOPE RANGE

© DeLorme

140

OREGON
NEVADA

LAKE COUNTY   HARNEY COUNTY
WASHOE COUNTY   HUMBOLDT COUNTY

OREGON
NEVADA

41°59'38"

Scale 1:300,000
1 inch represents 4.8 miles

Contour interval
600 feet (182.9 meters)

119°30'00"
119.5000°

119°10'00"
119.1667°

119°00'

Continue in DeLorme's
Nevada Atlas & Gazetteer

73

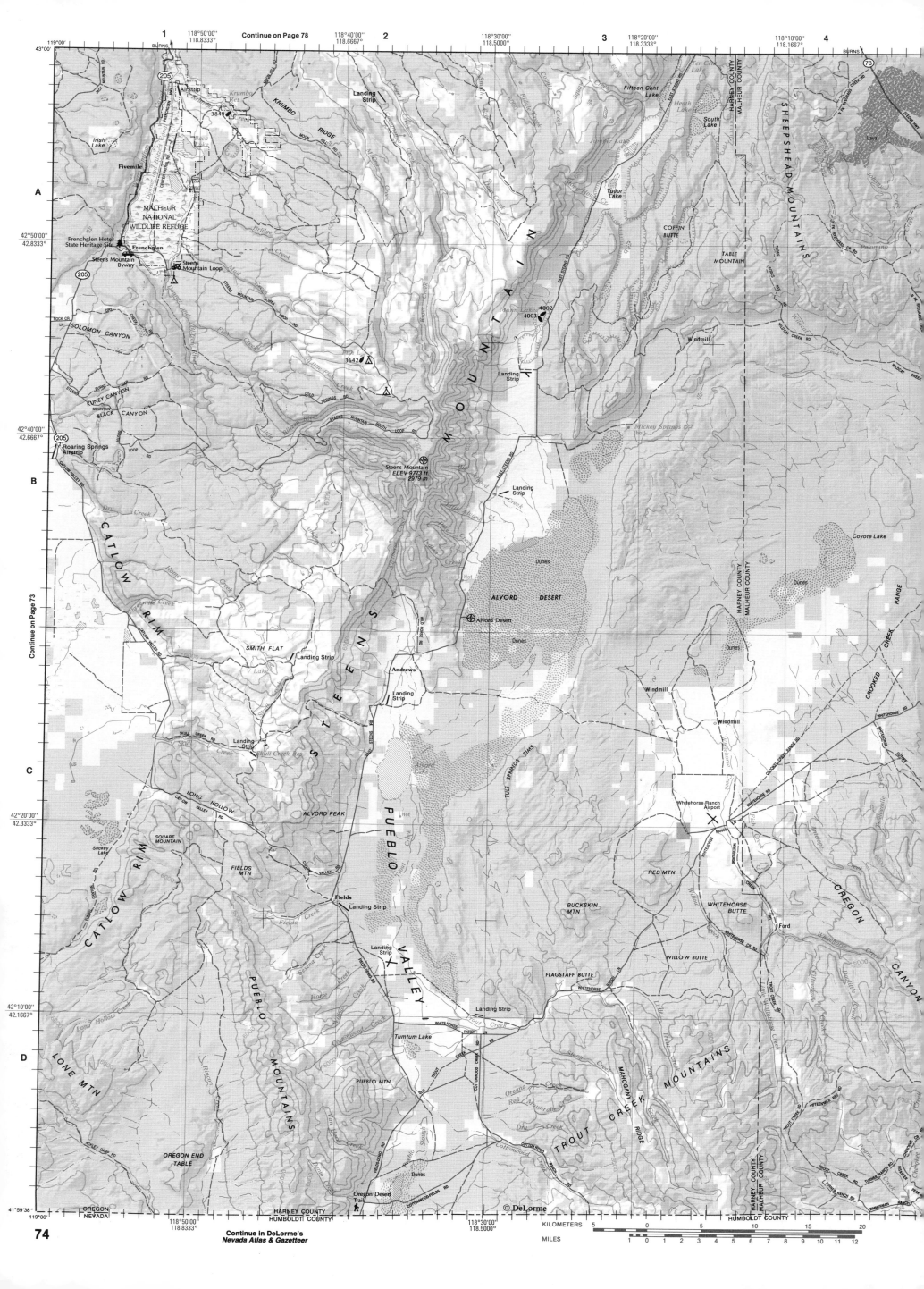

1   118°50'00"   118°40'00"   2   118°30'00"   3   118°20'00"   118°10'00"   4
118.8333°   118.6667°   118.5000°   118.3333°   118.1667°

43°00'

BURNS

A

MALHEUR NATIONAL WILDLIFE REFUGE

42°50'00"
42.8333°

Frenchglen Hotel State Heritage Site
Frenchglen
Steens Mountain Byway
Steens Mountain Loop

SOLOMON CANYON

KINEY CANYON
MOUNTAIN
BLACK CANYON

42°40'00"
42.6667°

Roaring Springs Airstrip

B

CATLOW RIM

Steens Mountain
ELEV 9773 ft
2979 m

42°00'

SMITH FLAT
Landing Strip

Andrews
Landing Strip

ALVORD DESERT

Alvord Desert

Dunes

C

LONG HOLLOW

Landing Strip
Skull Creek Rd

42°20'00"
42.3333°

ALVORD PEAK

SQUARE MOUNTAIN

Slickey Lake

PUEBLO

FIELDS MTN

Fields
Landing Strip

Landing Strip

42°10'00"
42.1667°

D

LONE MTN

PUEBLO MOUNTAINS

PUEBLO MTN

OREGON END TABLE

Oregon Desert Trail

41°59'38"

119°00'
118°50'00"
118.8333°

OREGON
NEVADA

HARNEY COUNTY
HUMBOLDT COUNTY

SHEEPSHEAD MOUNTAINS

Lava

Fifteen Cent Lake
Heath Lake
South Lake
Tudor Lake

COFFIN BUTTE

TABLE MOUNTAIN

Windmill

Coyote Lake

Dunes

Dunes

HARNEY COUNTY
MALHEUR COUNTY

Windmill

Windmill

Whitehorse Ranch Airport

RED MTN

WHITEHORSE BUTTE

Ford

WILLOW BUTTE

FLAGSTAFF BUTTE

BUCKSKIN MTN

TROUT CREEK MOUNTAINS

MAHOGANY RIDGE

CROOKED CREEK RANGE

OREGON CANYON

HARNEY COUNTY
MALHEUR COUNTY

118°30'00"
118.5000°

HUMBOLDT COUNTY

Continue on Page 73

Continue in DeLorme's
Nevada Atlas & Gazetteer

© DeLorme

KILOMETERS   5   0   5   10   15   20

MILES   1 0 1 2 3 4 5 6 7 8 9 10 11 12

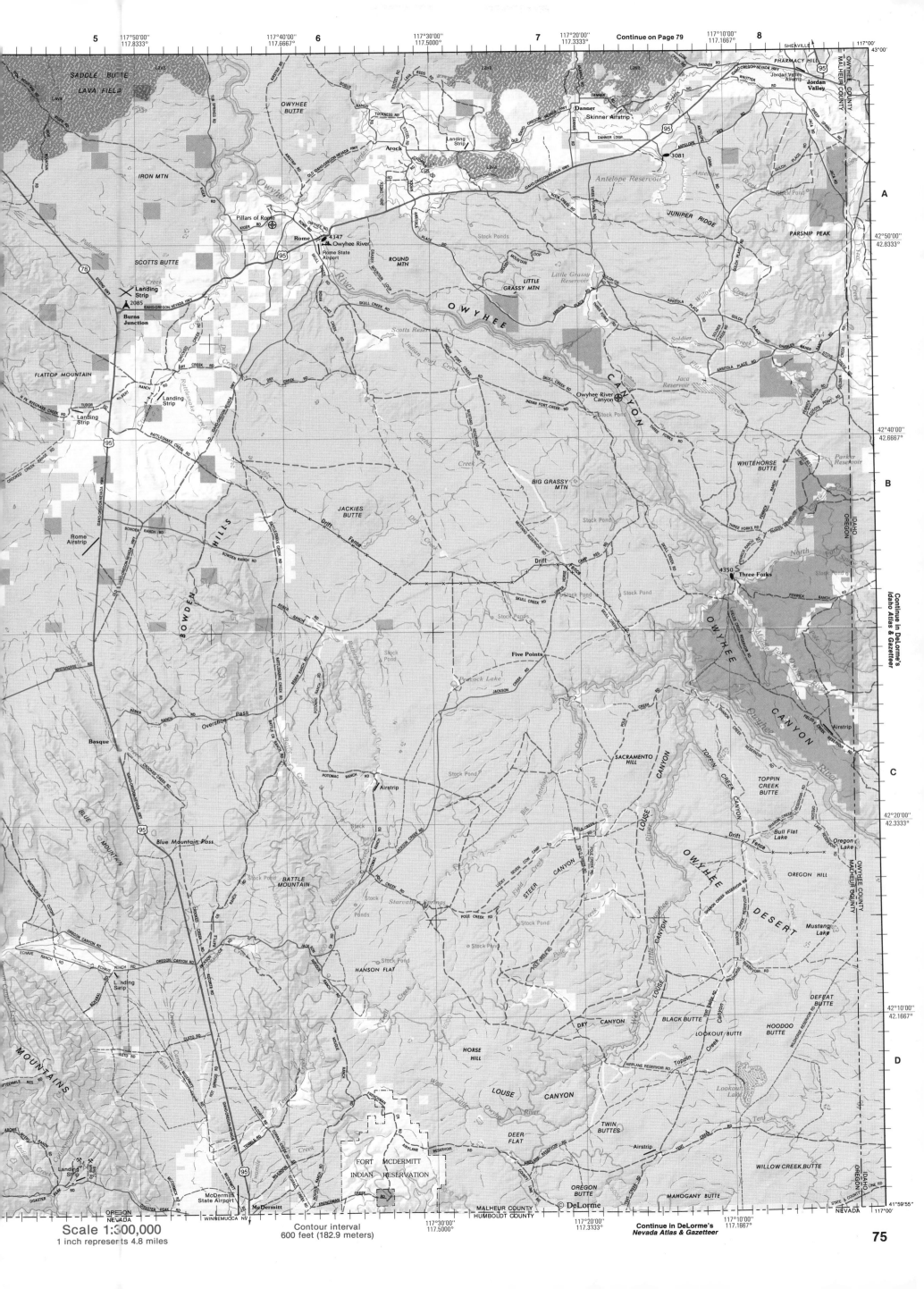

43°00'

SADDLE BUTTE
LAVA FIELD

Lava

OWYHEE
BUTTE

Lava

PHARMACY HILL

IDAHO-OREGON-NEVADA HWY
Jordan Valley
Airport
Jordan
Valley

OWYHEE COUNTY
MALHEUR COUNTY

SHERVILLE

Danner
Skinner Airstrip

IRON MTN

Tuckness
RANCH
Arock

Landing
Strip

3081

A

Pillars of Rome

JUNIPER RIDGE

42°50'00"
42.8333°

Rome
4347
Owyhee River
Rome State
Airport

ROUND
MTN

Antelope Reservoir

PARSNIP PEAK

SCOTTS BUTTE

LITTLE
GRASSY MTN
Little Grassy
Reservoir

Landing
Strip

2085

Burns
Junction

OWYHEE

Scotts Reservoir

Jaca
Reservoir

Owyhee River Canyon

FLATTOP MOUNTAIN

CANYON

Soldier
Creek

42°40'00"
42.6667°

B

Landing
Strip

Landing
Strip

WHITEHORSE
BUTTE

Parker
Reservoir

Rome
Airstrip

JACKIES
BUTTE

BIG GRASSY
MTN

Stock Pond

4350
Three Forks

Drift Fence

BOWDEN HILLS

Drift

IDAHO
OREGON

North

OWYHEE

Continue in DeLorme's
Idaho Atlas & Gazetteer

Bowden Ranch Rd

Five Points

Peacock Lake

CANYON

C

Basque

OveraBoe Pass

SACRAMENTO
HILL

LOUSE CANYON

TOPPIN CREEK CANYON

TOPPIN
CREEK
BUTTE

42°20'00"
42.3333°

Airstrip

Blue

BLUE MOUNTAIN

Potomac Ranch Rd

Bull Flat
Lake

Drift Fence

Oregon
Lake

Blue Mountain Pass

STEER CANYON

OWYHEE

OREGON HILL

Battle
Mountain

Starvation Springs

DESERT

Mustang
Lake

MOUNTAINS

HANSON FLAT

DEFEAT
BUTTE

42°10'00"
42.1667°

Landing
Strip

HORSE
HILL

DRY CANYON

BLACK BUTTE

LOOKOUT BUTTE

HOODOO
BUTTE

D

LOUSE CANYON

Lookout
Lake

Airplane Reservoir Rd

DEER
FLAT

TWIN
BUTTES

Airstrip

WILLOW CREEK BUTTE

FORT McDERMITT
INDIAN RESERVATION

OREGON
NEVADA

Little Owyhee River

MALHEUR COUNTY
HUMBOLDT COUNTY

DeLorme

OREGON
BUTTE

MAHOGANY BUTTE

IDAHO
OREGON

STATE LINE RD

NEVADA

41°59'55"

McDermitt
State Airport
McDermitt
WINNEMUCCA NV

Scale 1:300,000
1 inch represents 4.8 miles

Contour interval
600 feet (182.9 meters)

117°30'00"   117°20'00"   Continue in DeLorme's
117.5000°   117.3333°   Nevada Atlas & Gazetteer

117°10'00"
117.1667°   117°00'

75

121°00'   44°00'

CROOK COUNTY
DESCHUTES COUNTY
Landing Strip

BEAR CREEK BUTTES

OCHOCO NAT FOR

LOGAN BUTTE

RODMAN RIM

GERRY MTN

BEND

20

Millican
CENTRAL OREGON HWY

A

27

Lower Crooked River Byway

43°50'00''
43.8333°

MERRILL RD

Landing Strip

GRASSY BUTTE

Dry River

HAMPTON BUTTES

Continue on Page 45

23

PINE MOUNTAIN
Radio Tower

Brothers

20

CENTRAL OREGON HWY

FAN LAKE RD

Hampton Airstrip

MAHOGANY BUTTE

DESCHUTES

22

Sand Spring
Lavacicle Cave

ANTELOPE BUTTE
PLOT BUTTE

43°40'00''
43.6667°

EAST BUTTE

22

NATIONAL

23

Hampton

KO BUTTE
WATKINS BUTTE

FIRESTONE BUTTE
ROGERS BUTTE
QUARTZ MOUNTAIN
DESCHUTES COUNTY
LAKE COUNTY

FOX BUTTE

FREDERICK BUTTE

B

22

POT TOP BUTTE

Causeway

SIXTEEN BUTTE
DEAD LOG BUTTE

23

FOREST

BURNT BUTTE
SHORT BUTTE
ASPEN BUTTE

QUARTER BUTTE

Button Springs

HORSESHOE BUTTE
WIGTOP BUTTE

LONG BUTTE

SQUAW RIDGE

Glass Buttes

BUCK BUTTE
BUZZARD ROCK

SQUAW BUTTE

SQUAW MOUNTAIN

Benjamin Lake

43°30'00''
43.5000°

THE DEVILS GARDEN

Lava
Derrick Cave

HOGBACK BUTTE

LAVA BUTTE

Lava

Lava

Stauffer

Landing Strip

COUGAR MOUNTAIN
FRAZEE-FREDERICK BUTTE RD

Lava

MILLIGAN

Tired Horse Lake

GREEN MTN

BUNCHGRASS BUTTE

C

FORT ROCK RD
DERRICK CAVES RD

Lava

FOSSIL LAKE RD
LOST FOREST

Dunes

43°20'00''
43.3333°

FORT ROCK VALLEY

KING TUT RD

Crack-in-the-Ground

Alkali Flat

RAMS BUTTE

Radar Site

ELK MTN

Continue on Page 39

HORNING GAP
HAYES BUTTE

Christmas Lake

CONNLEY HILLS

CHRISTMAS VALLEY-WAGONTIRE RD

Christmas Valley

CHRISTMAS VALLEY-WAGONTIRE RD

CHRISTMAS LAKE

2625

Table Rock Airstrip

Christmas Valley Airport

VALLEY

BOWENS RD

LEHENNIE RIDGE

FANDANGO CANYON

CHRISTMAS VALLEY-WAGONTIRE RD

Sand Hills

43°10'00''
43.1667°

Paulina Marsh

Bottomless Lake

TABLE ROCK

KITTY LITTER RD

OLD LAKE RD

Thorn Lake

D

31

FREMONT

SILVER LAKE

Silver Lake

OLD LAKE RD

SHEEPLICK DRAW

ST PATRICK MOUNTAIN

JUNIPER CANYON

SAND CANYON

HORSE MOUNTAIN

3558

ST PATRICK MOUNTAIN

Murdock Reservoir

Cottonwood

SQUAW BUTTE

SHEEP ROCK

ALKALI BUTTES

FREMONT NATIONAL FOREST

31

CARLON RD

SUMMER LAKE

© DeLorme

121°00'

KILOMETERS   5   0   5   10   15   20
MILES   1 0 1 2 3 4 5 6 7 8 9 10 11 12

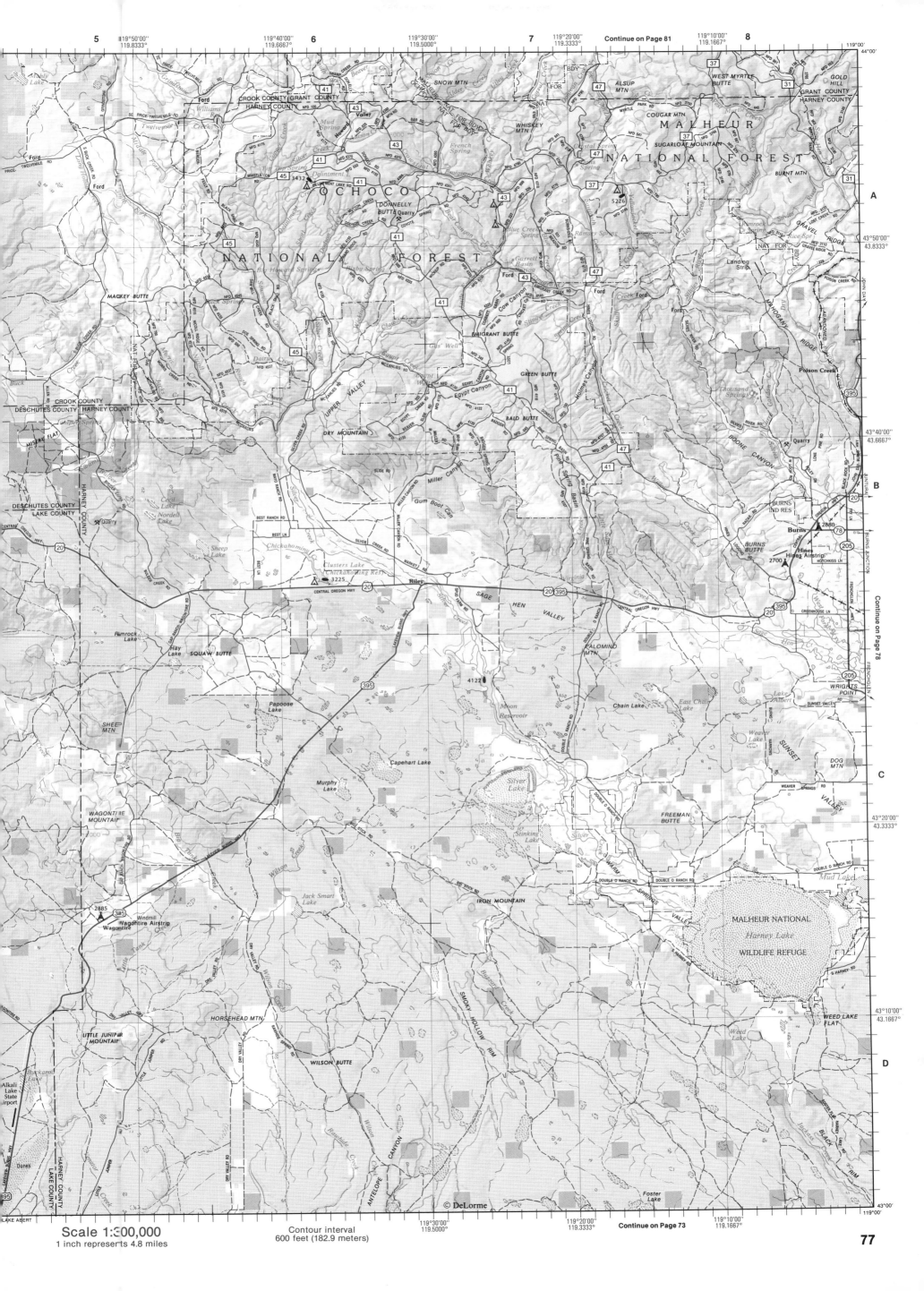

Scale 1:300,000
1 inch represents 4.8 miles

Contour interval
600 feet (182.9 meters)

© DeLorme

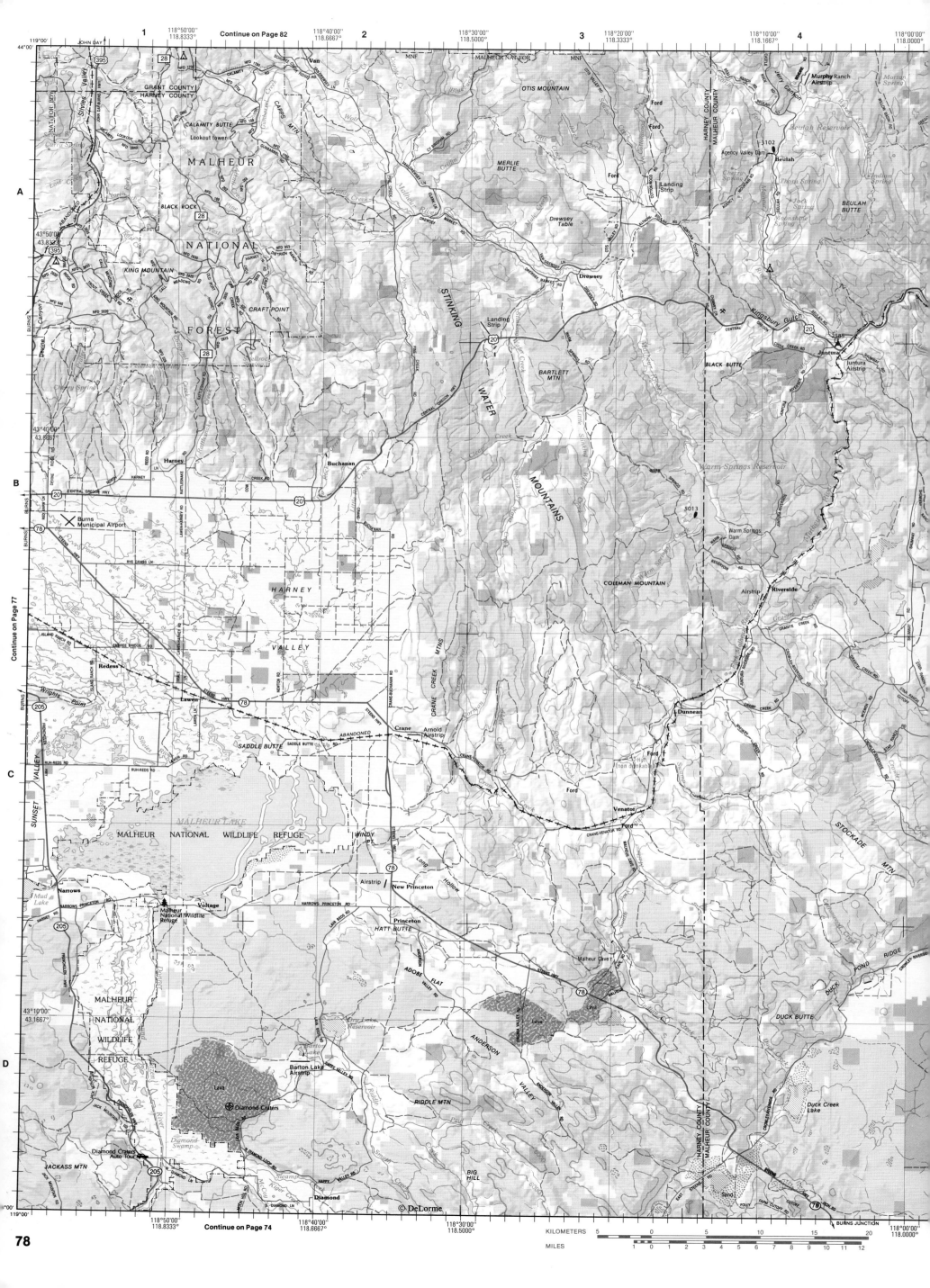

Continue on Page 77

Continue on Page 74

Scale 1:300,000
1 inch represents 4.8 miles

Contour interval
600 feet (182.9 meters)

© DeLorme

Continue in DeLorme's *Idaho Atlas & Gazetteer*

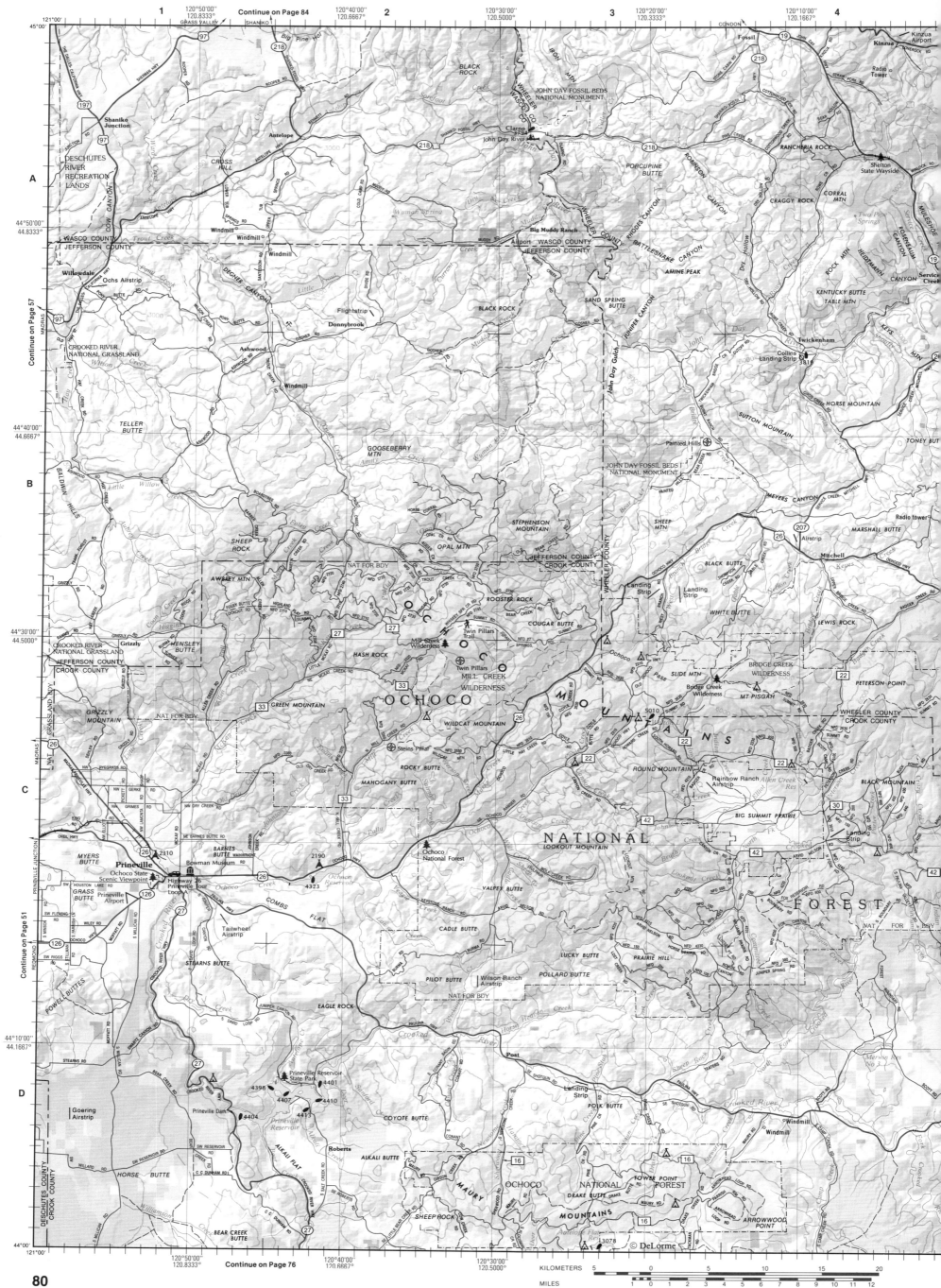

Continue on Page 84
Continue on Page 57
Continue on Page 51
Continue on Page 76

© DeLorme

KILOMETERS

MILES

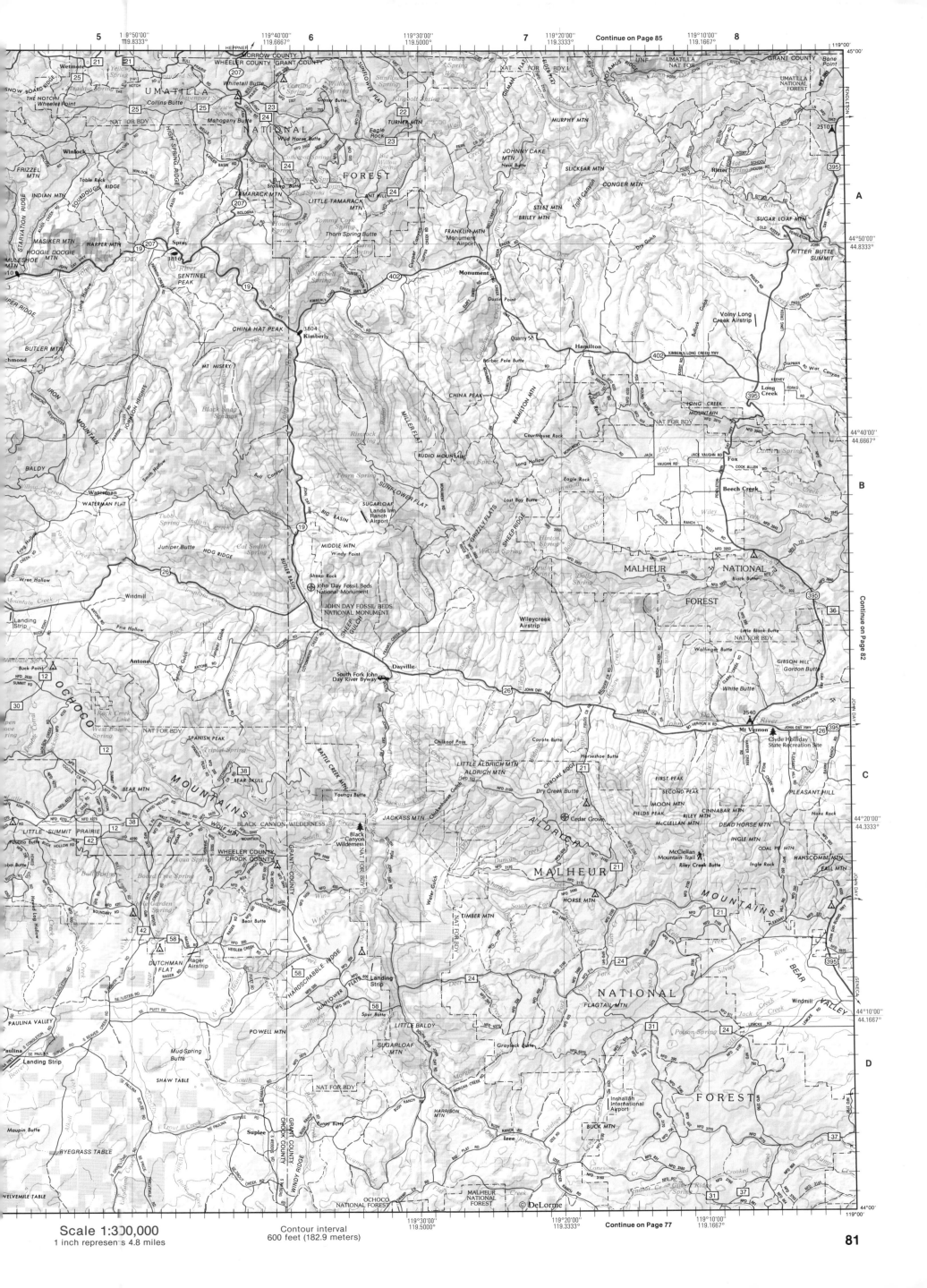

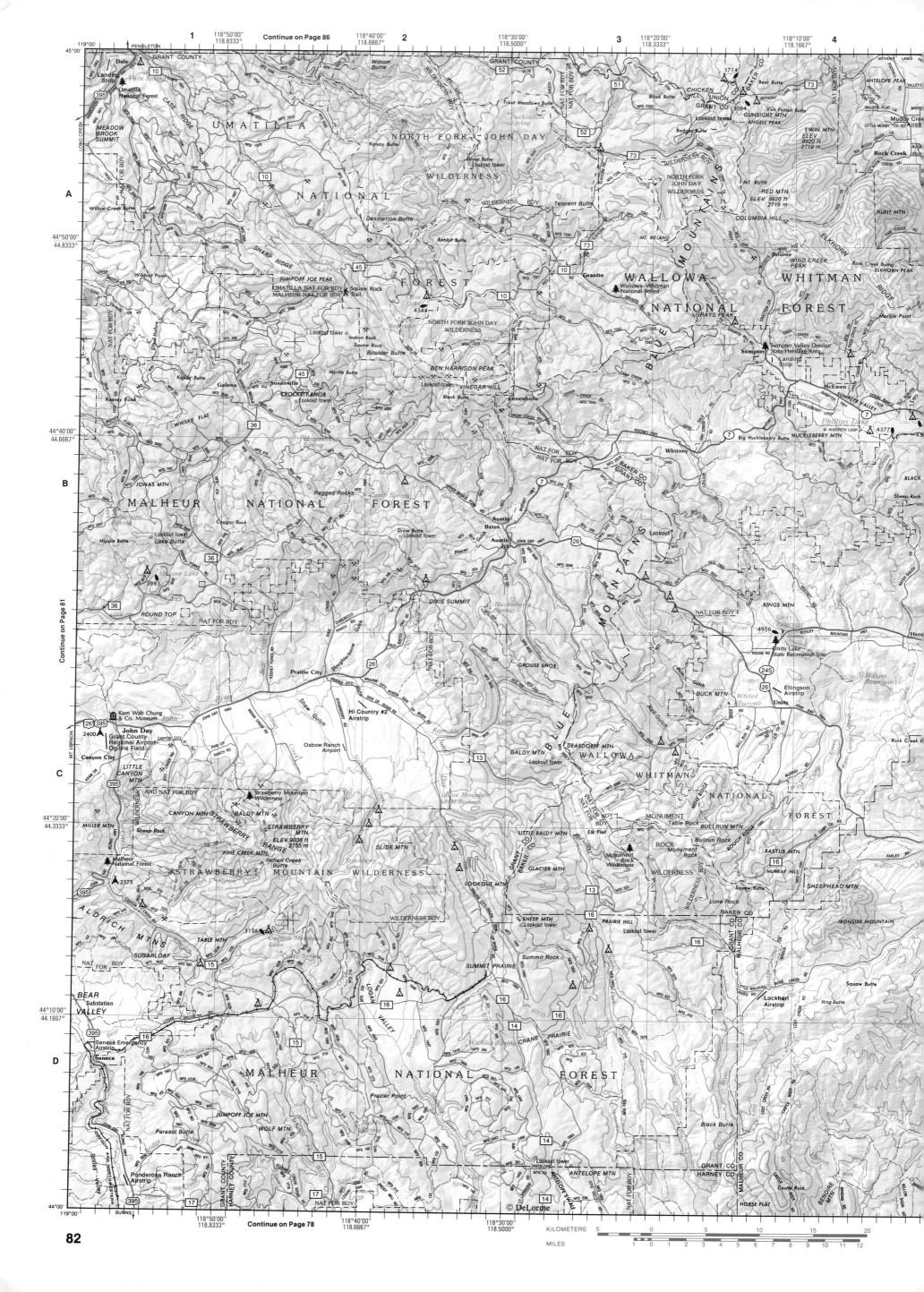

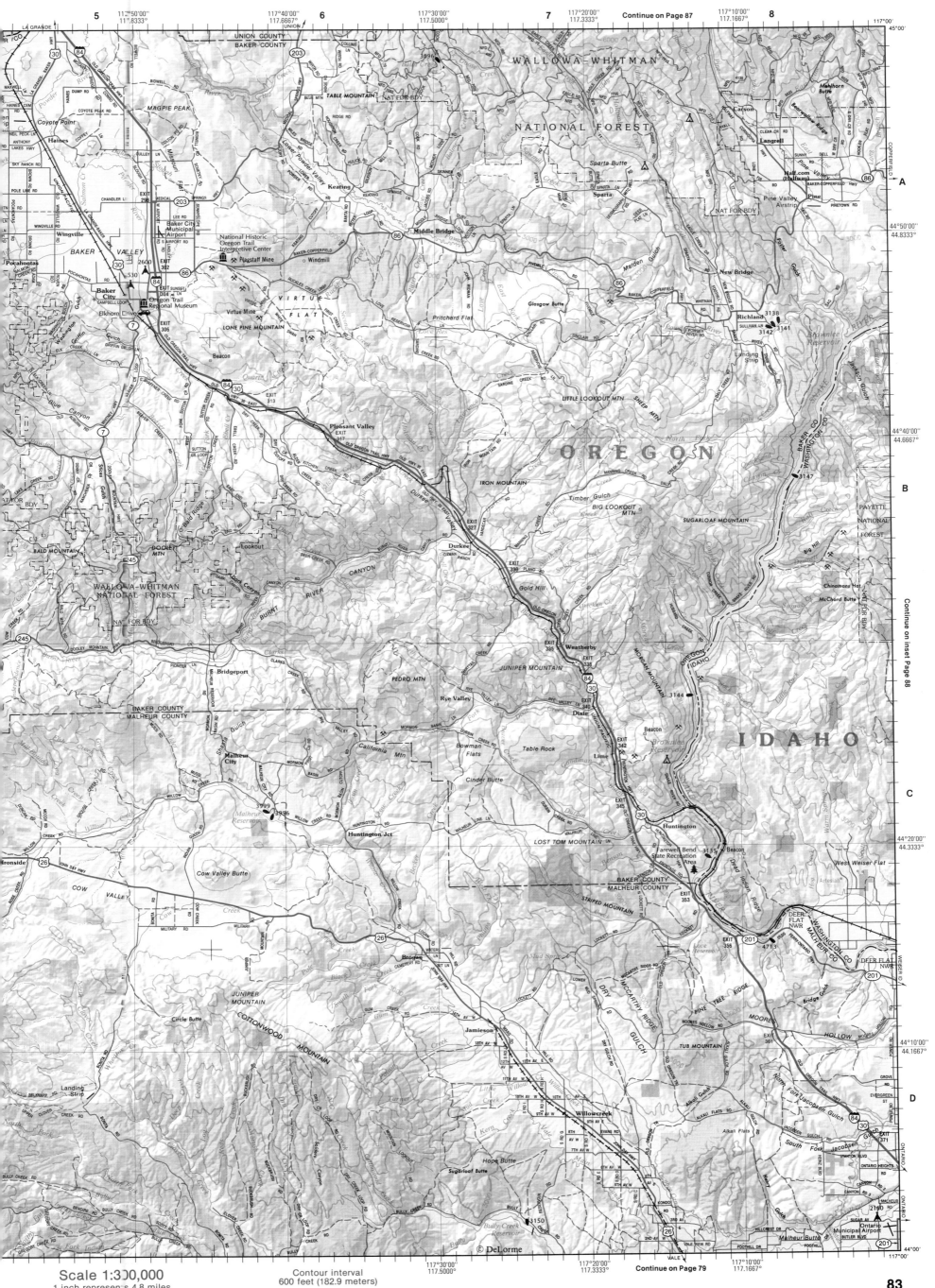

Continue on Page 87

Continue on inset Page 88

Continue on Page 79

© DeLorme

Scale 1:300,000
1 inch represents 4.8 miles

Contour interval
600 feet (182.9 meters)

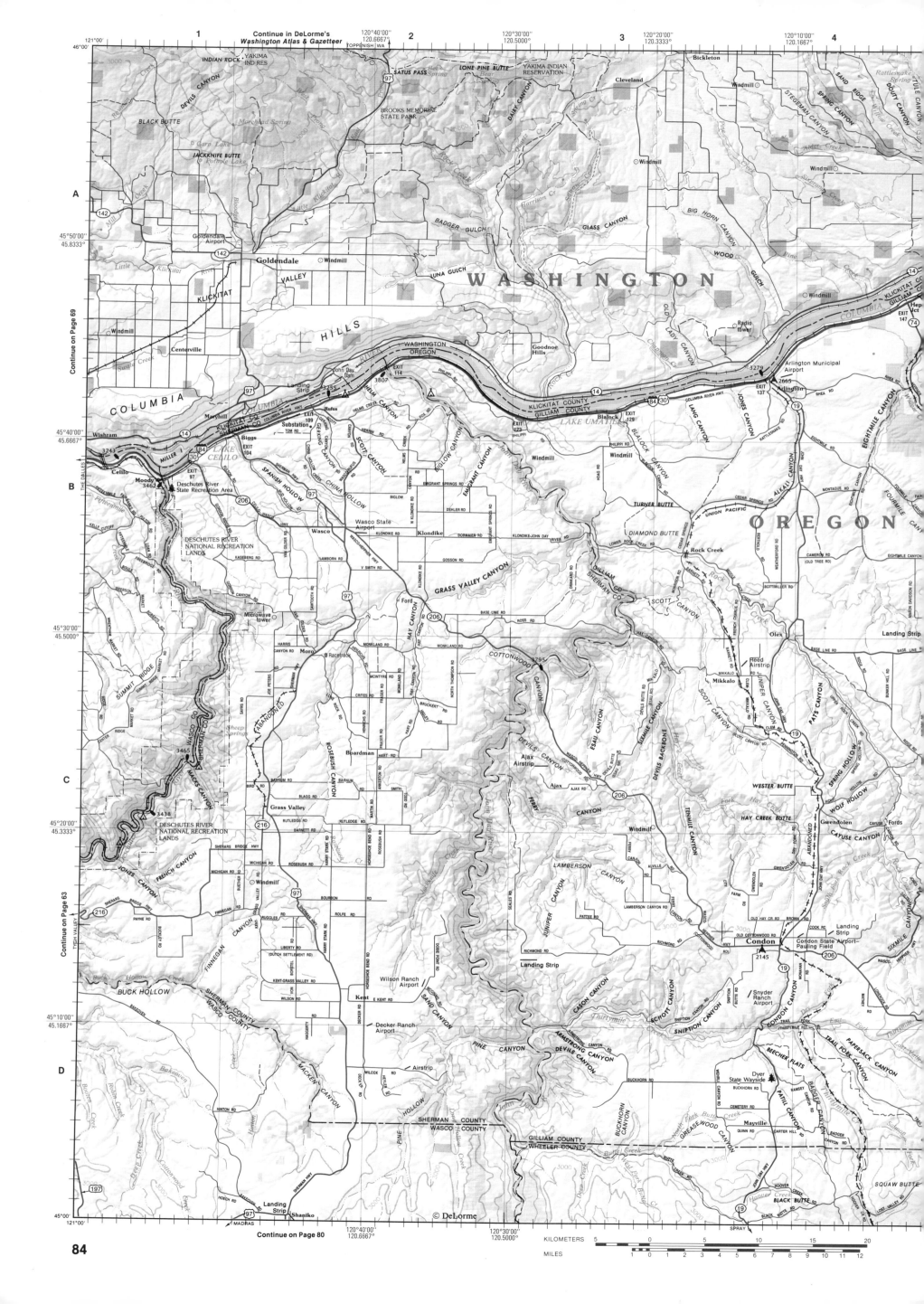

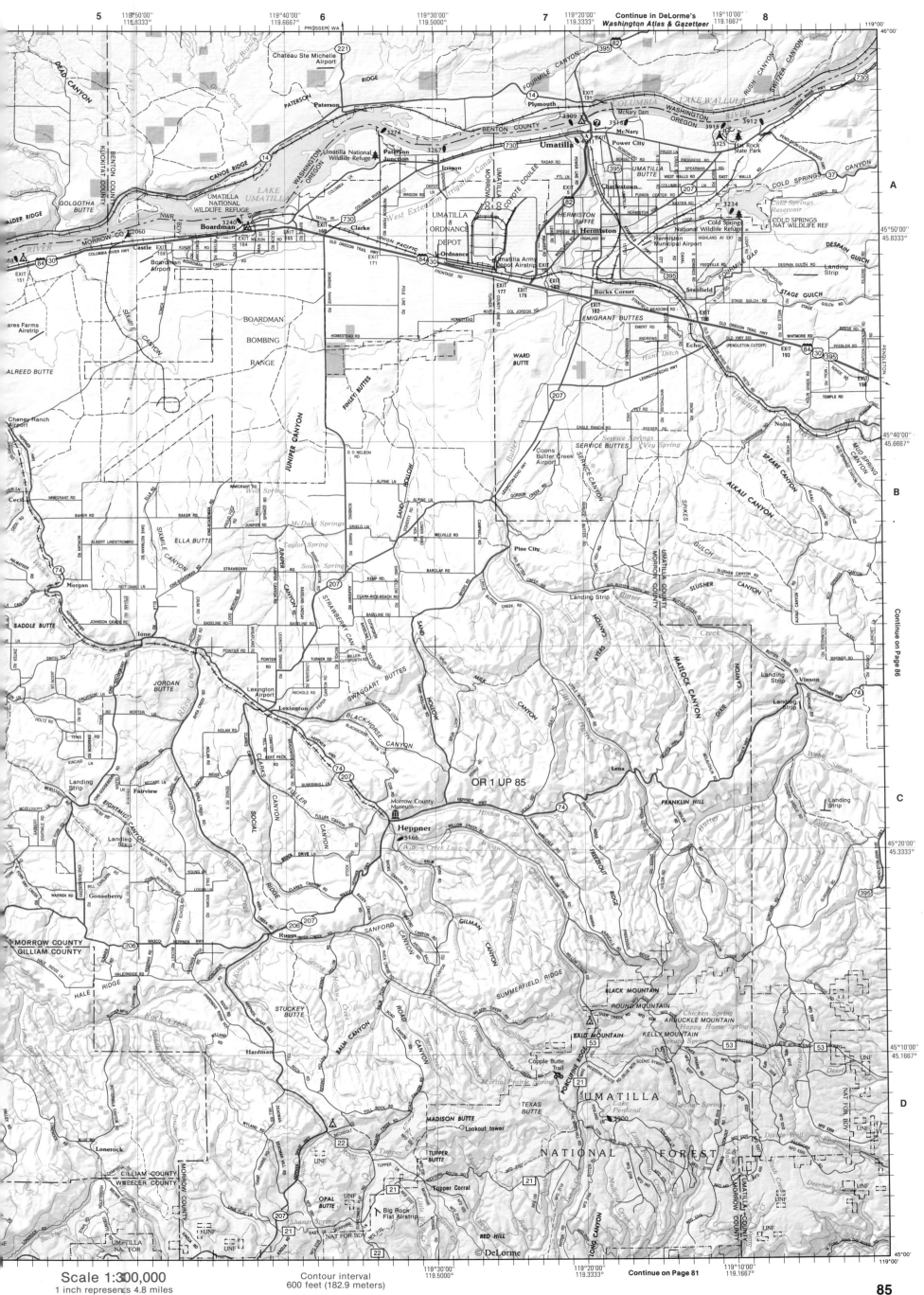

Continue on Page 86

OR 1 UP 85

Continue on Page 81

Scale 1:300,000
1 inch represents 4.8 miles

Contour interval
600 feet (182.9 meters)

©DeLorme

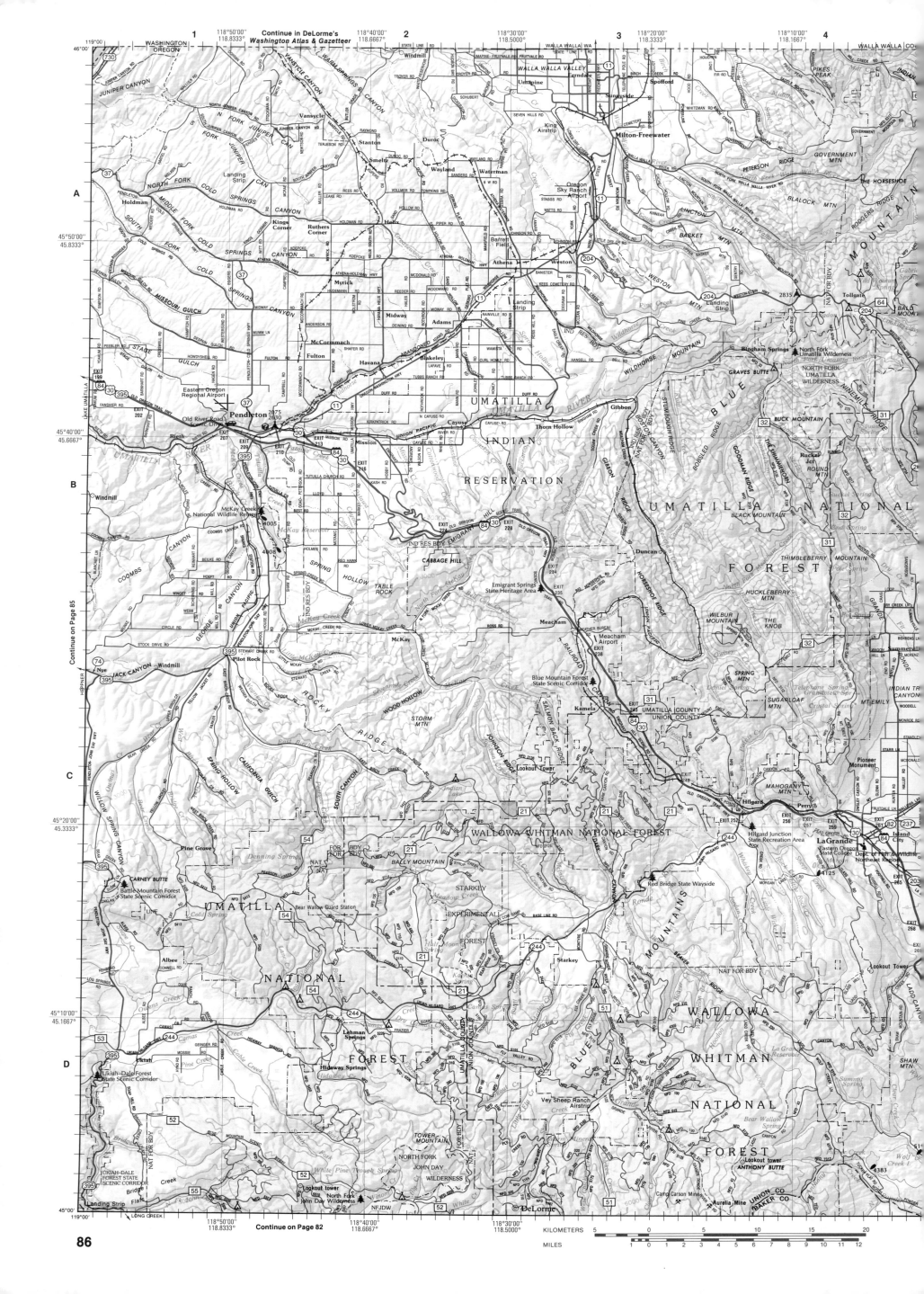

Continue in DeLorme's
Washington Atlas & Gazetteer

Continue on Page 85

Continue on Page 82

KILOMETERS   5   0   5   10   15   20

MILES   1   0   1 2 3 4 5 6 7 8 9 10 11 12

©DeLorme

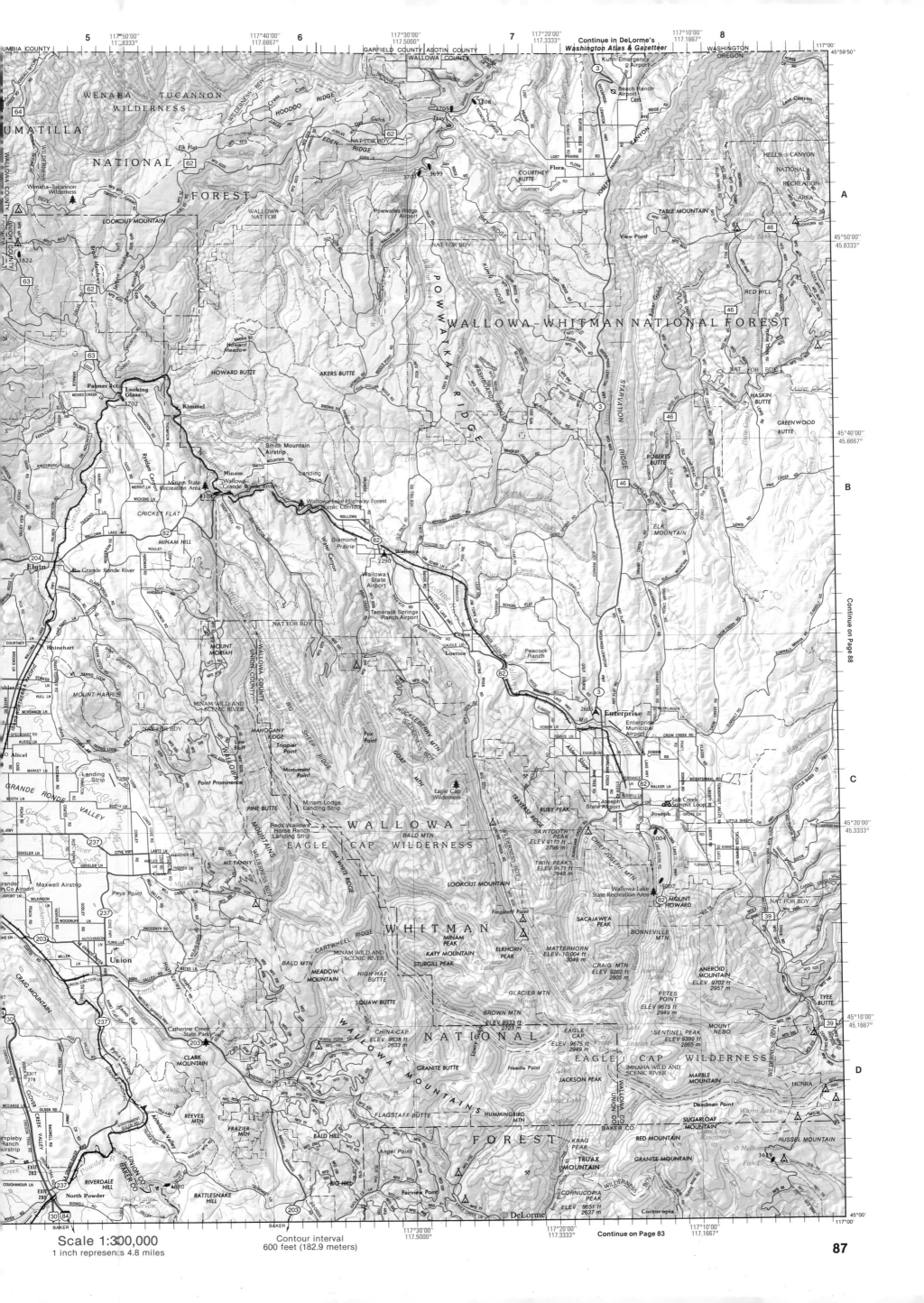

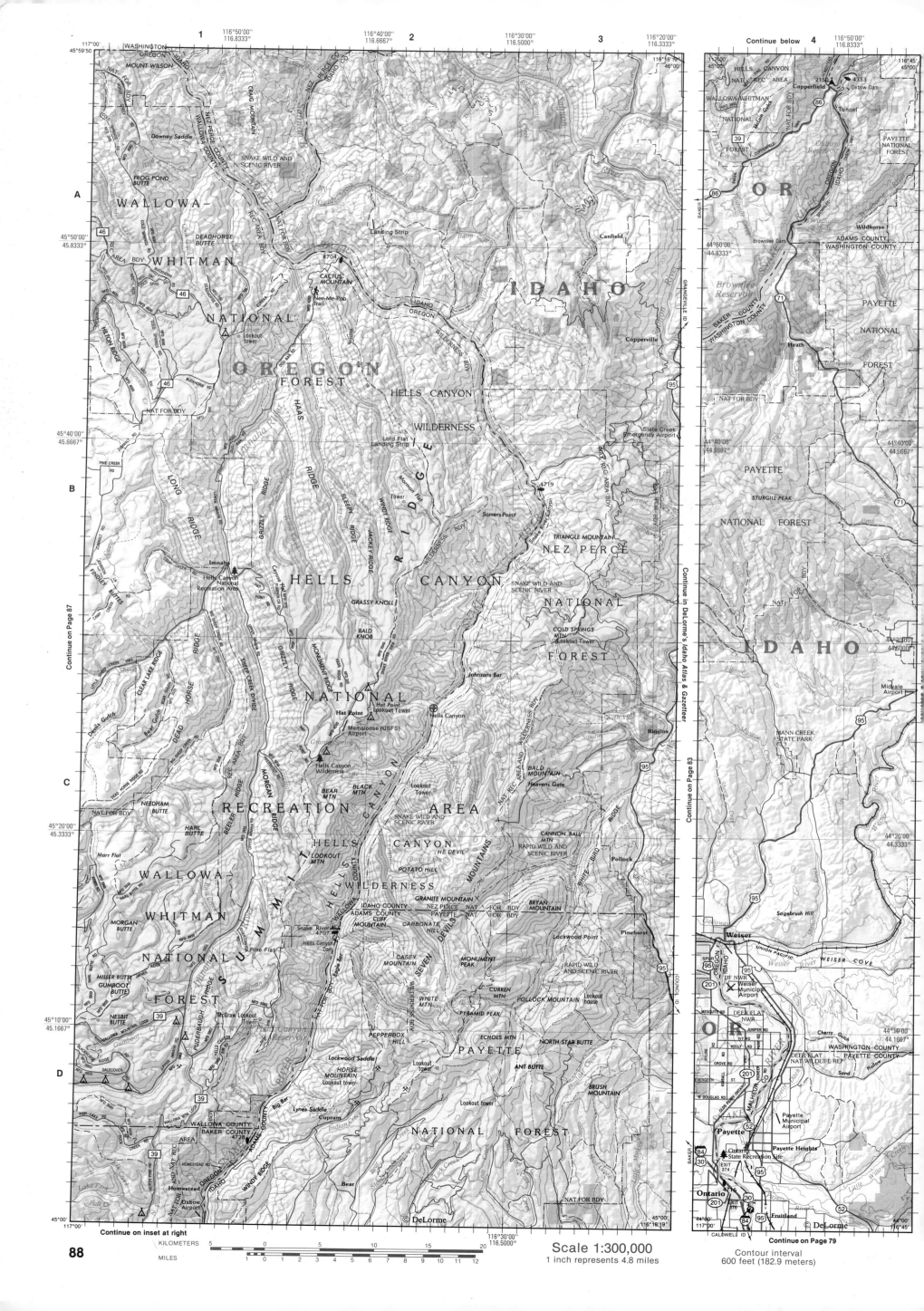

Continue below 4

Continue on Page 87

Continue in DeLorme's Idaho Atlas & Gazetteer

Continue on Page 83

Continue on inset at right

Continue on Page 79

KILOMETERS

MILES

Scale 1:300,000
1 inch represents 4.8 miles

Contour interval
600 feet (182.9 meters)

© DeLorme